SCHOOL LIBRARY MEDIA SERIES

Edited by Diane de Cordova Biesel

ABC BOOKS AND ACTIVITIES
From Preschool to High School

by
Cathie Hilterbran Cooper

School Library Media Series, No. 5

The Scarecrow Press, Inc.
Lanham, Md., & London

Please note: You are welcome to cut out and copy any pages in this book which are shown with a scissors symbol and dashed line. Permission to use other pages in the book must be sought through the publisher.

SCARECROW PRESS, INC.

Published in the United States of America
by Scarecrow Press, Inc.
4720 Boston Way
Lanham, Maryland 20706

4 Pleydell Gardens, Folkestone
Kent CT20 2DN, England

British Cataloguing-in-Publication Information Available

Library of Congress Cataloging-in-Publication Data

Cooper, Cathie Hilterbran 1953–
ABC books and activities: from preschool to high school /
by Cathie Hilterbran Cooper
P.   cm. — (School library media series; no. 5)
Includes bibliographical references and index.
1. English language—Alphabet—Textbooks. 2. Creative activities
and seatwork. I. Title. II. Series
LB 1525.65.C66 1995 372.4'145—dc 120 95-35325 CIP
ISBN 0-8108-3013-2 (cloth : alk. paper)

♾ ™The paper used in this publication meets the minimum requirements of
American National Standard for Information Sciences—Permanence of
Paper for Printed Library Materials, ANSI Z39.48–1984.
Manufactured in the United States of America

Printed on acid-free paper

CONTENTS

EDITOR'S FOREWORD

The School Library Media Series is directed to the school library media specialist, particularly the building-level librarian. The multifaceted role of the librarian as educator, collection developer, curriculum developer, and information specialist is examined. The series includes concise, practical books on topical and current subjects related to programs and services.

Destined to be the standard reference work in its field, this scholarly book is an in-depth analysis of alphabet books from their serious, religious beginnings to their funny, instructive, and artistic present.

Five hundred forty-two titles are listed with short annotations, suggested activities, and carefully crafted essays on each type (e.g., "Science, Technology, and the Alphabet").

As stated by the author, alphabet books are now "a genre that knows no age or subject boundaries." The text *clearly* demonstrates the author's vast knowledge of books of this type.

Diane de Cordova Biesel,
Series Editor

1. INTRODUCTION

Traditionally, alphabet books have been confined to use by preschoolers and beginning readers as a means of learning letters and sound relationships. From the early days of hornbooks and primers, children were expected to master the alphabet before they were permitted to learn how to read words or other materials, especially the Bible. While these early alphabet books were concerned with moral and religious instruction, they still managed to be a source of knowledge and delight for young children. Later when adults began to realize the importance of literature for children, alphabet books took on a more lighthearted approach.

While many of the alphabet books that are published now are still primarily picture books for young readers, today's publishers realize that a good alphabet book must appeal to both the young child and the adult reader. As a result, alphabet books have taken on a more sophisticated look both in illustrations and in contents. A profusion of new titles designed to fascinate and intrigue both children and adults is published each year. The range of subjects is never ending, and the artists use all kinds of media to produce illustrations that range from simple one-item pictures to sophisticated museum-quality art.

HISTORICAL PERSPECTIVE ON ALPHABET BOOKS

Lesson books, or "hornbooks," were the first type of children's materials to be influenced by the invention of printing. Lesson books first appeared in the 1450s in Europe and were the only instruction books for children for many years. They were later brought to America and used by the Puritans and the Colonial dame schools in teaching values and religion to children. In the early 1500s the alphabet was added to children's religious primers. The purpose of these early primers was to instruct children in moral and religious beliefs while letters were learned. *The New England Primer* (1683) included the alphabet in rhyme form, but it was designed for religious instruction rather than pleasure reading. The "calling of letters" was considered a serious matter not to be taken lightly or enjoyed. Children had to be able to recite the entire alphabet before being allowed to learn to read.

While alphabet books began being published in the 16th century, it was not until the 19th century in America that a more lighthearted approach to life and learning came into being. Alphabet books began to reflect this attitude, first seen in the Shaker abecedarius in 1882 (redesigned by Alice and Martin Provensen as *A Peaceable Kingdom: The Shaker Abecedarius* 1978). The Shakers used these alphabet animal rhymes to teach reading, but at the same time, the rhyme and meter in the verses made learning enjoyable. The Shakers considered singing and dancing a part of a child's school life, and the abecedarius served both as a source of learning and of fun.

Edward Lear's (1871) use of limericks and humorous illustrations for the presentation of the letters of the alphabet and Kate Greenaway's original woodblock designs of the rhyme "A Apple Pie" helped seal the transition from moral instruction alphabet books to the brightly-colored pleasurable books enjoyed by today's children. In 1898 William Nicholson's *Alphabet* was published with the distinction that it was not just an alphabet book for young children, but also a book for adults. In his alphabetical picture gallery of common types, Nicholson used direct engraving and squat block letters in the illustrations. The simple letters and clear pictures enticed the young child, while the content material appealed to adults.

By the early 20th century, alphabet picture books had become a well-established type of reading material for children. More and more artists became intrigued by the possibilities of taking a single letter and turning it into a dramatic statement, and as the century progressed the art and contents of alphabet books expanded to include a far-reaching range of subject matter. While children still need to "know the alphabet," the emphasis today is on reading of whole words in context so as to ascertain the meaning rather than a close familiarity with and recitation of the letters.

Although the alphabet books being published today include the traditional beginner alphabet book with all 26 letters (in upper and lower case) together with one or two familiar objects, there are many specialized types of alphabet books for all age levels. Many of the specialized ABC books currently being published look more like coffee table art books than beginning primers. The high quality in both text and illustration have made this genre one that knows no age or subject boundaries. Artists have adopted the genre as a playground for plying their imaginative works, and authors have adopted the ABC format as a means of presenting information. While the alphabetical sequence is still used, the resemblance to traditional ABC books stops there. Many different approaches including puzzles, games, and dictionary format, as well as detailed text, are often used in this new form of the alphabet genre. Specialized alphabet books range from the topical, such as Mary Azarian's *A Farmer's Alphabet* (1981) and James Rice's *Cowboy Alphabet* (1990), to specialized information in *The Extinct Alphabet Book* (1993) by Pallotta. What began as a simple reader for children has evolved into an appealing collection of illustrations, text, and information that is also fascinating.

CRITERIA FOR ALPHABET BOOKS

As a result of the current explosion in both beginning and specialized alphabet books for all ages, it is necessary to create two levels of criteria to evaluate alphabet books. One set is useful for books designed for young children, while a second set of criteria is needed to evaluate alphabet books designed for the older reader.

While most alphabet books fit one of two levels, it is important to realize that there are some books that know no age limit and can be enjoyed and used across the curriculum and with all grade levels. *Anno's Alphabet* is an example of a book that can easily be used by the youngest reader and also appreciated by the adult reader. Wordless text, a simple central illustration, and three-dimensional letters make this title one that children can use for identification. The complex decorative borders and the construction of wooden letters with changing perspectives offer a series of visual puzzles and optical illusions that older readers and adults can appreciate and understand better than a beginning reader.

Alphabet books designed for the early reader (from infancy through age seven) should be evaluated first for **clarity.** The background on each page should be simple and uncluttered with a typeface that is clear and easily read. The younger the reader, the larger the letters should be. Ornamented typefaces such as Old English make it difficult for young readers to recognize and identify letters. **Only one or two objects for each letter** should be used, and each object should be easily identified and consistent with the letter that it represents. **Only common words** that are easily known by young children should be used. **A picture should be easily identifible** as in "apple" or "ant" rather than "anaconda" or "arachnid." The illustration should match the key letter only with words that begin with the featured letter in its most commonly pronounced way. A as in ant, rather than A as in arm, would be the first word choice for a beginning alphabet book. Words that have several common names should not be used. For example, rabbit would not be a good choice for R, because young children often refer to rabbits as bunnies. The **text should be limited to only a few words,** with the illustration carrying the thrust of the "story." The illustrations should be consistent with the theme of the book and set its mood and pace. A simple identification type of alphabet book is the best for use with young children; that is not to say that they should not also be exposed to the more complex alphabet picture books. As with any set of rules or criteria, there are always exceptions.

Many alphabet books can be used with older readers (ages six to adult) not only as introductions to letters and sounds, but also as lessons in social studies, science, and art. They can also be used as a means of becoming familiar with other cultures and customs and as an introduction to poetry and poetic forms. Some books use a story format to present both the letters and other information. **Story alphabet books should be evaluated on the basis of how good the story is, whether the story naturally fits into the alphabetical structure, and whether there are any breaks in continuity because of the letter order.** *The Alphabet Soup* by Gabler is a good example of a story that uses the alphabetical stucture, holds the reader's interest, and has a smooth, even flow in the plot action. In this book, two witch children come home from school with the assignment of making alphabet soup. They proceed to throw all kinds of weird and unusual ingredients into their soup as a hidden schoolmate watches. Alphabet books that use a topical or thematic approach should also be evaluated on the basis of continuity and letter order. If the use of alphabetical letters interferes with the natural order of information, it can prove to be more of a hindrance than a help. Many of the science alphabet books by Jerry Pallotta, such as *The Ocean Alphabet Book,* are good examples of thematic alphabet books.

With the explosion of alphabet books on the market and the wide range of topics covered in them, there is no lack of ABC books for both the preschooler and the older reader. Each book should be evaluated on its own virtues of concept and design as well as the audience for which it is intended. By looking at the illustrations, design and layout of the page, and the content of the book, teachers and parents will be able to determine which ABC books meet their needs.

VALUE OF ALPHABET BOOKS

The English alphabet consists of 26 simple letters that can be grouped together in a variety of ways to form the 40 sounds that allow us to communicate with one another. Although the concept of 26 letters is a simple one, its value can not be underestimated. The letters of the alphabet are powerful tools that hold the keys to communication.

Early alphabet books were used solely as a means of instruction in letter recognition and as a prerequisite for reading, and they were considered valuable in that respect. Today that theory no longer holds true with the current proliferation of both simple and sophisticated alphabet books. The wide variety and number of ABC books that have been published in the past 50 years can be used as valuable resources in a wide range of curriculum areas and with a broad spectrum of age levels.

Perhaps the most valuable thing about alphabet books is that they expose the reader to the sounds of the language and show both the visual and auditory connection between letters and words. Alphabet books provide opportunities for readers to develop and enhance identification skills, to encourage letter recognition, to acquire and understand new words, to promote the mastery of letter forms, and to provide a variety of other learning experiences. Within the context of alphabet books, children are exposed to skills such as sequencing, matching, classification, discrimination of likenesses and differences, rhyming, recall, memory, drawing conclusions, and following directions. All of these are important life skills that lead to literacy.

Although some experts doubt the merits of rote learning, even the skeptics cannot deny that learning the alphabet is an important component in learning to read and to write. Frequent exposure to letters and their shapes and forms encourage children to become familiar with the names of letters and to learn about their special features. As a child becomes comfortable looking at and using letters, he or she also becomes adept at being able to identify and to distinguish special features of letters such as vertical and horizontal lines, curved shapes, and rounded features.

Like all other types of writing and literature, alphabet books provide students with models of literary forms. Alphabet books expose students of all ages to common literary forms such as plot, character development, setting, theme, style, and humor. An alphabet book may not be as complex as *Macbeth,* but it offers the same literary elements to the reader. In fact, many of the most basic alphabet books (or any picture book for that matter) offers teachers and parents a unique opportunity to expose children to basic literary elements and to provide opportunities for children to examine and to identify these elements. Older students can easily identify these elements in an alphabet book and then transfer the knowledge to more difficult literature.

Alphabet books are also valuable in providing an introduction to writing techniques and styles. Some authors favor a direct simplistic style while others offer complex word analogies. The simpler alphabet books are good for exposing children to direct writing styles and the effectiveness of a single word and picture in portraying a vivid image. Alphabet books with more complex text can show how words can be used to convey a variety of different images and to demonstrate how words and language can be twisted and turned to suit an author's fancy.

The interaction between a child and a book involves more than a familiarity with the letters on the page. The imaginative illustrations provide children with strong visual experiences and the opportunity to link vivid images to letters and words that match them. In addition, the letters and words teach them about communication and the power of language. While learning the alphabetical sequence is important, it is even more important to expose children to a variety of ABC books. Looking at and studying letters within the context of real books provides children with more meaningful and enriching language experiences than using rote drills and flashcards to teach only the letters. Alphabet books are valuable because they look at the whole rather than the part, and they provide the unique connection between written and oral language.

USE OF ALPHABET BOOKS

There was a time when alphabet books were primarily designed for use with preschool and primary age children, but that is no longer true today. The current explosion in the alphabet book genre has produced books that tackle more sophisicated themes, have clever intricate illustrations, and spark interest in persons of all age levels, from preschoolers to adults. ABC books can not only be used to teach letter recognition, shapes and sounds, but also as content resources in the language arts, science, social studies, art, and other subject areas.

For the youngest reader (infants and toddlers), only the simplest of alphabet books are best to use for letter and sound recognition. Board books, toddler books, and the beginning readers use only one or two easily recognizable objects on a plain uncluttered background to provide a visual and auditory connection. There are some artists, such as Brian Wildsmith, Lois Ehlert, and Bruno Munari, who have beginner alphabet books that are a bit more complex in content and illustration, but for the most part the early alphabet book is used as a simple exposure to books, words, and letters and as a means of combining entertainment with identification instruction.

At the preschool and primary levels, alphabet books can be used for a number of purposes including the following:

• to teach the alphabet and its sequential order
• to demonstrate the forms of letters (lower and upper case)
• to show sound and symbol relationship
• to teach visual and auditory discrimination
• to contribute to visual literacy and to help students organize graphic experiences
• to provide identification of familiar and not so familiar objects
• to provide information about people, places, and things
• to introduce different languages and forms of communication
• to explain concepts, such as gardening and paper folding
• to entertain and instruct at the same time
• to stimulate vocabulary development

Primary students can use alphabet books to explore reading and writing. Like other forms of literature, ABC books use literary conventions, such as plot, setting, and characters, and they can be used to introduce the young reader to some of the basic literary forms. When reading and examining an alphabet book, the parent or teacher can discuss where the story takes place, what characters are important, and the sequence of the book's action. Although preschoolers may not be ready for the critical analysis of literature, they are ready to tell you what happens next, who is in the story, and where it happens. In a gentle way, some alphabet books introduce issues that face children, such as cultural diversity, peace, and friendship. Many of the recent ABC books show children from all kinds of backgrounds working and playing together. ABC books also provide a structure for investigation and a model for invention. Some of the animal and science alphabet books encourage children to find out more information about a topic or challenge the reader to look for alphabet shapes in the world around them (as in *Archbet* and *Arlene Alda's ABC*). Exposure to words and how they can be turned, twisted, and manipulated into different meanings encourages a child to experiment with language and the offbeat possibilities for words, to manipulate words to create new visual images, and to extend their own learning experiences.

The potential for the use of alphabet books at the upper middle school and high school levels goes virtually unnoticed. While most alphabet books would not be suitable for use with older students, there are many that would be appropriate to use in a number of curriculum areas including science, English, social studies, and art. One way of presenting ABC books to older readers is to pair up books that cover similar topics. Readers can compare and contrast the illustrations and content materials to determine which book is more effective, why and how either title would be used, and whether the author achieved his purpose. Some titles that make good companion volumes include: 1. *Alphabet Garden* (Coats) and *Alison's Zinnia* (Lobel); 2. *Victory Garden Alphabet Book* (Pallotta) and *Eating the Alphabet* (Ehlert); 3. *A for the Ark* (Duvoisin) and *Aardvarks Disembark* (Jonas); 4. *The Z Was Zapped* (Van Allsburg) and *An Alphabet in Five Acts* (Andersen); 5. *A My Name Is Alice* (Bayer) and *I Love My Anteater with an A* (Ipcar); 6. *Anno's Alphabet* (Anno) and *Albert's Alphabet* (Tryon); and 7. *A Farmer's Alphabet* (Azarian) and *Farm Alphabet Book* (Miller). Dozens of other alphabet titles could also be paired for a closer look.

Alphabet books can be used with the middle grades to examine language and vocabulary, to explore other cultures and customs, to probe the world of nature and the environment, to study the techniques and media of artists, and to investigate for the pure enjoyment of reading. Teachers can introduce alphabet books and use them to help students hone their observational and discussion skills.

With preschoolers and primary age students, the best way to use an alphabet book is to read it and to discuss the information and illustrations in the book. With middle school students, you can take the discussion several steps higher by comparing and contrasting a wide assortment of ABC books. Bring in a wide variety of alphabet books from simple board books such as *Baby's ABCs* to the intricately illustrated ones like *The Annotated Ultimate Alphabet Book*. Divide the class into groups and examine the books. Talk about outstanding characteristics of the books including format, type of print, pictures, and art techniques. Develop a chart listing similarities and differences in ABC books that tackle comparable topics. Students can discuss their likes and dislikes of a particular title and evaluate it with a written or oral book review. Talk about the popularity of ABC books and let the students decide why they are so popular. These are only a few of the ways that you can use alphabet books with middle school students to develop critical thinking skills and for pure enjoyment.

On the high school level, alphabet books are excellent tools to use for vocabulary development, interest in language, and independent and creative thinking. Teachers will find them valuable sources for writing topics and techniques and as a means of encouraging an appreciation of art and illustration. ABC books provide a glimpse into the customs and cultures of people around the world and can be used to challenge students to look at the world from different perspectives. Other uses for alphabet books on the secondary level include an opportunity to provide a glimpse into the past and gain some historical insights, to serve as models for imaginative games, and to examine books for their scientific accuracy.

Perhaps the most obvious use of alphabet books on the high school and even the adult level is in the area of English and language arts. Alphabet books can be used as a means of encouraging students to discover words on their own and to increase their repertory of words based on their examination and perception of illustrations in books. They can be used as springboards for students to stretch the creativity and flexibility of their minds and imaginations. Several alphabet books concentrate on particular parts of speech or aspects of language, and they can be used to provide an interesting introduction to gerunds, nouns, adjectives, and curious words. Lecourt's *Abracadabra to Zigzag* is one of the best examples of curious or "ricochet" words and includes a glossary of the origins and meanings of such words as dilly dally, jeepers creepers, rolypoly and yoo-hoo. After looking at Lecourt's examples and their origins and meanings, students can create their own list of unusual words, slang, or colloquial terms.

Nouns, adjectives, and other parts of speech are usually considered boring topics by teenagers, but by using alphabet books as a means of livening up a discussion, teachers may find that their students take a real interest in the discussion. Sandra Boynton's *A is for Angry* is one alphabet book that transcends generations with whimsical animals and an alphabetical look at adjectives. The letter is the focal point of each page with one of Boynton's inventive beasts draped in and around it, demonstrating the adjective used in the sentence, such as the anteater appearing angry. Students can use her 26 examples as a springboard for creating their own list of alphabetical adjectives. In *Hosie's Alphabet,* Baskin combines a simple noun naming an animal with unusual descriptive adjectives such as furious fly and omnivorous swarming locust. Students can compare and contrast these two titles and discuss the use of adjectives to describe the illustrations, whether they are appropriate, and what other terms could be used instead of the ones the authors choose to use. The use of gerunds is another English concept that students are not particularly excited to learn about. But by using such books as *Busy ABC* by Hawkins and *ABC Say with Me* by Gundersheimer and demonstrating to students how gerunds can be integrated into stories and everyday language, learning becomes much more interesting. Another ABC book that is useful in a discussion on language and words is *Antics!* by Cathi Hepworth. In *Antics!,* the author uses a simple three-letter combination as the basis for her romp through the alphabet. Twenty-six unusual ants gambol through the pages and show the reader how three simple little letters can be a part of bigger words with a variety of meanings. This book is useful as a means of dissecting words and discussing how the combination of letters can create totally new words.

Alliterative rhyme and verse as well as poetic forms such as limericks and couplets are abundant in numerous alphabet books. They provide a unique opportunity for students to look at the ways that words can be put together to create unusual visual images. Many of the animal alphabet books as well as others use alliteration and tongue twisters as a means of conveying the alphabet in a fun and rhythmic manner. Everyone loves tongue twisters and such books as *Faint Frogs Feeling Feverish and Other Terrifically Tantalizing Tongue Twisters, Aster Aardvark's Alphabet Adventure,* and *All About Arthur* offer ample opportunites for children of all ages to test the strength of their read aloud skills. *Faint Frogs* features alliterative sentences describing animals engaged in unusual situations such as "Goats getting goggles." Carle's *All About Arthur* involves an ape crisscrossing the country meeting all kinds of new friends and places which are described in alliterative sentences, while *Aster Aardvark's Alphabet Adventure* is an unusual compilation of paragraphs of words all beginning with the same letter. After reading a page of Aster Aardvark's adventures aloud, the concept of alliteration will be permanently embedded in a student's memory.

Poetry and verse are evident in all kinds of alphabet books from nursery rhymes to Edward Lear, the master of the nonsense verse. X. J. Kennedy, Eve Merriam, and Sylvia Cassedy use free verse, rhyming couplets, and other poetic forms in their alphabet poetry books. High school students can study ABC books featuring alliteration and rhyme as models for writing their own verse and for a deeper understanding of the power of the written word in creating visual images.

Close examination of the words and word combinations in alphabet books can serve as a basis for writing topics and as examples of descriptive writing. *"C" is for Clown* by the Berenstains shows how words all beginning with the same letter can be built upon in a pyramid style. Students can make a list of words that go together and then build them up into a pyramid style. ABC books can provide all kinds of ideas for writing and vocabulary projects. Students can create their own literature-based dictionaries based on one work such as *The Scarlet Letter* or just focus on one letter and use that letter to create a list of words describing a particular character or event in a book. By examining the intricately detailed drawings in ABC books like *The Annotated Ultimate Alphabet* and *Dr. Moggle's Alphabet Challenge,* they can use the word identifications and find or write definitions for them. Divide the class into groups and assign each group a letter to investigate in one of these complicated books. Students can literally spend hours poring over the illustrations and trying to identify all the objects for the letter on each page. They can write definitions and sentences for different words and present their findings to the class as a whole. *Animalia* by Base is another title that is useful with high school students but is also one that middle school students would find fascinating. Another exercise to use with this type of alphabet book is to have students write descriptive paragraphs or essays describing all the items that they find on a particular page. Dozens of details found on each page could serve as story starters or as inspiration for descriptive writing.

High schools students can look at alphabet books like *A Peaceable Kingdom* and *The Folks in the Valley* to provide insights into the history of different areas of the country and the people who settled there. Other books like *Illuminations* and *Hieroglyphs from A to Z* take a look at the distant history, customs, and lifestyles of earlier time periods. Geography is the subject of alphabet books like *Alphabet Annie Announces an All-American Album, Texas Alphabet, A Northern Alphabet,* and *Antler, Bear, Canoe.* Students can use these books to trace the travels of a character or the locations mentioned in a story on a map. Alphabet books are an interesting and unusual resource to use to help students polish their map skills and geographic sense.

Alphabet books know no age boundaries and can be utilized in any area of study with a little imagination and creativity. The content, art, and illustration in alphabet books make them adaptable to a variety of curricular areas, as well as serving as vehicles for cooperative learning and as a basis for further research projects. They challenge readers to seek more information on their own and to develop their own alphabetical lists on a variety of topics. Students of all ages can write ABC books for their states or other geographic locations, for famous people, heroes, or their own families. They can study animals, plants, and marine life in alphabet books by Jerry Pallotta; research flowers and gardening techniques based on *A Garden Alphabet* or *Alison's Zinnia;* read about space travel in *Astronaut to Zodiac* and *Space Words;* learn about camouflage, adaptation, and symbiosis in *Under the Sea;* examine architectural features and building techniques in *Architects Make Zigzags* and *Albert's Alphabet;* and study the past in *Illuminations* and *ABC Book of Early America.* These alphabet books and over 500 more, many with related activities, are described in the following chapters.

2. FIRST ENCOUNTERS: ALPHABET BOOKS FOR BABIES, TODDLERS, AND PRESCHOOLERS

During the past 20 years research has shown that even infants can benefit from looking at and being read to from books. By being exposed to words and sounds from birth, a baby begins to understand sound patterns and to gradually develop comprehension skills that permit it to attach meaning to the sounds around it. Children who are exposed to books and to reading at a very early age are also developing skills that are essential for learning to read: skills such as how to handle books, beginning concepts about the printed word, and even the form and structure of stories. Young children respond to stimulation by and interaction with language, and research shows that early exposure to books and language, as well as time to discuss the contents of a book, are key elements in a child's road to literacy and to successful reading experiences. Researchers who support the idea that early exposure to language is effective include: Nancy N. DeSalvo in *Beginning with Books;* Laura B. Smolkin and David B. Yaden in "O is for Mouse" in *Language Arts,* October 1992; and Lea M. McGee and Donald J. Richgels in "K is for Kristen's" in *The Reading Teacher,* December 1989.

The publishing field has jumped into the market with an onslaught of baby's first books, board books, and chubby books for toddlers in order to fulfill the public's desire to acquaint the preschooler with words and pictures. The baby's first books are usually constructed of cloth, vinyl, or nontoxic plastic materials that are not harmful to babies who tend to chew on everything in sight and put sticky fingers on things. The sturdy "board" books and chubby books for toddlers are constructed of heavy laminated cardboard or plastic that can withstand the tearing onslaught of small fingers. In addition to these durable books, there are toy or mechanical books with pop-up figures, pull tabs, and lift-the-flaps as well as beginner books with simple identification text and pictures that are appropriate for the young preschool child. Board books, chubbies, and mechanical books are all welcome additions to the world of children's literature. Not only are they useful for encouraging language, cognitive learning, and direct interaction with the text and pictures, but they are also a pleasant introduction to a relationship with books that will hopefully extend into older childhood and adulthood.

Although there are literally hundreds of titles currently available for the early reader, there are only a dozen or so that are specifically labelled alphabet books. Most of these books have either little or no text and usually involve simple identification of objects on the pages with little or no background clutter to distract from the object being identified. Using photographs, especially of babies and small children doing familiar activities, is a popular trend in board and toddler books. Familiar characters such as the Muppet babies and the Richard Scarry animals are particularly good to use with babies and toddlers. *Thomas's ABC Book* is a good example of a beginner book that employs a familiar character to introduce the letters of the alphabet. The "Thomas the Tank Engine" series is popular with children, and the alphabet book featuring Thomas satisfies the fascination with trains while at the same time introducing the alphabet. The pages are sturdy enough to withstand heavy use by little ones, the text is simple, and the photographs are bright and cheerful. Two small board books for very young children (8 months and up) that feature familiar characters are *The Muppet Babies ABC* and *Richard Scarry's Cars and Trucks from A to Z.* In the first title, Miss Piggy, Kermit the Frog, and the rest of the Muppet baby gang use familiar objects to introduce the letters of the alphabet to children. Not only are these characters familiar by virtue of television, but they also use bright colorful pictures of objects like gloves, apples, and more to emphasize the featured letter. Richard Scarry's animal characters have been popular with children for several decades. In his board book, characters motor through the alphabet in all sorts of real and imaginary vehicles from an ambulance, jeep, and mail truck to an apple car, egg truck, peanut car, and zippermobile. The cartoonish characters and the silly vehicles will bring giggles to babies and toddlers alike.

In addition to the small board books designed for children from about 8 months and up, there are board books or "chubbies" that are designed especially for toddlers (ages 1½ to around 4). These books are made of the same sturdy laminated cardboard, but they are just a little bigger in size and include content materials more sophisticated than the early board books. One of the best of the toddler board books is *Alphabite* by Charles Reasoner and Vicky Hardt. The book is oblong in shape with an apple on the cover. The unique thing about this board book is that the apple as well as all of the pages have a large bite taken out of them. The bite starts on the front cover and goes all the way through the pages and back cover. Someone has been eating an alphabet of goodies, and it isn't until the very last page that the reader discovers who the culprit is. Children enjoy examining the bites from the foods as well as trying to guess who could possibly be eating them.

Rodney Peppe has created another unusual toddler board book in *Rodney Peppe: The ABC Index*. Along the right side of the book is a thumb index showing what letters are contained on each page. The child can choose to jump around the alphabet by using the thumb index. The text uses familiar objects for the two letters on each double page, but with the distinctive feature of making the letters interdependent upon one another. For example, apples are used for the letter A while on the B page the apples are found in a basket; O stands for octopus, and on the P page the octopus is in pajamas. In a third title designed for toddlers, *A is for Apple,* the cover is sturdy laminated cardboard, but the pages inside are paper. The drawings are almost childlike, using simple outlines and bright bold colors. All of the objects shown with the letters begin with the sound of the letter as well as the letter itself. This book is invaluable for prereaders in reinforcing sound and letter connections.

The creators of the colorful photographic Eyewitness series have an alphabet book entry of their own. *My First ABC Book* uses bright, colorful photographs of familiar objects on a stark white background to introduce the letters of the alphabet one by one. Alphie, the Alphabet Builder, is shown on the bottom of each page to help provide continuity throughout the book. Children love to look at colorful photographs and try to identify familiar objects. *From Apple to Zipper* by Nora Cohen is another new title that uses bright colorful pictures on a stark white background. In this book, however, the shape of the objects is integrated with the letter of the alphabet, providing familiar objects with an unusual twist. For example, A is an apple with a bite out of it, P is a pencil bent into the shape of the letter, S is formed from a seahorse, and Z is a zipper being unzipped. *ABC: An Alphabet Book* by Thomas Mattiesen was published almost 30 years ago, but it still is an excellent example of an alphabet book that is perfect to use with the preschooler. Using a plain background with color photographs of familiar objects, such as balloons, shoes, and an umbrella, along with clear letters and one-word identifications makes Mattiesen's book an excellent choice for the beginner. In addition to the one-word identification of the object in the photograph, Mattiesen also includes a brief paragraph describing the object and things to do with it. The paragraph is not necessary, but it does allow the teacher or parent to extend the use of the book to primary age children. All three of these titles, *From Apple to Zipper, ABC: An Alphabet Book,* and *My First ABC Book* provide ample opportunity for the preschooler to practice letter recognition and identification skills of real objects.

The wordless alphabet book *Still Another Alphabet Book* by Chwast and Moskof offers an unusual look at the entire alphabet on each page. A frieze of letters appears on each page, but the letters that make up the word of the featured object are highlighted in a different color. For example, on the Q page a queenly character appears in the center, while in the alphabet frieze the letters that make up the word "queen" appear in a different color than the rest of the letters.

Children are fascinated by mechanical books like the pop-up, lift-the-flap, and pull-tab books. They stimulate a child to interact with the pictures and the words on the page and to speculate about what is under the flap or tab. Children's curiosities are aroused as they speculate on the hidden objects, and they enjoy trying to guess what is under a flap before lifting or pulling to discover whether their guesses are correct. These mechanical books are useful in providing early reading experiences for the young child. As is evident from professional journal and review sources, the number of mechanical books being published are ever increasing. *Marie Angel's Exotic Alphabet* is an unusual lift-the-flap alphabet book that includes a collection of exotic creatures on one side and a 9-foot-long decorative frieze that folds out from the book. Although all kinds of animals are shown in the jungles around the world, it is only when the flap is lifted that the child finds a letter and a word to identify a creature for each of the 26 letters. A fold-out frieze is also a part of Tracy Pearson's *A Apple Pie*. Pearson focuses on a huge apple pie that makes its way down a long dinner table where all kinds of things happen to it, from T trodding on it to Y yearning for it. The book unfolds to reveal the table and all the children that the apple pie encounters.

Another atypical lift-the-flap alphabet book is Chuck Reasoner's *A Big Alphabet Book*. Instead of creating a page-turning A to Z guide to animals, Reasoner has filled an oversized cardboard backing with rows of letters that when lifted reveal humorous creatures cavorting underneath. With four letter flaps across and seven down, the reader can lift his way to a humorous trip through the alphabet from artistic alligator, friendly fox, and kissing kangaroo to tiger tails and zebras catching zzzz's. Robert Crowther has designed an interesting mechanical book, *The Most Amazing Hide-and-Seek Alphabet Book,* that uses both pull tabs and pop-ups to help develop letter concepts. Young readers must follow the arrows on the letters to discover what is hidden beneath each letter.

In the pop-up category, David Pelham's *A is for Animals* is one that stands out above the rest. The child need only lift a flap for the animal to pop up and greet him. Bright colorful pictures are used to present familiar and some not so familiar animals. The only drawback to this book and to most mechanical type books is that they are not very durable and are quickly torn and broken.

Jan Pienkowski always produces books that are child appealing, but in *ABC Dinosaurs and Other Prehistoric Creatures* she has produced an extraordinary volume. Not only is the topic of dinosaurs ever popular, but the combination of bold colors and computer-generated graphics with pull tabs and pop-up dinosaurs is guaranteed to rouse the interest of children of all ages. The computer graphics on the pages challenge the reader to find the featured letter shown as the initial letter of the name of the dinosaur, from allosaurus to zephyrosaurus.

In addition to all the ABC board books, mechanical books, and beginner books, many publishers are also producing small versions of picture book alphabet books. *Chicka Chicka Boom Boom* is available in two formats; one is the original picture book style, and a second is a board book version of this very popular title. *Animalia* is another title that has been printed in a small-format edition so that even the youngest reader can enjoy its intricately designed illustrations and menagerie of familiar and exotic creatures.

Books for the youngest readers are basically identification books with little or no text. The pictures should be simple and familiar to the preschooler, and the child should be able to give their version of the contents of the illustrations. Common terms, not confusing ones, should be used—cat and not kitty. Even the mechanical books such as pop-ups, lift the flaps, and pull tabs should follow the simple identification format. Research in the past twenty years has shown that children begin learning from infancy, and early exposure to language and activities can help children develop the story sense they need for reading skills, as well as contributing to language development. Alphabet books are one type of reading material that can be used to stimulate interaction with language, and the earlier a child is exposed to words the better their reading and language skills will become. By using board and toddler books as well as the mechanical ABC books, parents and teachers can help children get an early start on the road to literacy.

FIRST ENCOUNTERS: BIBLIOGRAPHY

A is for Apple. Illustrated by Lynn N. Grundy. Auburn, Maine: Ladybird Books, 1990. ISBN 0-7214-5052-0.
  The 26 letters of the alphabet are illustrated with bold pictures and one-word text.
TODDLER. Upper case.
ABC. New York: Lexicon Publications, Inc., 1990. ISBN 0-7172-4588-8.
  Twenty-six children and the things they love are used to introduce the alphabet.
BOARD BOOK. Upper case.
ABC in the Woods. Illustrated by Barbara Leonard Gibson. Washington D.C.: National Geographic, 1990. ISBN 0-7922-1832-9.
  This small board book provides an alphabetical look at the inhabitants of the woods.
BOARD BOOK. Upper and lower case.
ABC Just for Me. Illustrated by Mary Hildebrandt. The Unicorn Publishing House, 1992. ISBN 0-88101-246-7.
  The alphabet is introduced with bright colorful comic illustrations of familiar objects.
BEGINNER. Upper and lower case.
Angel, Marie. *Marie Angel's Exotic Alphabet*. New York: Dial Books for Young Readers, 1992. ISBN 0-8037-1247-2.
  An unusual lift-the-flap alphabet book that includes a bestiary of exotic creatures from the jungles of the world as well as a 9-foot-long decorative frieze.
LIFT-THE-FLAP BOOK. Upper and lower case.
The Animal's ABC. Mahwah, New Jersey: Troll Associates, 1988. ISBN 0-8167-1443-6.
  Animals from A to Z perform an array of tricks and stunts.
POP-UP BOOK. Upper case.
Awdry, Rev. W. *Thomas's ABC Book*. New York: Random House, 1990. ISBN 0-679-80362-9.
  An illustrated alphabet book about Thomas the tank engine and all of his friends.
BEGINNER BOOK. Upper case.
Baby's ABC. Illustrated by Bettina Paterson. New York: Grosset and Dunlap, Inc., 1992. ISBN 0-448-40130-4.
  Babies and toddlers can find their favorite things in this sturdy alphabet book.
BOARD BOOK. Upper case.
Baby's ABC. Photographs by Anita and Steve Shevett. New York: Random House, 1986. ISBN 0-394-87870-1.
  Photographs of very familiar objects such as apples, ball, crayons are used to introduce the alphabet.
BOARD BOOK. Upper and lower case.
Baby's First ABC. New York: Platt & Munk, 1992. ISBN 0-448-40864-3.
  Photos of familiar objects on sturdy pages are used to introduce the youngest readers to the alphabet.
BOARD BOOK. Upper case.
Boynton, Sandra. *A to Z*. New York: Little Simon, 1984. ISBN 0-671-49317-5.
  A simple ABC book of animals engaged in a variety of activities.
BOARD BOOK. Upper case.
Bunting, Jane. *My First ABC Book*. New York: Dorling Kindersley, 1993. ISBN 1-56458-403-8.
  Alphie, the Alphabet Builder, assembles the alphabet letter by letter in this photographic book of first words for the very young.
BEGINNER BOOK. Upper and lower case.
Charles, Donald. *Letters from Calico Cat*. Chicago, Illinois: Childrens Press, 1974. ISBN 0-516-03519-3.
  Calico Cat introduces the alphabet with simple text and words.
BEGINNER BOOK. Upper and lower case.
Chwast, Seymour, and Martin Stephen Moskof. *Still Another Alphabet Book*. New York: McGraw Hill, 1969.
  The letters of the alphabet appear in a frieze on each page with the letters of the word for the featured object highlighted in the frieze.
BEGINNER BOOK. Upper case.
Cleaver, Elizabeth. *ABC*. New York: Macmillan, 1985. ISBN 0-689-31072-2.
  Bright bold pictures and simple text are used to feature the letters of the alphabet and objects that begin with each letter.
BEGINNER BOOK. Upper and lower case.
Cohen, Nora. *From Apple to Zipper*. Illustrated by Donna Kern. New York: Aladdin Books, 1993. ISBN 0-689-71708-3.
  An alphabet book that combines rhyming text with pictures that form the letter that they represent.
BEGINNER BOOK. Upper case.
Crowther, Robert. *The Most Amazing Hide-and-Seek Alphabet Book*. New York: Viking, 1977. ISBN 0-670-48996-4.
  Using pop-ups and pull tabs, the letters of the alphabet and objects are introduced to the young reader.
POP-UP/PULL TAB BOOK. Upper and lower case.

Demi. *The Peek-A-Boo ABC*. New York: Random House, 1982. ISBN 0-394-85418-7.
   In this ingenious book, the young reader not only reads the simple text but also opens doors to find the drawings within drawings behind them.
LIFT-THE-FLAP BOOK. Upper and lower case.
Disney Babies A to Z. New York: Golden Press, 1989. ISBN 0-307-12317-0.
   Disney babies including Mickey, Donald, and the gang, introduce the alphabet in this sturdy board book.
BOARD BOOK. Upper case.
Dreamer, Sue. *Circus ABC*. Boston, Massachusetts: Little, Brown and Company, 1985. ISBN 0-316-1919-5.
   A parade of circus performers and animals demonstrate the letters of the alphabet.
BOARD BOOK. Upper case.
Dubin, Jill. *Little Bitties ABC*. New York: Barron's, 1991. ISBN 0-8120-6266-3
   Easily identifiable objects and bright colorful pictures present the alphabet in this "just right for little fingers" book.
BOARD BOOK. Upper and lower case.
Hatay, Nona. *Charlie's ABC*. New York: Hyperion Books for Children, 1993. ISBN 1-56282-353-1.
   Black and white photographs with spot hand coloring show a small child as he introduces the alphabet with very common objects.
BEGINNER BOOK. Lower case.
Hawkins, Colin, and Jacqui Hawkins. *I Spy: The Lift-The-Flap ABC Book*. Boston, Massachusetts: Little, Brown & Co., 1989. ISBN 0-316-35105-9.
   In this unusual alphabet book the reader is invited to lift the flap and spy some amazing things.
LIFT-THE-FLAP. Upper and lower case.
Hyman, Trina Schart. *A Little Alphabet*. New York: Morrow, 1980, 1993. ISBN 0-688-12034-2; 0-688-12035-0 (lib bdg)
   Updated version of a special wordless book that introduces 26 small worlds of everyday things.
BEGINNER BOOK. Upper case.
Jones, Lily. *Baby Kermit's Playtime ABC*. Illustrated by David Prebenna. Racine, Wisconsin: Western Publishing Company, Inc., 1992. ISBN 0-307-10024-3.
   Baby Kermit and the other Muppets present the ABC's through playthings and activities.
BEGINNER BOOK. Upper case.
Kightley, Rosalinda. *ABC*. Boston, Massachusetts: Little, Brown & Co., 1986. ISBN 0-316-49930-7.
   With bold bright pictures and simple text, the reader is introduced to the alphabet.
BEGINNER BOOK. Upper and lower case.
A Little ABC Book. New York: Little Simon, 1980. ISBN 0-671-41342-2.
   Rhyming sentences and familiar objects introduce the alphabet to the young reader.
TODDLER BOOK. Upper case.
Mattiesen, Thomas. *ABC: An Alphabet Book*. New York: Platt and Munk, 1966. ISBN 0-8228-1050-6.
   Full color photos of familiar objects from A to Z together with brief descriptions comprise this alphabet book.
BEGINNER BOOK. Upper and lower case.
Mickey's Daytime-Nighttime ABC. Philadelphia, Pennsylvania: Running Press, 1992. ISBN 1-56138-153-5.
   Mickey and his friends frolic through a daytime alphabet, and then the reader flips the book over for a view of the Disney characters as they go through a nighttime alphabet.
BOARD BOOK. Upper and lower case.
The Muppet Babies featuring Jim Henson's Muppets. New York: Random House, 1984. ISBN 0-391-86363-1.
   Kermit, Miss Piggy, and the rest of the Muppet babies gang introduce the letters of the alphabet.
BOARD BOOK. Upper case.
Murphy, Chuck. *My First Book of the Alphabet*. New York: Scholastic, Inc., 1992. ISBN 0-590-46304-7.
   Tiny little mice help lead the reader to discover the alphabet of simple things by simply lifting a flap.
LIFT-THE-FLAP/POP-UP BOOK. Upper and lower case.
My ABC. Illustrated by Anne and Mike Ricketts. Newmarket, England: Brimax Books, Ltd., 1991. ISBN 0-86112-776-5.
   In rhyming text, familiar objects and animals illustrate the letters of the alphabet.
TODDLER BOOK. Lower case.
My ABC's at Home. Illustrated by Maryann Cocca-Leffler. New York: Grosset and Dunlap, Inc., 1990. ISBN 0-448-02257-5.
   In an unusual twist, familiar objects from around the house such as gate, lamp, and refrigerator are used to introduce the alphabet.
BOARD BOOK. Upper case.
Oxenbury, Helen. *Helen Oxenbury's ABC of Things*. New York: Delacorte Press, 1971. ISBN 0-385-29290-2; 0-385-29291-0 (lib bdg).
   Oxenbury shows all kinds of familiar objects in her introduction to the alphabet for the very young reader.
BEGINNER BOOK. Upper and lower case.

Patrick, Denise Lewis. *Animal ABC's*. Illustrated by Kate Gleeson. Racine, Wisconsin: Western Pub. Co., Inc., 1990. ISBN 0-307-06127-2.
  Little Beasties use familiar objects to introduce the alphabet.
TODDLER BOOK. Upper case.
Patterson, Bettina. *Merry ABC*. New York: Grosset & Dunlap, 1993. ISBN 0-448-40553-9.
  Collage artwork is used to highlight the alphabet as it introduces the joyous celebrations of Christmas in alphabetical sequence.
BOARD BOOK. Upper case.
Pearson, Tracy Campbell. *A Apple Pie*. New York: Dial Press, 1986. ISBN 0-8037-0252-3.
  A huge apple pie makes its way down a dinner table and encounters all kinds of A to Z activities.
FOLD-OUT BOOK. Upper case.
Pelham, David. *A is for Animals*. New York: Simon and Schuster, 1991. ISBN 0-671-72495-9.
  In this unique alphabet book the author presents some familiar and some not-so familiar animals in pop-up format.
POP-UP BOOK. Upper and lower case.
Peppe, Rodney. *Rodney Peppe: The ABC Index*. New York: Bedrick/Blackie, 1991. ISBN 0-87226-441-6.
  With a side thumb index, familiar objects and animals are used to introduce the alphabet.
TODDLER BOOK. Upper and lower case.
Pienkowski, Jan. *ABC*. New York: Little Simon, 1973. ISBN 0-671-68133-8.
  Bright colorful illustrations of easily identifiable objects introduce the alphabet to the youngest reader.
BOARD BOOK. Upper and lower case.
———. *ABC Dinosaurs and Other Prehistoric Creatures*. New York: Lodestar Books, 1993. ISBN 0-525-67468-3.
  Pienkowski provides an ingenious pop-up alphabet book on the ever popular topic of dinosaurs.
POP-UP/PULL TAB BOOK. Upper case.
Piper, Watty. *The Little Engine That Could: Let's Sing ABC*. Illustrated by Cristina Ong. New York: Platt and Munk, 1993. ISBN 0-448-40509-1.
  The famous Little Blue Engine goes on a trip to find familiar objects A to Z.
LIFT-THE-FLAP BOOK. Upper case.
Pragoff, Fiona. *Alphabet from A-Apple to Z-Zipper*. Garden City, New York: Doubleday & Co., Inc., 1985. ISBN 0-385-24171-2.
  Photographs of everyday objects from A to Z are used in this beginning alphabet book.
BOARD BOOK. Upper and lower case.
Reasoner, Charles, and Vicky Hardt. *Alphabite! A Funny Feast from A to Z*. Los Angeles, California: Price Stern Sloan, Inc., 1989. ISBN 0-8431-2361-3.
  In this funny feast of ABCs, someone is eating an alphabet of goodies.
TODDLER BOOK. Upper and lower case.
Reasoner, Chuck, and Cary Pillo Lassen. *A Big Alphabet Book*. Los Angeles, California: Price Stern Sloan, Inc., 1993. ISBN 0-8431-3552-2.
  All kinds of whimsical creatures from A to Z are hiding under the flaps in this alphabet book.
LIFT-THE-FLAP BOOK. Upper case.
Ricklen, Neil. *Baby's ABC*. New York: Little Simon, 1990. ISBN 0-671-69540-1.
  Photographs of toddlers and familiar objects are used to introduce the alphabet.
TODDLER BOOK. Upper and lower case.
Ross, Anna. *Little Ernie's ABC*. Illustrated by Norman Gorbaty. New York: Random House, 1992. ISBN 0-679-82240-2.
  Using rhyming text and colorful pictures the Sesame Street characters introduce the alphabet from apple to zipper.
TODDLER BOOK. Upper and lower case.
Scarry, Richard. *Richard Scarry's ABC's*. Racine, Wisconsin: Western Publishing Company, Inc., 1991. ISBN 0-307-11515-1; 0-307-66515-1.
  When Charlie Chipmunk invites Big Hilda Hippo to dinner, he goes on an alphabet search for the proper foods to feed her.
TODDLER BOOK. Upper and lower case.
———. *Richard Scarry's Cars and Trucks from A to Z*. New York: Random House, 1990. ISBN 0-679-80663-6.
  Both real and imaginary vehicles are used in this trip through alphabet land.
BOARD BOOK. Upper and lower case.
Silverman, Marcia. *Baby's Book of ABC*. Illustrated by Kate Gleeson. Racine, Wisconsin: Western Publishing Company, Inc., 1993. ISBN 0-307-06037-3.
  A nontoxic, durable baby ABC book that uses simple, colorful animal illustrations to introduce the alphabet.
BOARD BOOK. Upper case.

————. *Bunny's ABC Box*. Illustrated by Ellen Blonder. New York: Grosset and Dunlap, 1986. ISBN 0-448-01464-5.
  Bunny and his friend discover all kinds of things from A to Z when they open a box layer by layer.
BOARD BOOK. Upper and lower case.
Tallarico, Tony. *Preschool Can You Find ABC Picture Book*. New York: Tuffy Books, 1992. ISBN 0-448-40426-5.
  This wordless alphabet book invites the reader to locate items A to Z in the pictures.
TODDLER BOOK. Upper and lower case,
Wynne, Patricia. *The Animal ABC*. New York: Random House, 1977. ISBN 0-394-83589-1.
  In this very simple beginner book the reader encounters all kinds of animals from A to Z.
BOARD BOOK. Upper case.

FIRST ENCOUNTERS: ACTIVITIES

While letter recognition and alphabetical order are items that may be beyond a baby or toddler's comprehension, recognition of familiar items and their names is not. Cut out large pictures of animals and objects that very young children could easily recognize. The pictures should be as simple as possible with very few complicated details. Mount the pictures on cardboard or heavy colored paper. In large print write the beginning letter for each object on the back. Laminate the pictures and use them as ABC Photograph flash cards.

After sharing *Animal ABC's* by Patrick, give the children precut simple outline shapes of some of the Little Beasties featured in the book. Children can color, paint, or decorate the beasties and make their own animal ABCs.

Richard Scarry's Cars and Trucks from A to Z is one board book that is popular with children of ages. The silly vehicles, bright colors, and cute animal characters are sure to bring smiles and giggles from the toddler age crowd. After reading and talking about the book, ask the children to make their own kind of motor vehicles from familiar objects (picklemobile, lollipop car, etc.). Have the child describe the vehicle (color, size, etc.) and if possible draw a picture of it.

Another activity to use with toddlers and preschoolers is to make scrambled ABC puzzles. Using bold colors, print each letter on a 6″ square of cardboard. On the back of the cardboard, mount a picture of a familiar object that begins with that letter. Laminate the cardboard ABC squares, and then cut them apart into four to six puzzle pieces. As the children put them back together they can practice identifying both the objects and the alphabet letters.

Scrambled letters is another alphabet activity that is good to use with preschoolers as a means of differentiating between lower and upper case letters. Use 3″–6″ squares and write upper case letters on the top half of the card and lower case letters on the bottom half. Laminate the cards and cut them apart. Mix up the cards and let the children put them back together matching the upper and lower case versions of each letter. When they are finished, have them put the entire set into ABC order.

Many types of activities involving letter and sound recognition, alphabetizing skills, and other alphabet adventures can be found in teachers' resource books. Several of these books are listed in the bibliography at the end of this book.

3. ANIMALS AND ALPHABET BOOKS

Animals are the most popular topic for alphabet books. There are literally dozens of animal alphabet books available on the market. They vary greatly in their approach: the simple letter and animal on a page, the complicated text and intricately detailed illustrations, and the alphabetical story adventure. Animal alphabet books contain a wide variety of animals from the real to the imagined. They include fictional characters such as Winnie the Pooh, familiar real animals that are easily recognized and labelled, unfamiliar animals with unusual names, and fictional animals with little resemblance to real creatures. Animals give an added dimension to a book while introducing the letters, telling a well-known story, or teaching a rhyme or song. Because animals offer a familiar, comforting tone to a book, their use in alphabet books is a natural extension of teaching reading skills. The use of animals in board, mechanical, and beginner books has already been discussed in the "First Encounters" chapter. Animal alphabet books are also discussed in other chapters in this book.

Familiar animals that are easily recognized and identified by children of all ages are used in the most popular type of animal alphabet book. They include those that use drawings of familiar animals such as bears, dogs, and cats as well as those that include photographs or detailed realistic drawings of unfamiliar animals such as cockatoos and voles. Many of the animal books used with preschoolers utilize colored drawings such as *The Big Golden Animal ABC* by Garth Williams, *Animal Parade* by Jakki Wood, or *Where Is Everybody? An Animal Alphabet* by Eve Merriam. Color drawings entice children to look closely at the pictures and attempt to identify the characters on the pages.

Other animal books that can be used for all ages include those that employ photographs of animals or exactingly realistic drawings of unfamiliar animals. *A is for Animals* by Gayle Shirley uses drawings and paragraphs of factual information to present a portrait of the diversity of animal life on earth. On the left side of the double page spread is a colored illustration of one animal and a fanciful rhyme about it. On the facing page is a paragraph or two giving factual information about the animal and one to three other animals whose names begin with the featured letter. The other animals are black and white sketches accompanied by all kinds of facts about them. Hope Ryden has two volumes, *Wild Animals of Africa ABC* and *Wild Animals of America ABC*, that use color photographs to present an alphabetical account of animals from two regions of the world. *The Alphabet in Nature* by Judy Feldman is another title that uses colored photographs to present an alphabetical roll call of animals in nature. All of the animal alphabet books by Jerry Pallotta (listed in the science section, chapter 7) use detailed realistic colored illustrations to show animals in their natural habitat. By using photographs and intricate, realistic drawings of real animals to introduce the alphabet, children have the opportunity to not only practice letter recognition but to also develop a familiarity with uncommon animals.

The Shakers used an abecedarius (26 lines of rhymed verse) about animals to teach the alphabet, and there are two books that used an illustrated abecedarius to present the alphabet to today's readers. *A Peaceable Kingdom* by Alice and Martin Provensen is an illustrated version of the abecedarius that was published in the Shaker Manifesto in July 1882 under the title "Animal Rhymes." Each of the 26 lines contains the names of four animals, and each line begins with each successive letter of the alphabet. Michele Clise has adapted the Shaker abecedarius, changed a few words, and used black, white, and gray sketches for illustrations to create her alphabet version in a fold-out frieze. The singsong rhyming verse makes both titles good to use with young children just learning their ABC's.

Animal Alphabet by Bert Kitchen is one of the best all-around alphabet books to use with any age. This oversized book meets the criteria for the perfect alphabet book for the youngest child. Each page has only a very large letter and an animal whose name begins with that letter. A plain white background, familiar animals, and clear letters make this a good book to use with the very young. Older students can use the illustrations as a means of identifying animals or for visual art appreciation. A list of the names of the animals is found in the back of the book.

Kate Duke's *The Guinea Pig ABC* follows a simple alphabet form. Very large upper case letters dominate the page with guinea pigs in and around the letter demonstrating a simple concept such as awake, clean, greedy, etc. The concepts are simple, the letters are highly visible, and the illustrations are easily identified. *Ape in a Cape* by Fritz Eichenberg is another simple identification alphabet book, but instead of one word a rhyming phrase is used to identify each animal (e.g. Mouse in a blouse, Goat in a boat). This book was selected as a Caldecott Honor Book in 1953. The illustrations are pen and ink sketches with some color shading. Sandra Boynton also uses the single letter animal format in her *A is for Angry*. A large brightly colored upper case letter is in the center of the page. Usually one but sometimes two animals whose names begin with the featured letter are draped in and around the letter and are shown demonstrating the adjective used to describe it. For example, E is for energetic with an elephant energetically holding up the letter E. The clever use of bright colors and alliteration make Boynton's book one that can be enjoyed over and over again.

Hosie's Alphabet by Leonard Baskin is a rather unusual alphabet book. Each watercolor illustration, along with descriptive text that uses some unusual and unfamiliar adjectives to describe the animals, covers a full page. The text in this book is better listened to than read by the young child. For example, the locust used for the letter L is described as "the omnivorous swarming" locust, and the zebra for Z is labelled a "ruminating" zebra. The text is more suitable for older children, and it would require some explanation with preschoolers. *Hosie's Alphabet* is one alphabet book that would be particularly useful with upper middle school and high school students in a discussion on descriptive adjectives and vocabulary expansion. Baskin received a Caldecott Honor Award for *Hosie's Alphabet* in 1973.

Although at first glance, *Ed Emberley's ABC* would appear to be a simple letter alphabet, a second look shows that it is more complex. Not only is the letter shown, but a series of four pictures across the page demonstrates how it is formed. An ant in an airplane skywrites the letter across the page, and a bear watches as a bug uses blueberries from a basket to build a letter step by step. Emberley's alphabet book is useful to share with children just learning to make their letters and to help them develop their own alphabet stories.

One of the most popular alphabet books with both children and adults is *Animalia* by Graeme Base. Base uses very detailed—almost three dimensional—lush colored illustrations in his oversized alphabet book on animals. The text uses alliterative sentences to describe each animal, but dozens of other animals and objects beginning with each letter are found in the densely packed illustrations. As an added bonus, Base tells the reader on the title page that if they look carefully, they can find a small boy (supposedly Base) hidden somewhere in the illustrations. Finding all the alphabet objects in the rich opulent illustrations and the hidden boy provides intrigue and entertainment for all ages for hours. *The Cow Is Mooing Anyhow* by Laura Geringer is another alphabet book that uses a kind of puzzle and animals to present the alphabet. Although not as intricately illustrated or as colorful as *Animalia,* this title does provide an interesting change of pace for the alphabet. On two pages, in the front and in the back of the book, all of the letters and animals are shown in alphabetical order. The letters of the alphabet also border the pages, and as a featured letter is presented in the text, it is highlighted in the border. As a little girl eats her breakfast, a parade of animals in scrambled ABC order join her. The alphabet is presented in mixed up order rather than in the traditional A to Z fashion.

From Albatross to Zoo by Patricia Borlenchi is a multilingual alphabet book. When a little bird searches in a jungle, he finds an alphabetical array of animals. The animals' names are given in five different languages, handwritten so as to capture the distinctive style of the language. English, German, French, Spanish, and Italian words for each animal are listed on the pages.

Cats galore is the only way to describe the number of alphabet books featuring cats of all sizes, shapes, and breeds. Some feature only one cat who takes the reader on a alphabetical tour of his day and life, such as *ABC Cat* by Jewell, *Annie's ABC Kitten* by Steiner, and *Sue Boettcher's Black Cat ABC*. Jewell's book follows a mischievous cat through a day's activities while a black cat in Boettcher's book shows the reader all the different personalities and traits of a cat such as guilty cat, scavenging cat, and jealous cat. *Annie's ABC Kitten* is the story of a little girl who finds a cat on her doorstep and decides to take it in. *Miss Hindy's Cats* employs the same 'lost cat looking for a home' theme, but in this case Miss Hindy finds herself with 26 stray cats and a new home. *Alphabet Cat* by Floyd Black is all about a detective cat who goes in search of a kidnapped Countess. Rats are responsible, and the reader is asked to identify objects beginning with the letters of the alphabet as well as the multitude of cliches in the humorous story. Three other cat alphabet books, *The Kittens ABC, A Cat Alphabet,* and *Comic and Curious Cats* include all kinds of cats and kittens introducing the letters of the alphabet. *Comic and Curious Cats* uses an old game, "I love my . . ." to introduce a cat and the reasons to want it. All three of these titles show the ordinary lives of all kinds of cats as they chase birds and insects, sleep, play, and eat.

Ipcar also uses the old "I love my . . ." game as part of her alphabet book, *I Love My Anteater with An A.* Ipcar uses full color illustrations in shades of purple, maize, brown, and black, and a five line poem describing why the animal is loved and hated as well as the name, food, location, and occupation of the animal. All of this is done using the featured letter.

Isabelle Brent's *An Alphabet of Animals* is more than just a simple animal alphabet book. Each double page spread includes the letter of the alphabet and one word identifying the animal and a colorful picture trimmed in gold. Along with the letter and animal's name, there is detailed information such as the physical features, eating habits, and habitat of the animal. Brent's book serves as good reference source on 26 different animals as well as a simple animal book for the young child.

Demi's Find the Animal ABC is both an animal and a guessing game alphabet book, and it is an excellent resource to use with children of all ages. A small box identifies the animal that represents the letter of the alphabet. It also serves as a reference point for the reader to find that animal in the box in the larger picture on the page. The larger picture is usually an outline of the animal (e.g., E-elephant) with dozens of small animals drawn within it. The child has to locate the exact replica of the small animal in the box within the larger animal. Black and white pages are alternated with color pictures. Demi's book is available in Big Book format which makes it easier to use with large groups of children.

In *As I Was Crossing Boston Common* by Norma Farber, all sorts of uncommon but real creatures are used to introduce the alphabet. The line-up includes both alphabetical and zoological names of these unusual animals. A glossary in the back gives pronunciation and background details on the animals named in the story.

The most popular fictional introducers of the alphabet are teddy bears. There are no less than four titles that use teddy bears and their activities to present the letters of the alphabet. Of the four titles, Kathleen Hague's *Alphabears* is the best. The illustrations are bright and colorful, the rhyming couplets include the letter of the alphabet in large print, and the description of the special quality for each bear is delightful. *The Teddy Bear ABC* by Laura Rinkle Johnson uses softer colors and rhyming text to show some of the activities and characteristics of teddy bears, while Susanna Gretz's entry in the field, *Teddy Bear ABC,* uses an adventure story format to present five bears whose alphabetical adventures often turn into mishaps (fleas start hopping, a giraffe has a sore throat, a yak won't budge). *Teddy Bears ABC* uses brief rhyming text, bold bright colors, and unrealistic round-body bears to introduce bear activities from A to Z to the very youngest readers. While all of these titles vary in their methods of presenting the ABCs of teddy bears, they all have one thing in common: they appeal to very young children through the use of a comfortable topic.

Using animals to integrate the alphabet into a story line is one way to introduce the letters to children. Although alphabet stories are dealt with in another section in this book, there are several animal alphabet stories that are best dealt with here and now. Wanda Gag's *The ABC Bunny* has been around for a long time, but it is still popular with children. A bunny runs away when an apple falls on him, and on his adventure he meets all kinds of animals from A to Z. The oversized black and white lithographs still appeal to children. On a more humorous note, *Alligator Arrived with Apples* by Crescent Dragonwagon is the tale of a Thanksgiving feast with animals bringing all kinds of food from A to Z. The comic, colorful illustrations and rhythmic text make for a great holiday read-aloud as well as an interesting way to introduce the alphabet. Victoria Chess integrates all kinds of A to Z words and animals in her story, *Alfred's Alphabet Walk.* On his walk, Alfred meets lots of animals doing a variety of alphabetical activities. While Chess does not formally present the letters of the alphabet, they are emphasized as a part of the text. Noted artist Eric Carle presents a humorous tale of a lonely ape named Arthur in his unusual alphabet book, *All About Arthur (An Absolutely Absurd Ape).* Carle intersperes linoleum cuts of Arthur and his friends with color photographs of the letters of the alphabet. The photographs are of the letters in natural settings on brick walls, signs, billboards, sweaters, sidewalks, etc. Arthur travels from city to city and meets all kinds of musical animals from a banjo-playing bear to a bewhiskered walrus and a zany yak who plays a zither. The alliterative text and linocuts ensure that generations of children will enjoy reading about Arthur over and over again.

Animals are an integral part of the story of Noah's ark, and two alphabet picture books take very different approaches to presenting this legend. In *A for The Ark* by Roger Duvoisin, the story of Noah and the flood is told as the animals enter the ark in alphabetical order. The story line becomes more complex with a retelling of previous events each time a new letter is introduced. *Aardvarks Disembark!* by Ann Jonas begins with the end of the flood and the animals descending from the ark in backwards alphabetical order. Duvoisin's illustrations are pen and ink with some bright primary colors, while Jonas's book shows a multitude of animals in bright, colorful watercolor illustrations. Roger Duvoisin includes one or two familiar animals for each letter of the alphabet; Jonas's book is a litany of unfamiliar animals. After the familiar animals disembark, Noah realizes that he doesn't know the names of the animals left on board. As they descend in backwards ABC order, their names and a drawing are shown on the pages. In the back is a glossary identifying each of the familiar and unfamiliar animals that existed in Noah's time as well as codes marking the animals that are now extinct or endangered.

Dozens of animal alphabet books are available for use with students of all ages and sizes. They range from the comfortable teddy bear tales to a parade of unusual creatures crossing Boston Common. Although the contents may vary, the purpose of each of these animal books remains the same: to entertain and amuse the reader while presenting words and objects for the letters of the alphabet.

ABC. Illustrated by Colin Twinn. New York: Viking Press, 1989. ISBN 0-7232-3604-6.
   Based on famous rabbit characters created in the 1930's, this is the A to Z story of twin bunnies and their first day at school.
AGES 3–7.

Argent, Kerry. *Animal Capers*. New York: Dial Books for Younger Readers, 1989. ISBN 0-8037-0718-5; 0-8037-0752-5 (lib bdg).
   A parade of animals from anteater to zebra greet the reader in the pages of this alphabet book.
AGES 4–7. Upper and lower case.

Arnosky, Jim. *Mouse Numbers and Letters*. New York: Harcourt Brace Jovanovich, 1982. ISBN 0-15-256022.
   A mouse attempts to construct letters of the alphabet from twigs that he found.
AGES 3–6.

———. *Mouse Writing*. New York: Harcourt Brace Jovanovich, 1983. ISBN 0-15-256028-9.
   Two small mice on ice skates trace the letters of the alphabet in cursive writing.
AGES 3–6. Upper and lower case.

Barry, Robert. *Animals Around the World*. New York: McGraw-Hill Books Co., 1967.
   Through verse and black and white illustrations, a presentation from A to Z of animals from around the world.
AGES 5–9.

Base, Graeme. *Animalia*. New York: Harry N. Abrams, Inc., 1986. ISBN 0-8109-1868-4.
   Alliterative sentences and lavishly colored pictures are used to introduce all kinds of animals and objects from A to Z.
ALL AGES. Upper case.

Baskin, Leonard. *Hosie's Alphabet*. Pictures by Leonard Baskin; words by Hosia Tobias, Lisa Baskin. New York: The Viking Press, 1972. ISBN 0-670-37958-1.
   With abstract watercolors and unique adjectives, the reader is treated to all kinds of animals from A to Z.
PRESCHOOL–GRADE 4. Upper case.

Biondi, Janet. *D is for Dolphin*. Text by Cami Berg. Illustrations by Janet Biondi. Sante Fe, New Mexico: Windom Books, 1991. ISBN 1-879244-01-2.
   Using blue water as a background and simple text, an alphabetical guide to dolphin life.
ALL AGES. Upper case.

Black, Floyd. *Alphabet Cat*. Illustrated by Carol Nicklaus. New York: Gingerbread House/Elsevier-Dutton, 1979.
   Detective alphabet cat is on a search for the kidnapped Countess and must find the culprits somewhere in the alphabet.
AGES 6–9. Upper and lower case.

Blackwell, Deborah. *An ABC Bestiary*. New York: Farrar, Straus, Giroux, 1989. ISBN 0-374-30005-4.
   In bright fluorescent colors, the animals line up to show their ABC's, from aardvark arranging art to x-marked yak zooming.
AGES 3 AND UP. Upper and lower case.

Boettcher, Sue. *Sue Boettcher's Black Cat ABC*. London, England: Souvenir Press, 1991. ISBN 0-285-63062-8.
   A black cat leads the way through the alphabet and shows the different sides and traits of a cat.
AGES 3–7. Upper case.

Borlenchi, Patricia. *From Albatross to Zoo: An Alphabet Book in Five Languages*. Pictures by Piers Harper. New York: Scholastic, 1992. ISBN 0-590-45483-8.
   A little bird searches a special jungle and finds all kinds of animals from A to Z, in five different languages.
AGES 4 AND UP. Upper and lower case.

Boynton, Sandra. *A is for Angry*. New York: Workman Publishing, 1983, 1987. ISBN 0-89480-453-7; 0-89480-507-X (soft).
   From an angry anteater to a zany zebra, a host of alliterative animals introduce the letters of the alphabet.
AGES 4 AND UP. Upper case.

Brent, Isabelle. *An Alphabet of Animals*. Boston, Massachusetts: Little, Brown & Co., 1993. ISBN 0-316-10852-9.
   An alphabet of exotic animals, birds, and insects illustrated in colorful pictures are accompanied by a potpourri of facts about each creature in this informative alphabet book.
ALL AGES. Upper case.

Broomfield, Robert. *The Baby Animal ABC*. New York: Penguin, 1968. ISBN 0-14-050006-5 (soft).
   Baby animals are used to introduce the letters of the alphabet.
AGES 3 AND UP. Upper and lower case.

Buckman, Mary. *The Alphagate*. San Mateo, California: Mary Bee Creations, 1992. ISBN 1-879414-104
   When a green creature eats groups of letters, all kinds of crazy activities happen in his stomach.
AGES 4 AND UP.

Bunnies' ABC. Illustrated by Garth Williams. Racine, Wisconsin: Western Publishing Company, Inc., 1957, 1954. ISBN 0-307-03050-4; 0-307-60328-8
   In this Little Golden book, familiar animals are used to introduce the letters of the alphabet.
AGES 2–6. Upper and lower case.
Carle, Eric. *All About Arthur (An Absolutely Absurd Ape)*. New York: Franklin Watts, 1974. ISBN 0-531-02662-0.
   Arthur, the lonely ape, goes on an alphabetical tour of U.S. cities and makes all kinds of new friends.
ALL AGES. Upper case.
Carter, Angela. *Comic and Curious Cats*. Illustrated by Martin Leman. New York: Harmony, 1979.
   Full color illustrations and verses explaining why "I love . . ." introduce the ABC's and all kinds of cats.
AGES 5 AND UP.
Charles, Donald. *Shaggy Dog's Animal Alphabet*. Chicago, Illinois: Childrens Press, 1979. ISBN 0-516-03574-2.
   Shaggy dog presents a list of animals from A to Z.
AGES 3–5. Upper case.
Chwast, Seymour. *The Alphabet Parade*. Orlando, Florida: Harcourt Brace Jovanovich, 1991. ISBN 0-15-200351-7.
   As a parade of animals and other characters go by, over 300 items can be found in the pictures from A to Z.
AGES 4 AND UP. Upper and lower case.
Chouinard, Roger, and Mariko Chouinard. *The Amazing Animal Alphabet Book*. Illustrated by Roger Chouinard. Garden City, New York: Doubleday and Co., Inc., 1988. ISBN 0-385-24099-5; 0-385-24030-9.
   Through a series of alliterative phrases the reader is introduced to some unusual animals and the letters of the alphabet.
PRESCHOOL–GRADE 3. Upper and lower case.
Clise, Michele Durkson. *Animal Alphabet Folding Screen*. San Francisco, California: Chronicle Books, 1992. ISBN 0-8118-0152-7.
   In lilting, singsong rhythmic verse, an array of animals is revealed as the book unfolds into a frieze.
AGES 4 AND UP.
Demi. *Demi's Find the Animal ABC*. New York: Putnam, 1985. ISBN 0-448-18970-4
   Demi combines simple animal identification with a seek-and-find guessing game for animals from A to Z.
ALL AGES. Upper and lower case.
Dragonwagon, Crescent. *Alligator Arrived with Apples: A Potluck Alphabet Feast*. Pictures by Jose Aruego and Ariane Dewey. New York: Macmillan Publishing Company, 1987. ISBN 0-689-71613-3 (soft);
   A multitude of animals celebrate Thanksgiving with a grand feast from Alligator's apples to Zebra's zucchini.
ALL AGES. Upper case.
Duke, Kate. *The Guinea Pig ABC*. New York: E.P. Dutton, 1983. ISBN 0-440-84571-8.
   The guinea pigs use the alphabet to introduce simple concepts such as awake, clean, juicy, greedy, and others.
AGES 2–6. Upper case.
Duvoisin, Roger. *A for the Ark*. New York: Lothrop, 1952.
   Duvoisin presents a retelling of the legend of Noah, the flood, and the ark as the animals enter the ark.
AGES 4 AND UP. Upper case.
Edens, Cooper, Alexandra Day, and Welleran Poltarnees. *An ABC of Fashionable Animals*. San Diego, California: The Green Tiger Press, Inc., 1989. ISBN 0-88138-122-5.
   The animals in this alphabet book are dressed in very fashionable clothing.
AGES 3–7. Upper case.
Eichenberg, Fritz. *Ape in a Cape: An Alphabet of Odd Animals*. New York: Harcourt Brace Jovanovich, 1952. ISBN 0-15-607830-9.
   Rhyming phrases are used to identify the animals used for each letter of the alphabet.
AGES 3–7. Upper case.
Emberley, Ed. *Ed Emberley's ABC*. Boston, Massachusetts: Little, Brown, and Co., 1978. ISBN 0-316-23408-7.
   In this almost wordless book the animals engage in a variety of activities to introduce the letters of the alphabet.
AGES 5–7. Upper case.
Falls, Charles B. *ABC Book*. Garden City, New York: Doubleday & Co., Inc. 1923. ISBN 0-385-08097-2.
   From antelope to zebra, colorful woodcuts are used to introduce an alphabet of animals.
AGES 4 AND UP. Upper case.
Farber, Norma. *As I Was Crossing Boston Common*. Pictures by Arnold Lobel. New York: E.P. Dutton & Co., 1975. ISBN 0-525-25960-0.
   From A to Z, Farber gives a rhyming account of some unusual animals that are seen crossing Boston Common.
ALL AGES.
Feldman, Judy. *The Alphabet in Nature*. Chicago, Illinois: Childrens Press, 1991. ISBN 0-516-05101-6.
   In this exploration of the alphabet, photographs of animals and nature are used to present the letters of the alphabet.

ALL AGES.

Felix, Monique. *The Alphabet*. Mankato, Minnesota: Creative Editions, 1992. ISBN 1-56846-003-1.

A tiny mouse trapped in a book discovers the alphabet and eats his way through all 26 letters.

AGES 2–6. Upper and lower case.

Ferguson, Don. *Winnie the Pooh's A to Zzzz*. Illustrated by Bill Langley and Diana Wakeman. New York: Disney Press, 1992. ISBN 1-56282-015-X.

All of the characters of the Hundred Acre Wood help introduce the ABC's.

AGES 4 AND UP. Upper case letters.

Fortey, Richard. *The Dinosaur's Alphabet*. Illustrations by John Rogan. New York: Barron's, 1990. ISBN 0-8120-6206-7.

Through funny verses and comic illustrations, kids are introduced to facts and figures about dinosaurs from Allosaurus to Zephyrosaurus.

AGES 4 AND UP. Upper and lower case.

Gag, Wanda. *The ABC Bunny*. New York: Coward-McCann, Inc., 1933. ISBN 0-698-20000-4; 0-698-20465-4 (soft).

When an apple falls off a tree, bunny runs away and meets all kinds of animals from A to Z.

ALL AGES. Upper case.

Geringer, Laura. *The Cow Is Mooing Anyhow: A Scrambled Alphabet Book to Be Read at Breakfast*. Pictures by Dirk Zimmer. New York: HarperCollins, 1991 ISBN 0-06-021986-6.

As a little girl eats her breakfast, all kinds of animals appear in scrambled ABC order to join her.

AGES 5 AND UP. Upper case.

Goennel, Heidi. *Heidi's Zoo: An Un-alphabet Book*. New York: Tambourine Books, 1993. ISBN 0-688-12109-8; 0-688-12110-1 (lib bdg).

In this unusual alphabet zoo, the animals, people, and objects are scrambled in unexpected and humorous pairs.

AGES 6–10.

Gretz, Susanna. *Teddy Bears ABC*. New York: Four Winds Press, 1986. ISBN 0-02-738130-7.

Five small bears go off on a series of adventures from A to Z.

AGES 2–6. Upper case.

Hague, Kathleen. *Alphabears: An ABC Book*. Illustrated by Michael Hague. New York: Henry Holt and Co., 1984. ISBN 0-8050-0841-1.

This is a rhyming ABC book of 26 lovable teddy bears with a description of each bear's special qualities.

AGES 2 AND UP. Upper case.

Heide, Florence Parry. *Alphabet Zoop*. Illustrated by Sally Mathews. New York: The McCall Publishing Co., 1970. ISBN 0-8415-2017-8.

From Alexander the alligator to Zelda the zebra, the reader is treated to an alphabetical menagerie of animals and the foods they like.

AGES 3–8. Upper case.

Hepworth, Cathi. *Antics! An Alphabetical Anthology*. New York: Putnam and Grosset Group, 1992. ISBN 0-399-21862-9.

The *antics* of 26 ants and their zany activities are used to introduce the alphabet.

AGES 3–7. Upper case.

Holabird, Katharine. *The Little Mouse ABC*. Pictures by Helen Craig. New York: Little Simon, 1983. ISBN 0-671-47733-1.

In this small book, all kinds of mice are engaged in an alphabet of activities.

AGES 4 AND UP. Upper case.

Ipcar, Dahlov. *I Love My Anteater with an A*. New York: Alfred A. Knopf, 1964.

Ipcar uses an old wordplay game, "I love my . . ." to introduce animals from A to Z.

ALL AGES.

Jernigan, Gisela. *Agave Blooms Just Once*. Illustrated by E. Wesley Jernigan. Tucson, Arizona: Harbinger House, 1989. ISBN 0-943173-46-9; 0-943173-44-2 (soft).

In rhyming verse the plants and animals of the desert are presented in alphabetical order.

AGES 6 AND UP. Upper case.

Jewell, Nancy. *ABC Cat*. Pictures by Ann Schweninger. New York: Harper and Row, 1983. ISBN 0-06-022847-4; 0-06-022848-2 (lib bdg).

Jewell follows a mischievous cat through his day and his A to Z antics.

AGES 4–7. Upper case.

Johnson, Laura Rinkle. *The Teddy Bear ABC*. Illustrated by Margaret Landers Sanford. New York: Green Tiger Press, 1982. ISBN 0-671-74979-X; 0-671-75949-3 (soft).

The letters of the alphabet are introduced along with some of the activities and characteristics of teddy bears.

AGES 3 AND UP. Upper case.

Johnson, Odett, and Bruce H. Johnson. *Apples, Alligators and Also Alphabets*. New York: Oxford University Press, 1991. ISBN 0-19-540757-1.

Colorful clay illustrations of animals in humorous situations introduce the letters of the alphabet.
AGES 3–9.

Jonas, Ann. *Aardvarks Disembark!*. New York: Greenwillow Books, 1990. ISBN 0-688-07206-2; 0-688-07207-0 (lib bdg).

After many familiar animals have left the ark, Noah discovers that there are dozens of animals left on board whose names he does not know.
AGES 4 AND UP. Lower case.

King-Smith, Dick. *Alphabeasts*. Illustrated by Quentin Blake. New York: Macmillan Publishing Co., 1990. ISBN 0-02-750720-3.

An alphabet extravaganza of animals of all shapes and sizes from the anaconda to the zambra.
AGES 5 AND UP. Upper case.

Kitchen, Bert. *Animal Alphabet*. New York: Dial Books, 1974. ISBN 0-8037-0431-1 (soft)

The alphabet is introduced through the use of very large letters, one animal per page.
ALL AGES. Upper case.

Leedy, Loreen. *The Dragon ABC Hunt*. New York: Holiday House, 1986. ISBN 0-8234-0596-6.

When 10 little dragons complain of boredom, their mother sends them on a scavenger hunt for objects A to Z.
AGES 4 AND UP. Upper and lower case.

McPhail, David. *David McPhail's Animals A to Z*. New York: Scholastic, Inc., 1988. ISBN 0-590-40715-5.

A wordless alphabet book in which the reader may search the pictures for objects that begin with each letter of the alphabet.
AGES 2–7. Upper case.

Mayer, Marianna, and Gerald McDermott. *The Brambleberrys Animal Alphabet*. Honesdale, Pennsylvania: Bell Books, 1987. ISBN 1-878093-78-9.

A variety of animals introduce objects of the alphabet.
AGES 3–7. Upper case.

Mendoza, George. *Alphabet Sheep*. Illustrated by Kathleen Reedy. New York: Grosset & Dunlap, 1982. ISBN 0-448-12220-0.

When a shepherd loses one of his sheep, he goes on an alphabetical search for it.
AGES 5–8.

Merriam, Eve. *Goodnight to Annie: An Alphabet Lullaby*. Illustrated by Carol Schwartz. New York: Hyperion Books for Children, 1992. ISBN 1-56282-205-5; 1-56282-206-3 (lib bdg).

As Annie falls asleep, so do a variety of creatures from alligators in mud to zebras in a zoo.
AGES 2 AND UP. Upper case.

———. *Where Is Everybody? An Animal Alphabet*. Illustrations by Diane de Groat. New York: Simon and Schuster, 1989. ISBN 0-671-64964-7; 0-671-77821-8 (soft).

A humorous litany of animals from A to Z as they engage in human activities from alligator in the attic and elephant on the escalator to tiger in the taxi and zebra at the zoo.
AGES 4–8. Upper case.

Miller, Edna. *Mousekin's ABC*. Englewood Cliffs, New Jersey: Prentice-Hall, Inc., 1972. ISBN 0-13-604389-5; 0-13-604371-2 (soft)

As Mousekin goes through the forest, he investigates the ABC's of the woods including acorns, bats, quails, yellow jackets, and zephyr.
ALL AGES. Upper case.

Miller, Elizabeth, and Jane Cohen. *Cat and Dog and the ABC's*. Illustrated by Victoria Chess. New York: Franklin Watts, 1981. ISBN 0-531-03532-8; 0-531-04294-4 (lib bdg)

After he eats too much food, Dog dreams of an around-the-world animal alphabet adventure.
AGES 3 AND UP. Upper case.

Newberry, Clare Turlay. *The Kittens ABC*. New York: Harper & Row, 1964. ISBN 0-06-024451-8.

Using bright yellow letters and rhyming verse, Newberry introduces the world of kittens from A to Z.
AGES 4–6. Upper case.

Obligado, Lilian. *Faint Frogs Feeling Feverish and Other Terrifically Tantalizing Tongue Twisters*. New York: The Viking Press, 1983. ISBN 0-670-30477-8.

This alphabet book features all kinds of animals in unusual situations such as "Gorilla greeting galloping Giraffe" and "Goat getting goggles."
ALL AGES. Upper case.

Olesky, Patti. *The ABC of Living Things*. Illustrated by Arline and Marvin Oberman. New York: Young Reader Press, 1972.

Each page in this alphabet book features a verse about a special living thing as well as other objects beginning with each letter.
ALL AGES. Upper and lower case.

Owens, Mary Beth. *A Caribou Alphabet*. Brunswick, Maine: The Dog Ear Press, 1988. ISBN 0-937966-25-8.

This unique alphabet book tells all about the world of the caribou, North America's reindeer.
ALL AGES. Upper case.

Palazzo, Tony. *A Cat Alphabet: A Tony Palazzo ABC Book*. New York: Duell, Sloan and Pearce, 1966.
   Twenty-six cats in rhyme and verse as well as objects associated with cats are used to introduce the alphabet.
AGES 5–7. Upper case.
———. *A Monkey Alphabet: A Tony Palazzo ABC Book*. New York: Duell, Sloan and Pearce, 1962.
   Palazzo provides an alphabetical tour of the lives of monkeys, their habits, behaviors, and lifestyles.
AGES 5–7. Upper case.
Piatti, Celestino. *Celestino Piatti's Animal ABC*. Text by Jan Reid. New York: Atheneum, 1966.
   Full page colored illustrations of animals and rhyming verse are used to introduce the alphabet.
AGES 4–8. Upper case.
Pittman, Helena Clare. *Miss Hindy's Cats*. Minneapolis, Minnesota: Carolrhoda Books, 1990. ISBN 0-87614-368-0.
   Miss Hindy takes in one stray cat, then another, until she has a houseful of cats.
AGES 4–9. Upper and lower case.
Provensen, Alice and Martin Provensen. *A Peaceable Kingdom: The Shaker Abecedarius*. New York: The Viking Press, 1978.
   ISBN 0-670-54500-7.
   In this version of the Shakers Abecedarius, an alphabetical menagerie of 100 real and fanciful animals march across the
pages.
AGES 4 AND UP.
Roe, Richard. *Animal ABC*. New York: Random House, 1984. ISBN 0-394-96864-6.
   A variety of familiar animals from alligator to zebra represent each letter of the alphabet.
AGES 2 AND UP. Upper and lower case.
Rojankovsky, Feodor. *Animals in the Zoo*. New York: Alfred A. Knopf, 1962.
From A to Z, the reader goes on a visit through the alphabet and the zoo.
ALL AGES. Upper and lower case.
———. *Wild Animals of Africa ABC*. New York: Lodestar Books, 1989. ISBN 0-525-67290-7.
   Large color photographs present wild animals found in different parts of Africa.
ALL AGES.
Ryden, Hope. *Wild Animals of America ABC*. New York: Lodestar Books, 1988. ISBN 0-525-67245-1.
   Color photos present an alphabetical roll call of animals from all parts of North America.
ALL AGES.
Sendak, Maurice. *Alligators All Around: An Alphabet*. New York: Harper & Row, Publishers, 1962. ISBN 0-06-025530-7; 0-
   06-443254-8 (soft).
   Sendak presents an A to Z jamboree of alligators engaging in their favorite activities.
AGES 2 AND UP. Upper case.
Shirley, Gayle C. *A is for Animals*. Illustrated by Constance R. Bergum. Helena, Montana: Falcon Press, 1991. ISBN 1-56044-
   025-2.
   From anteater to zebra, *A is for Animals* celebrates the diversity of animal life on earth.
AGES 7 AND UP. Upper and lower case.
Small, Terry. *Tails, Claws, Fangs and Paws: An Alphabeast Caper*. New York: Bantam Books, 1990. ISBN 0-553-05852-5.
   Through rhyming text and colorful illustrations, the reader is introduced to all kinds of animals from A to Z.
ALL AGES. Upper and lower case.
Steiner, Charlotte. *Annie's ABC Kitten: An Alphabetical Story about Annie and Her Pet*. New York: Alfred A. Knopf, 1965.
   Annie finds a kitten at her door and decides to take care of it.
AGES 4–7.
Sutton, Rosalind. *The Mouse Family ABC*. Illustrated by Pamela Storeys. Newmarket, England: Brimax Books, 1989. ISBN 0-
   86112-586-X.
   From A to Z, a family of mice have all kinds of adventures from gathering apples to going zigzagging on the ski slopes.
AGES 3–5.
Tallon, Robert. *Zoophabets*. Indianapolis, Indiana: The Bobbs Merrill Co., Inc., 1971.
   Tallon takes us through a fun-filled trip through the alphabet with 26 very unusual creatures.
ALL AGES. Upper case.
Thornhill, Jan. *The Wildlife A-B-C: A Nature Alphabet Book*. New York: Simon & Schuster, 1988. ISBN 0-671-67925-2.
   North American animals are used to introduce the letters of the alphabet.
ALL AGES. Upper and lower case.
Williams, Garth. *The Big Golden Animal ABC*. Racine, Wisconsin: Western Publishing Co., Inc., 1957, 1954. ISBN 0-307-
   10457-5.
   Soft watercolors and familiar animals present the alphabet.
AGES 3–6. Upper and lower case.
Wood, Jakki. *Animal Parade*. New York: Bradbury Press, 1993. ISBN 0-02-793394-6.

A parade of animals march nose-to-tail across the pages introducing the alphabet.
AGES 3–7. Upper and lower case.

Wormell, Christopher. *An Alphabet of Animals*. New York: Dial Books, 1990. ISBN 0-8037-0876-9.
    Handcut linoleum prints were used to print animals for each letter of the alphabet.
PRESCHOOL–AGE 7. Upper and lower case.

Yolen, Jane. *All in the Woodland Early: An ABC Book*. Illustrations by Jane Breskin Zalben. Honesdale, Pennsylvania: Caroline House, 1979. ISBN 1-878093-62-2.
    This unusual alphabet book provides a cumulative tale of a woodland hunt for animals A to Z.
AGES 6–9. Upper case.

ANIMALS AND ALPHABET BOOKS: ACTIVITIES

After reading *Hosie's Alphabet,* discuss some of the descriptions of the animals to help the children understand what the adjectives mean and how they fit the animal. Have each child select a person, object, or animal and write their own descriptive phrase to fit.

Explain to the students what alliteration is and give some examples such as those in *The Amazing Animal Alphabet Book*. Have each child choose an animal, write an alliterative phrase describing something the animal is doing, and then draw an illustration of the animal. Bind the drawings into a class alphabet book or use them as a display in the classroom. Other books using alliterative phrases include: *Alligator Arrived with Apples* by Crescent Dragonwagon; *Faint Frogs Feeling Feverish and other Terrifically Tantalizing Tongue Twisters* by Lilian Obligado; *Tails, Claws, Fangs and Paws: An Alphabeast Caper* by Terry Small.

Read the story *A is for Angry* by Sandra Boynton to the class without using the adjectives. Explain the term alliteration to the class and give a few examples. Write the names of the animals in alphabetical order in a column on the blackboard, and have the children suggest alliterative adjectives to describe the animals. After they have made up a list, go back and read the story again, but this time use the adjectives Boynton wrote in the text. Compare your list of adjectives with the ones that Boynton used.

After reading several animal alphabet books to the class, have each student compile a list of five favorite animals. Give each child a copy of the fact sheet (pg. 28) and have them locate information about their favorite animals. Find five to seven facts about the animal, list the facts, then rewrite the information in paragraph form. Draw sketches of each of the five animals and compile the sketches and facts into a pamphlet.

Demi's Find the Animal ABC is an interesting book to use with large or small groups of children. The Big Book version is especially helpful with large groups where the children try to find the hidden animal. After using this book, have the children make an ABC list of animals not mentioned in the book. Using that list, show the children how to do animal calligraphy, and let them create their own word creatures. In animal calligraphy, the name of the animal becomes the animal itself. An activity sheet shows how to turn a word into an animal (pg. 29).

A different way to present the alphabet story *Alligator Arrived with Apples* might be to use the flannelboard. The animals and foods can be easily created in felt figures. Make a large felt table to place in the center of the flannelboard, and as you read the story aloud place the animals and the foods that they bring in and around the table. A combination of flannelboard and read-aloud of this alphabet tale is a good way to help the children remember the visual sequence of events. Afterwards take all the pieces except the table off of the board, and ask the children to re-create the events as they occurred in the story. Follow-up activities might include making a list of more foods and animals that could have joined the feast and having the children bring some kind of food item to school to have your own A to Z holiday feast.

The Guinea Pig ABC by Kate Duke is a simple animal alphabet book, but it presents some interesting possibilities in terms of follow-up activities. After reading the book, go over the activities of the guinea pigs. Discuss the concepts one by one. Explain words that the children don't understand and ask questions, draw pictures, etc. to throughly teach the concepts. For example, with the word juicy, you could have the children name some juicy foods and draw pictures of them; for clean, discuss baths and bubbles, etc. Bring in a real guinea pig for the children to look at, touch, and talk about. Discuss the foods, care, and habits of the animal. What other kinds of pets do the children have? Choose another kind of pet and have the class help make up a list of A to Z activities for it.

Both *A for the Ark* and *Aardvarks Disembark* retell the legend of Noah's ark and the great flood. Use these two books as companions to present two different views of the alphabet (forwards and backwards). Several activities can be used to reinforce the two stories including:

1. Rewrite the legend of Noah in a different setting other than the ark or even using an unusual page shape.
2. Use clay or playdough to create some of the animals on the ark. Older children can fingermold their animals. Use cookie cutters to make animal shapes with very young toddlers or preschoolers. Let the children create their animals and then use nontoxic paints and glaze to add features to the animals.
3. Make a chart of the animals on the ark (pg. 30). In one column list a desirable quality of the animal and in a second column list an undesirable quality of the animal. Have the children defend their answers.

Using any of the alphabet books that present unusual alphabeasts (*Ape in a Cape* by Eichenberg, *Alphabeasts* by King-Smith, *Zoophabets* by Tallon) have the children create their own alphabeasts. Choose a letter of the alphabet and make up a creature for it. Describe the creature (physical features, coloring, size, foods, enemies, friends, habitat, etc.) and then draw a sketch of the animal.

Ed Emberley's ABC provides some interesting ways to introduce the alphabet and the construction of letters to beginning readers. After reading the book, use the chart in the back to give children practice in constructing their own letters using all kinds of materials. Give the children crackers (round and square), pretzels, cereal, etc. By nibbling around the foodstuffs, children can create their names and letters of the alphabet. Use other kinds of materials such as popcorn, shelled corn, yarn, clay, or plasticene to mold and shape the letters of the alphabet.

The ABC Bunny by Wanda Gag is a classic alphabet tale to share with children. Afterwards, have the students create a list of other animals and/or events that the bunny might have encountered.

After sharing *Heidi's Zoo,* go through the illustrations and discuss the relationship between the two animals that are paired together in the book.

Teddy bears are very popular, especially with young children, and they are also a popular topic with alphabet books. Plan a teddy bear day and use any or all of these ABC books as a part of the celebration. Prior to the day tell the children to bring in their favorite bears for the festivities. Some of the activities include:

1. ABC searches for the 26 bears in *Alphabears* by Kathleen Hague (pg. 31).
2. Role-play one of the bears in the books. Have the students describe the bear that they choose to pretend to be. Tell about his/her size, physical features, favorite foods, and more. Make up a story about the bear.
3. After reading *Alphabears,* have the class make up a class Alpha animal story such as Alphadinosaurs, Alphacats, etc. and illustrate it. Each child can choose a letter, draw their alpha animal, and tell about it.
4. Make potpourri bears from felt shapes sewn together or from brown paper bags. Decorate the bear shapes and fill with potpourri.
5. Have the children make up alliterative names for themselves. Pick a name and then give yourself another one that begins with the same letter.
6. Have Teddy grahams and apple juice for refreshments.
   Bear alphabet books include *Alphabears* by Kathleen Hague, *Teddy Bears ABC* by Susanna Gretz, *The Teddy Bear ABC* by Laura Rinkle Johnson, and *Teddy Bears ABC.*

Mice are nice, especially in small alphabet books like Katharine Holabird's *The Little Mouse ABC* which is designed for the preschooler and early reader. Give out precut mice shapes. The children decorate the mice, glue sticks to the back to create mice puppets, and then tell the class all about the ABC mice including their names and the activities that they are doing. Explain that each child should choose a letter of the alphabet for the mouse's name and its actions.

What else would be the perfect extension activity for *The Dragon's ABC Hunt* by Leedy than to have your own alphabet scavenger hunt. Before sharing the story with the students, hide A to Z items around the room. After the story, divide the group into pairs and give them a list of items to find. When all 26 things have been found, have everyone say their ABC's together. For older children, make the list using clues that have to be deciphered instead of a list of the items.

In *Alphabet Sheep,* a shepherd goes on an alphabet search to find his lost sheep. Have the students make up their own alphabet "lost" stories, using a variety of locales such as a zoo, school, cruise ship, ranch, etc.

Use *Goodnight to Annie* by Eve Merriam as a bedtime story. As you read the story, have the children mimic the action in the story as the alligators sleep, bees swarm, etc. Afterwards, make a list of animals (naturally A to Z) that were not used in the story. Have the students help write a phrase or sentence that tells how the animal sleeps or gets ready to sleep.

For *Where Is Everybody? An Animal Alphabet* have the children make a list of other animals not mentioned in the book. Make up phrases where those animals are engaged in human activities and draw sketches of the animals.

Hope Ryden's two volumes on wildlife and Judy Feldman's *The Alphabet in Nature* are excellent volumes to use to share photographs of real animals with children. Make available a variety of old magazines that have pictures of animals and nature photographs. Have the children find pictures of animals A to Z and compile a classroom animal alphabet book.

After sharing *Alligators All Around: An Alphabet* have the students draw pictures of themselves as alligators doing their favorite things. Add an alphabet phrase that describes the alligator's antics. Use the drawings for a class mural or bulletin board display.

Zoophabets by Robert Tallon is a wacky adventure through a zoo filled with some very strange fictional creatures. Read the text to the children without showing them the pictures. Have them draw their rendition of what the residents of Zoophabets really look like. Then give each child a card with a letter of the alphabet. They are to make up their own zoo animal, write a description of it (eating habits, location, size, etc.), and draw a picture of it. Use chalk on black construction paper to give the creature a look like Robert Tallon's.

After sharing some of the cat alphabet books, discuss cats with the children. Make a list of cat facts from A to Z. The list might include things that cats eat, games they play, how they sleep, etc.

After sharing several animal alphabet books with the children, play "Animal Alphabet Bingo" with them. Give each child a sheet of paper with a blank Bingo card printed on it. The children fill in the nine blanks with a letter from the alphabet. As you pull names of animals from a box, select a child each time to make up an alliterative name for the animal. For example, a "D" for dog might include the name "Dainty dancing dog."

Animals Facts!!!!!

What is your favorite animal? Find 5 facts about the animals and write them in the spaces below.

FACTS I FOUND:

1. _____
2. _____
3. _____
4. _____
5. _____

Use the five facts and your imagination to write a paragraph about the animal.

Animal Calligraphy

Create your own word creature by turning the name of an animal into a picture of it.

For example: A N T becomes:

Make a list of some of the animals that were on the ark. List one desirable or good trait and one undesirable or bad trait for the animal.

NAME OF ANIMAL	DESIRABLE OR "GOOD" TRAIT	UNDESIRABLE OR "BAD" TRAIT
EXAMPLE: Elephant	Has a long trunk that can reach things in very high places	Is very large and takes up a lot of space

An Alphabet of Bears

Now that you have met the 26 Alphabears, see if you can find their names in the puzzle below. Names can be found up and down, across or diagonally. Circle the names as you find them.

Amanda	Gilbert	Nikki	Ursula
Bryon	Henry	Ollie	Vera
Charles	Ivan	Pam	William
Devon	John	Quimby	X
Elsie	Kyle	Robert	York
Freddie	Laura	Sarah	Zak
	Marc	Tammy	

```
W  I  L  L  I  A  M  I  O  R  U  R  S  U  L  A  G  N  V

G  F  T  W  E  D  A  I  P  N  O  V  E  D  U  I  M  C  G

I  R  U  T  C  N  R  O  L  O  R  E  L  T  I  O  M  N  F

L  E  U  Z  T  A  C  H  A  R  L  E  S  K  A  I  X  D  S

B  D  J  K  S  M  I  E  U  Y  R  V  I  O  P  H  V  T  E

E  D  I  O  A  A  M  N  R  B  L  N  E  I  Q  E  E  A  M

R  I  U  E  R  M  X  R  A  L  Q  D  R  O  B  E  R  T  N

T  E  R  T  A  M  M  Y  O  R  K  W  E  T  Z  V  A  M  B

J  N  J  O  H  N  A  H  G  A  Y  B  M  I  U  Q  X  C  D

Y  W  R  Z  V  M  P  N  Z  O  L  L  I  E  M  N  I  O  W

U  R  M  Z  U  E  W  I  P  I  E  A  M  F  D  S  T  R  Y
```

4. RHYME AND REASON: ALPHABET BOOKS AND LANGUAGE

Words and language are certainly a major part of alphabet books, but there are many ABC books that use special forms of language and words. Rhyme, alliteration, tongue twisters, nursery rhymes, and nonsense verse can be found in many of the ABC books on the market today. In addition to rhyme and verse in alphabet books, there are titles available that present the alphabet using only certain parts of speech, sign language, or more than one language or that provide a dictionary style guide to the alphabet with dozens of words for each letter.

Because nursery rhymes are so much a part of our heritage, it is only natural that there are alphabet books that use classic rhymes to introduce the letters. Joan Walsh Anglund's charming whimsical illustrations accompany some well known Mother Goose rhymes in *In a Pumpkin Shell*. Each verse is preceded by a letter of the alphabet and a key word from the rhyme. *The Real Mother Goose ABCs* uses the same principle of nursery rhymes to introduce the letters along with pictures containing several objects that begin with each featured letter. The illustrations and typeface are duplicates of those used in a classic nursery rhyme book, *The Real Mother Goose*. *A Was an Angler* by Domanska uses only one Mother Goose rhyme to present the alphabet, rather than a series of verses.

One of the most popular alphabet rhyme stories available today is *Chicka Chicka Boom Boom* by Bill Martin and John Archambault. The bright, bold graphics and the pleasing rhyme about the day the letters climbed to the top of the coconut tree make this book one that children request over and over again. Not only does the story provide ample opportunities for letter and sound recognition, but the rhymthic nature of the verse is also very easy to remember and returns long after putting the book away. The entertainment value of *Chicka Chicka Boom Boom* insures it a permanent niche in the field of picture books.

Another popular alphabet story rhyme is *Old Black Fly* by Jim Aylesworth. A pesky old black fly bothers a family who spend the day chasing the fly all the way through the alphabet to a surprise ending. The illustrations are in bright vibrant colors using lots of hot pink, sky blue, luminous yellow, and fluorescent green. The family characters and animals all have exaggerated features with humorous faces, hair, and bodies. The fly is also comical looking with large oversized eyes and exagerrated body parts. The pesky fly gets into all kinds of mischief flittering his way through the house and getting into everything from A to Z. After reading aloud the refrain "shoo fly! shoo fly! shoo" once or twice, the children will begin to repeat it after you. Both *Chicka Chicka Boom Boom* and *Old Black Fly* are stories that children love to hear numerous times, not only because of the humorous story line but also because of the rhythm of the words used in the story.

Some of the alphabet books that deal specifically in rhyme and verse have set language patterns and follow them throughout the entire book. One of the best alphabet rhyme books is *A My Name Is Alice* by Jane Bayer. Bayer used a well-known jump rope rhyme as the basis for her alphabet book. Every verse contains a girl's name, boy's name, place, and some object all beginning with the same letter. As you read the story aloud, a singsong tone develops. In addition to the easily memorized rhyme, Steven Kellogg's humorous detailed illustrations offer the reader even more objects to identify than just those mentioned in the text. The combination of rhythmic verse and attractive illustrations make Bayer's rendition of a traditional alphabet rhyme a delightful contribution to the genre.

Like *A My Name Is Alice,* Ipcar uses a set language pattern for her alphabet poems in *I Love My Anteater with an A*. The author selected animals as the subject of her "I love" poems, and she uses a five-line set pattern to write about each one. She tells why she loves then hates the animal, the animal's name and home, and an occupation for the animal. After reading two or three of the letter poems, children will soon pick up the pattern and be ready to

33

write their own "I love" poems. By studying the language patterns established in both of these books, it is very easy to have students of any age duplicate the set patterns and write their own alphabet verses.

The best of the nonsense alphabet verse is by the much acclaimed master, Edward Lear. All kinds of poetic forms and subject matter can be found in alphabet poetry books. Many different versions of his classic rhymes are available, and every child delights in these humorous alphabet rhymes. Sylvia Cassedy chose to use rooms and things that go as the topic for her two humorous alphabet books, *Roomrimes* and *Zoomrimes*. Eve Merriam chose things associated with Halloween as her topic. The spooky illustrations by Lane Smith make such things as a skeleton, mask, fiend, bat, and trap even more realistic. Truly rotten, horrible children is the theme of David Elliott's *An Alphabet of Rotten Kids*. Comic colorful pictures by Oscar de Mejo are used to show some of the mean, nasty, terrible things that these children do. These titles are only a sampling of the many topics that have been used to create alphabet poems.

Tongue twisters are not only a lot of fun to say, but they are also a very special way to introduce letters. The Berenstains are a perennial favorite with young children, and in *The Berenstain's B Book,* they have outdone themselves. Only the letter B is used throughout the book, but it is a fascinating introduction to the letter. The Berenstains do the same thing for the letter "C" in *"C" Is for Clown.* A cumulative plot line shows a circus balancing act and its impossible load. The text is very easy to read and follows a pyramid style as the balancing act grows bigger. While the text and illustrations make *"C" Is for Clown* ideal for beginning readers, it is also a good title to use to show middle and high school students how they can build words into a pyramid style by using words beginning with the same letter or even words that have some other kind of connection such as a series of gerunds, adjectives, or adverbs.

For a more advanced tongue twister treat, try *Peter Piper's Alphabet.* The alliterative verse in this book is guaranteed to make your tongue twist as tight as a rubber band. The text is taken from a volume originally published by J. Harris in London in 1813. Marcia Brown's cartoonish illustrations lend just the right touch to this unusual collection. Without a doubt the king of all tongue twister alphabet books is Steven Kellogg's *Aster Aardvark's Alphabet Adventures.* The illustrations are hilarious and so full of details that it would take hours to see and identify all the objects on each page. As for the text, even the best adult readers would have problems stopping their tongues from giving out when reading about Aster Aardvark's adventures. The text is not just one simple little line; in some cases it is whole paragraphs of words all beginning with the same letter. Good luck with your reading and be sure to rest between letters.

In *Nedobeck's Alphabet Book,* the author uses alliterative sentences to introduce a host of alphabet animals. Instead of going across the page, however, the sentence is in a line down the page with one word per line. The featured letter is printed darker than the rest of the word. Nedobeck's book is a good example of alliteration with an unusual twist that both young and adult readers find entertaining.

Three other examples of alliterative language or tongue twisting sentences can be found in *Animalia* by Graeme Base, *Alphabet Soup* by Scott Gustafson, and *The Z Was Zapped* by Chris Van Allsburg. All of these titles are discussed in other chapters, but it is important to discuss them in terms of the way the words are presented in each of them. While *The Z Was Zapped* does not contain long sentences, each sentence involves the use of words beginning with the same letter, e.g. "The F was firmly flattened." *Animalia* and *Alphabet Soup* use the same language pattern as well as the same lushly detailed, realistic illustrations. Both authors provide the reader with pictures that are almost real enough to reach out and touch, and the text in both books follows a similiar pattern. The text in *Animalia* is shorter and more direct than that of *Alphabet Soup.* Base includes all kinds of alliterative animals and objects for each letter in his illustrations, while Gustafson's illustrations reflect the action expressed in the text. In Gustafson's book, animals are also the subject, but they are shown and described as they bring some kind of food to create an alphabet soup. An example of one of the alliterative sentences found in *Alphabet Soup* is "Armadillo and Asparagus. Armadillo was an award winning author who aimed asparagus arrows into the pot." The illustration reflects the action in the text.

Alphabet books can be useful in identifying parts of speech and for looking at word origins. *Abracadabra to Zigzag* by Nancy Lecourt presents a lively alphabetical introduction to some unusual and curious words. Bright colorful pictures are used to show examples of such words as abracadabra, itsy bitsy, and pitter patter. A glossary on the last page of the book explains the origins and meanings of the words. Colin and Jacqui Hawkins use only gerunds in their *Busy ABC.* The illustrations reflect the action of the word such as opening (with a boy opening a box) and ordering (a boy ordering a dog to roll over). *ABC Say with Me* by Karen Gundersheimer is another book that uses only gerunds as the text. A teeny tiny girl romps through the pages of this small book performing a variety of activities such as asking, hiding, and ignoring.

Antics! by Cathi Hepworth takes a look at parts of words and how one simple three-letter word can be a part of 26 very different words. The word *ant* is shown as part of the beginning, middle, and end of a multitude of words. Humorous drawings of ants in a variety of situations complete this unusual alphabet book,

In *A is for Angry* by Sandra Boynton, descriptive adjectives and nouns are used for the text, which includes an angry anteater and zany zebra. Many other animal books are useful for studying nouns and adjectives. *Have You Ever Seen?* by Beau Gardner uses interesting word combinations to portray objects and letters of the alphabet. Gardner asks the question, "Have you ever seen?" and then proceeds to give some interesting examples of animals including an alligator with antlers, a banana with buttons, a candy cane cat's tail, an octopus eating oatmeal, and a zipper on a zebra. With bright colorful illustrations and simple text, *Have You Ever Seen?* is excellent to use with young children as a humorous alphabet book and with older students as examples of ways to create interesting images with words. Patricia and Frederick McKissack use all kinds of colorful comic bugs to introduce the upper and lower case letters of the alphabet in *The Big Bug Book of the Alphabet*. Big bug clowns show how letters are formed by twisting their bodies into letter shapes while other bugs demonstrate ways in which letters can be combined and found in other letters.

Although numerous books on sign language exist, only a few would qualify as alphabet books in the true sense of the word. Laura Rankin's *The Handmade Alphabet* is one of the best books available on American Sign Language, and it is a perfect introduction to both the written and the sign alphabets. Beautiful colored pencil drawings of hands signing are linked to a word that begins with a corresponding letter of the written alphabet. For example, the hand that signs a V is holding a Valentine; G is wearing a glove; and R is intertwined with a ribbon. *I Can Sign My ABC's* by Susan Gibbons Chaplin is another guide to sign language that includes both the written and manual alphabet as well as a picture that begins with the featured letter. The illustrations are in bright primary colors with clearly defined outlines.

In *Alphabet Art: Thirteen ABCs from around the World* Leonard Fisher provides a guide to the alphabets of thirteen different peoples. Not only does he provide an illustrated guide to these different alphabets, but he also gives a brief history and explanation of each of the different alphabets. The alphabets include Arabic, Cherokee, Cyrillic, Eskimo, Gaelic, German, Greek, Hebrew, Japanese, Sanskrit, Thai, and Tibetan. While this book is not suitable for young children, it serves as a reference source for middle graders and high school students. Along with Fisher's guide to different alphabets, a teacher could use one of several alphabet books using different languages as part of a study on language. Ruth Brown uses the alphabet as a means of introducing both the letters and words from four languages in *Alphabet Times Four*. Lush, textured paintings are used for the illustrations, and a pronunciation guide is found on each page. A word for each letter is presented in English, Spanish, French and German. Mahji Hall includes both an English and a Spanish word for each letter of the alphabet in *"T is for Terrific"*. She was only a middle school student when she wrote this alphabet guide. *The ABCs of Origami* combines the alphabet with the craftsmanship of the Japanese art of paperfolding. One of the unusual facets of this book is that each paper figure is identified in a trilingual caption of Japanese, French, and English. Japanese writing also appears under each color photograph. More about this title can be found in the chapter on art and illustration.

In addition to the alphabet books that feature rhymes and verse, there are many that list dozens of words for each letter along with illustrations of all the objects. Richard Scarry's books have literally hundreds of pictures in them, all of which are clearly identified with one letter or another. *Annie's ABC* by Annie Owens presents over 500 tiny word pictures (all in rows) together with a one-sentence text at the bottom of each page identifying the objects (e.g., V is for volcanoes, violets, violins, and vans). *Oliver's Alphabet* by Lisa Bruce provides an unusual twist to the alphabet. Eight different aspects of Oliver's world (friends, house, friends with toys, animals, orchestra, people who work in his town, holiday and birthday parties) are shown in the book. Twenty-six words are listed in each of these eight areas together with detailed illustrations. Many more dictionary style alphabet books are listed in the annotations at the end of this chapter.

Alphabet books provide an excellent medium to use with students of all ages in studying language, word combinations, and rhyme. The wide variety of high quality ABC books on the market today provides ample resources to use with students in exploring, experimenting, and creating words and verse of their own.

Students can examine set language patterns in *A My Name Is Alice,* and *I Love My Anteater with an A;* study examples of alliteration in *Animalia* and *Aster Aardvark's Alphabet Adventure;* look at parts of speech in *Busy ABC* and *A is for Angry;* play with unusual words and puns in *Abracadrabra to Zigzag* and *Alphabatty Animals and Funny Foods;* examine poetic forms such as couplets, limericks, and free verse; and look at alphabet books like *Oliver's Alphabets* that provide a comprehensive look at words and letters.

By examining alphabet books that focus on the rhythm of language, students can create their own alliterative sentences, develop dictionaries of unusual or foreign words, or write plays, poems, or dialogue based on the alphabet. The possibilities for using alphabet books in language development go beyond simple identification by preschoolers to opening doors to vocabulary enrichment and language growth with all grade and age levels.

ABCs and Other Learning Rhymes. Selected by Sally Emerson. Illustrated by Colin and Moira MacLean. New York: Kingfisher Books, 1993. ISBN 1-85697-899-0.
    This collection of traditional early learning rhymes includes both alphabet and counting rhymes.
AGES 2 AND UP.

ABC in English and French. Illustrated by Beatrice Rich. New York: Sayre Publishing, Inc., 1982.
    A word in both English and French is shown for each letter of the alphabet.
ALL AGES. Upper and lower case.

Anglund, Joan Walsh. *In a Pumpkin Shell: A Mother Goose ABC.* New York: Harcourt Brace & Co., 1960. ISBN 0-15-238269-0.
    Anglund uses a collection of Mother Goose rhymes to present objects from A to Z.
ALL AGES. Upper case.

Asch, Frank. *Little Devil's ABC.* New York: Charles Scribner's Sons, 1979. ISBN 0-684-16096-X.
    Humorous little devils with tiny little illustrations introduce the alphabet.
AGES 4–9. Upper and lower case.

Ashton, Elizabeth. *An Old-Fashioned ABC Book.* Illustrations by Jesse Wilcox Smith. New York: Viking, 1990. ISBN 0-670-83048-8.
    Simple two-line verses together with old-fashioned art from the illustrator Jesse Wilcox Smith introduce the alphabet.
ALL AGES.

Aylesworth, Jim. *Old Black Fly.* Illustrations by Stephen Gammell. New York: Henry Holt and Co., 1992. ISBN 0-8050-1404-2.
    A family chases a pesky old fly through the day and the alphabet before arriving at a surprise ending.
ALL AGES. Upper case.

Barnes, Djuna. *Creatures in an Alphabet.* New York: The Dial Press, 1982. ISBN 0-385-27797-0.
    In this sophisticated book of alphabet rhymes all kinds of creatures are shown.
AGES 8 AND UP.

Base, Graeme. *Animalia.* New York: Harry N. Abrams, Inc., 1986. ISBN 0-8109-1868-4.
    Alliterative sentences and intricate pictures are used to introduce animals and objects from A to Z.
ALL AGES. Upper case.

Bayer, Jane. *A My Name Is Alice.* Illustrated by Steven Kellogg. New York: Dial Books, 1984. ISBN 0-8037-0123-3; 0-8037-0124-1 (lib bdg).
    An old jump rope rhyme uses the alphabet to introduce animals, places, and things from A to Z.
ALL AGES. Upper case.

Berenstain, Stan, and Jan Berenstain. *The Berenstain's B Book.* New York: Random House, 1971. ISBN 0-394-82324-9; 0-394-926243 (lib bdg).
    The Berenstain Bears provide a humorous look at lots of "B" things.
ALL AGES.

———. *"C" is for Clown: A Circus of "C" Words.* New York: Random House, 1972. ISBN 0-394-82492-X; 0-394-92492-4 (lib bdg).
    Only "c" words are presented in this story of a circus balancing act and its impossible load.
AGES 3–8.

Blake, Quentin. *Quentin Blake's ABC.* New York: Alfred A. Knopf, 1989. ISBN 0-394-84149-2; 0394-94149-7 (lib bdg).
    With rhyming text and wacky illustrations, Blake shows objects from A to Z.
ALL AGES. Upper and lower case.

Boynton, Sandra. *A is for Angry.* New York: Workman Publishing, 1983, 1987. ISBN 0-89480-453-7.
    Descriptive adjectives coupled with names of animals are used to show the alphabet.
AGES 4 AND UP. Upper case.

Brown, Marcia. *Peter Piper's Alphabet: Peter Piper's Practical Principles of Plain and Perfect Pronunciation.* New York: Charles Scribner's Sons, 1959.
    Alliterative verse is used to present all kinds of people from A to Z.
AGES 7 AND UP.

Brown, Ruth. *Alphabet Times Four: An International ABC.* New York: Dutton Children's Books, 1991. ISBN 0-525-44831-4.

In this ingenious alphabet book, a word for each letter of the alphabet is presented in four languages.
ALL AGES. Upper and lower case.
Bruce, Lisa. *Oliver's Alphabets*. Illustrated by Debi Gliori. New York: Bradbury Press, 1993. ISBN 0-02-735996-4.
　　In a twist to the traditional ABC book, this title presents the eight aspects of Oliver's world with a list of 26 items for each area.
ALL AGES. Upper and lower case.
Cassedy, Sylvia. *Roomrimes*. Illustrations by Michelle Chessare. New York: Thomas Y. Crowell, 1987. ISBN 0-690-04466-6; 0-690-04467-4 (lib bdg).
　　A collection of 26 poems describing a place from attic to zoo provides a new look at the alphabet.
ALL AGES.
―――. *Zoomrimes: Poems about Things That Go*. Pictures by Michele Chessare. New York: HarperCollins, 1993. ISBN 0-06-022632-3; 0-06-022633-1 (lib bdg).
　　Using all kinds of poetic forms, Cassedy has written 26 poems about things that go from ark to zeppelin.
ALL AGES.
Chaplin, Susan Gibbons. *I Can Sign My ABC's*. Illustrated by Laura McCaul. Washington D.C.: Kendall Green Publicatons, 1986. ISBN 0-930323-19-X.
　　This illustrated guide includes the manual alphabet handshape, a picture, and the name and sign of an object beginning with all the letters of the alphabet.
ALL AGES. Upper and lower case.
Dareff, Hal. *Fun with ABC and 123: An Alphabet and Counting Book in Rhyme*. Illustrated by Marylin Hafner. New York: Parent's Magazine Press, 1965.
　　In rhyme and verse, the author presents a litany of objects from A to Z.
AGES 6 AND UP. Upper case.
Delaunay, Sonia. *Sonia Delaunay's Alphabet*. New York: Thomas Y. Crowell Co., 1970. ISBN 0-690-75258-X.
　　A combination of rhymes from classic children's literature and modern paintings are used to present the alphabet.
ALL AGES.
Domanska, Janina. *A Was an Angler*. New York: Greenwillow Books, 1991. ISBN 0-688-06990-8; 0-688-06991-6 (lib bdg).
　　A nonsense rhyme based on a traditional nursery rhyme shows the alphabet from Angler to Zebra.
AGES 3–7. Upper case.
Elliott, David. *An Alphabet of Rotten Kids*. Art by Oscar de Mejo. New York: Philomel Books, 1991. ISBN 0-399-22260-X.
　　From Agatha to Zazu, the reader learns about a menagerie of 26 children who are the most devilish, ornery, mischievous, hateful children that you have ever met.
ALL AGES. Upper case.
Fisher, Leonard Everett. *Alphabet Art: Thirteen ABCs from around the World*. New York: Four Winds Press, 1978. ISBN 0-590-07520-9.
　　Reproductions of 13 alphabets in use around the world are included in this book.
ALL AGES. Upper and lower case.
Gardner, Beau. *Have You Ever Seen . . . ? An ABC Book*. New York: Dodd, Mead & Co., 1986. ISBN 0-396-08825-2.
　　Using bright colorful graphics and some amusing word combinations, the author presents an array of alphabetical creations.
AGES 3 AND UP. Upper and lower case.
Gorey, Edward, illustrator. *The Eclectic Abecedarium*. New York: Adama Pub Inc., 1983. ISBN 0-915361-31-0.
　　Short couplets and small black and white drawings are used to introduce the alphabet in this title for the older readers.
AGES 10 AND UP. Upper case.
Greenaway, Kate. *A Apple Pie*. New York: Derrydale Books, 1993. ISBN 0-517-09302-2.
　　Using Kate Greenaway's drawings, this rendition of the classic nursery rhyme follows the fortunes of an apple pie.
ALL AGES. Upper case.
Gundersheimer, Karen. *ABC Say with Me*. New York: Harper and Row Publishers, 1984. ISBN 0-06-022174-7; 0-06-022175-5 (lib bdg).
　　A teeny tiny girl romps through the alphabet performing all kinds of familiar activities.
AGES 2 AND UP.
Gustafson, Scott. *Alphabet Soup: A Feast of Letters*. Chicago, Illinois: Calico Books, 1990. ISBN 0-8092-4299-0.
　　Otter has a housewarming party and invites his friends to bring ingredients for alphabet soup.
AGES 4–10. Upper case.
Hall, Mahji. *"T is for Terrific": Mahji's ABC's*. Seattle, Washington: Open Hand Publishing Inc., 1989. ISBN 0-940880-22-9.
　　Written by a teenager, this book includes both an English and a Spanish word for each letter of the alphabet.
ALL AGES. Upper and lower case.
Hawkins, Colin, and Jacqui Hawkins. *Busy ABC*. New York: Viking Kestrel, 1987. ISBN 0-670-81153-X.

Cartoon-like characters are shown performing all kinds of alphabetical acts in this humorous look at gerunds and the alphabet.
ALL AGES. Lower case.

Hepworth, Cathi. *Antics! An Alphabetical Anthology*. New York: Putnam and Grosset Group, 1992. ISBN 0-399-21862-9.
The zany activities of 26 *ant*s are shown in this unusual ABC book.
AGES 3–7. Upper case.

Hillman, Priscilla. *A Merry Mouse Christmas ABC*. Garden City, New York: Doubleday & Co., Inc., 1980. ISBN 0-385-15596-4; 0-385-15597-2.
The ABC's of Christmas are introduced through rhyming verse and bright-eyed little mice.
ALL AGES. Upper case.

Hoberman, Mary Ann. *Nuts to You and Nuts to Me*. Illustrated by Ronni Solbert. New York: Alfred A. Knopf, 1974. ISBN 0-394-82742-2; 0-394-92742-7.
A collection of humorous poetry introduces the letters of the alphabet.
ALL AGES. Upper case.

Ilsley, Velma. *M is for Moving*. New York: Henry Z. Walck, Inc., 1966.
Told from a child's point of view, this is an alphabetical rhyme about moving day and all that it entails.
AGES 3–7. Upper case.

Ipcar, Dahlov. *I Love My Anteater with an A*. New York: Alfred A. Knopf, 1964.
From A to Z, the author tells all about the animals that she loves and why.
ALL AGES.

Jacobs, Leland B. *Alphabet of Girls*. Pictures by John E. Johnson. New York: Holt, Rinehart and Winston, 1969. ISBN 0-03-076305-3.
Infectious rhymes about girls from Arabella, Araminta, and Ann to Zepha and Zelda provide a humorous look at the alphabet.
ALL AGES. Upper case.

Johnson, Audean. *A to Z Look and See*. New York: Random House, 1989. ISBN 0-394-86127-2.
All kinds of familiar objects are shown in this easy to read alphabet book.
AGES 4–8. Upper case.

Kellogg, Steven. *Aster Aardvark's Alphabet Adventure*. New York: William Morrow & Co., 1987. ISBN 0-688-07256-9. 0-688-07257-7 (lib bdg).
Comic illustrations and alliterative text lead the reader through the adventures of animals from A to Z.
ALL AGES. Upper case.

Kennedy, X. L. *Did Adam Name the Vinegarroon?* Illustrated by Heidi Johanna Steig. Boston, Massachusetts: David R. Godine Pub., Inc., 1982. ISBN 0-87923-357-5.
Kennedy has written twenty-six alphabet rhymes about real and mythological creatures.
AGES 6 AND UP.

King-Smith, Dick. *Alphabeasts*. Illustrated by Quentin Blake. New York: Macmillan Pub. Co., 1990. ISBN 0-02-750720-3.
From Anaconda to Zambia, humorous verse is used to introduce a plethora of animals of all shapes and sizes.
ALL AGES. Upper case.

Lalicki, Barbara (compiler). *If There Were Dreams to Sell*. Illustrated by Margot Tomes. New York: Lothrop, Lee & Shepard Books, 1984. ISBN 0-688-03821-2; 0-688-03822-0 (lib bdg).
A variety of poems from Mother Goose to Keats and Dickinson are used to show the letters of the alphabet.
ALL AGES. Upper and lower case.

Lear, Edward. *A Was Once an Apple Pie*. Illustrated by Julie Lacome. Cambridge, Massachusetts: Candlewick Press, 1992. ISNB 1-56402-000-2.
This tome is a new picture book version of Edward Lear's classic alphabet nonsense verse.
ALL AGES.

———. *An Edward Lear Alphabet*. Illustrated by Carol Newsom. New York: Lothrop, Lee & Shepard Books, 1983. ISBN 0-688-00964-6; 0-688-00965-4 (lib bdg).
A new edition of Edward Lear's classic nonsense verses provides an introduction to the letters of the alphabet.
ALL AGES.

———. *A New Nonsense Alphabet*. Edited by Susan Hyman. London: Bloomsbury Publishers, Ltd., 1988. ISBN 0-7475-0320-6.
A reproduction of an alphabet that Edward Lear created in 1862 for the granddaughter of a friend is the topic of this book.
ALL AGES. Upper and lower case.

Lecourt, Nancy. *Abracadabra to Zigzag*. Pictures by Barbara Lehman. New York: Lothrop, Lee and Shepard Books, 1991. ISBN 0-688-09481-3; 0-688-09482-1 (lib bdg).
Twenty-six curious words and phrases of the English language are presented in this lively ABC book.

ALL AGES. Upper and lower case.

McKissack, Patricia, and Frederick McKissack. *The Big Bug Book of the Alphabet*. Illustrated by Bartholomew. St. Louis, Missouri: Milliken Publishing Company, 1987. ISBN 0-88335-764-X.

Using Big Book format, a series of comic colorful bugs introduce the alphabet and demonstrate how letters are formed from other letters and combined.

AGES 4–9. Upper and lower case.

Martin, Bill, Jr., and John Archambault. *Chicka Chicka Boom Boom*. Illustrated by Lois Ehlert. New York: Simon and Schuster, 1989. ISBN 0-617-67949-X.

This alphabet rhyme tells the story of the day that the letters climbed to the top of the coconut tree.

AGES 2–8. Upper and lower case.

Mazzarella, Mimi. *Alphabatty Animals and Funny Foods: Alphabet and Counting Rhymes*. Deerfield Beach, Florida: Liberty Publishing. Co., 1984. ISBN 0-89709-045-4.

In this beginning alphabet book, the reader is exposed to all kinds of puns about animals such as a chocolate mousse, catty cat, and alert alligator.

ALL AGES.

Merriam, Eve. *Halloween ABC*. Illustrations by Lane Smith. New York: Macmillan Publishing Co., 1987. ISBN 0-02-766870-3.

Macabre illustrations accompany this collection of 26 poems that convey the A to Z world of spooky, shivery Halloween.

ALL AGES. Upper case.

Nedobeck, Don. *Nedobeck's Alphabet Book*. Chicago, Illinois: Childrens Press, 1988. ISBN 0-516-09220-0.

Through alliterative sentences, the reader meets all kinds of animals from A to Z.

ALL AGES. Upper case.

Oliver, Robert S. *Cornucopia*. Drawings by Frederick Henry Belli. New York: Atheneum, 1978. ISBN 0-689-30626-1.

Short poems about real animals from A to Z is the subject of the cornucopia.

ALL AGES.

Owen, Annie. *Annie's ABC*. New York: Alfred A. Knopf, 1987. ISBN 0-394-89590-8; 0-394-99590-2 (lib bdg).

Over 500 tiny word pictures are used to show objects for each letter of the alphabet.

AGES 2 AND UP.

Rankin, Laura. *The Handmade Alphabet*. New York: Dial Books, 1991. ISBN 0-8037-0974-9; 0-8037-0975-7 (lib bdg).

Beautifully illustrated drawings are used to accompany this unique presentation of the manual alphabet.

ALL AGES. Upper case.

The Real Mother Goose ABCs. Illustrated by Patty McCloskey-Padgett. New York: Checkerboard Press, 1992. ISBN 1-56288-303-8.

Through classic nursery rhymes and old-fashioned illustrations, the alphabet is introduced letter by letter.

ALL AGES. Upper and lower case.

Reeves, James. *Ragged Robin*. Pictures by Emma Chichester Clark. Boston, Massachusetts: Little, Brown & Co., 1961, 1990. ISBN 0-316-73829-8.

Ragged Robin takes the reader through a magical tour of the alphabet using ballads, rhyming couplets, and nonsense verse.

ALL AGES. Upper case.

Rosenberg, Amye. *A to Z Busy Word Book*. Racine, Wisconsin: Western Publishing Company, Inc., 1988. ISBN 0-307-60517-5.

From A to Z, the reader is introduced to dozens of words beginning with each letter of the alphabet.

AGES 4 AND UP. Upper and lower case.

Sarasas, Claude. *The ABCs of Origami: Paper Folding for Children*. Rutland, Vermont: Charles E. Tuttle Co., Inc., 1964, 1990. ISBN 0-804-0000-6.

Sarasas gives explicit directions for creating origami figures from A to Z along with trilingual captions for each figure.

AGES 8 AND UP. Upper case.

Scarry, Richard. *Richard Scarry's ABC Word Book*. New York: Random House, 1971. ISBN 0-394-82339-7; 0-394-92339-1 (lib bdg).

Using a short story for each letter of the alphabet, Scarry introduces many objects for each letter.

AGES 3–8. Upper and lower case.

———. *Richard Scarry's Find Your ABC's*. New York: Random House, 1973. ISBN 0-394-82683-3.

Detectives Sam and Dudley go in search of the letters of the alphabet.

AGES 3 AND UP. Upper and lower case.

Seeley, Laura L. *The Book of Shadowboxes: A Story of the ABCs*. Atlanta, Georgia: Peachtree Publishing., 1990. ISBN 0-934601-65-8.

The letters of the alphabet are seen through a shadowbox containing rhyming verses and a collection of objects for each letter.

AGES 6 AND UP. Upper case.

Steig, Jeanne. *Alpha Beta Chowder*. Pictures by William Steig. New York: HarperCollins, 1992. ISBN 0-06-205006-0; 0-06-205007-9.

From A to Z, 26 verses tell a laugh-aloud tale, full of interesting words and unusual people.

AGES 6 AND UP.

Szekeres, Cyndy. *Cyndy Szekeres' ABC*. New York: Golden Press, 1983. ISBN 0-307-62120-0.

This colorful alphabet book shows examples of all kinds of animals and other things.

AGES 3–8. Upper and lower case.

Van Allsburg, Chris. *The Z Was Zapped*. Boston, Massachusetts: Houghton Mifflin Co., 1987. ISBN 0-395-44612-0.

A theatrical presentation of the letters of the alphabet as they suffer a series of mishaps.

ALL AGES. Upper case.

Williams, Jenny. *Everyday ABC*. New York: Dial Books for Younger Readers, 1991. ISBN 0-8037-1079-8.

Illustrations of ordinary everyday objects that make up a child's world are used in this alphabet book.

AGES 3–7.

Winik, J. T., and Lauren Pashunk. *Fun from A to Z*. Durkin Hayes Pub, 1985. ISBN 0-88625-105-2.

These easy to read poems take the reader through the alphabet.

ALL AGES.

Zen ABC. Illustrated by Amy Zerner and Jessie Spicer Zerner. Boston, Massachusetts: Charles E. Tuttle Co., Inc., 1993. ISBN 0-8048-1806-1.

Through classical haiku, koans, and contemporary poems, an alphabetical exploration of the history and spirituality of Zen.

ALL AGES. Upper case.

RHYME AND REASON: ACTIVITIES

After reading *Old Black Fly* aloud, have the children create their own old black fly face masks from paper plates. Draw and color the shape of the fly and facial features on the plate. Cut out the face mask, punch holes on either side and use elastic thread attached to either side to complete the mask. Another activity to use with this book is to have the class recreate the fly's alphabetical pilgrimage through the house through a large mural. Use a large piece of white paper for the background of the mural. Students can draw objects from A to Z on the background, then use the same type of bright colors and splatter paint techniques to recreate the illustrations. After sharing the book with younger children, give them an activity sheet to trace the fly's adventures.

A My Name Is Alice by Jane Bayer is a book that inspires a number of follow-up activities including the following: 1. Have each child choose a letter of the alphabet and write a verse about a character. Follow the language pattern established in the book. Illustrate the verse and combine the verses into a class book; 2. Choose one of the animals in the book, and find some facts about the animal. Make a face mask of the animal from a paper plate.

The Berenstain's B Book serves as an inspiration for more tongue twisters with "B" words. Make a list of even more "B" words and write some B tongue twisters.

Share *Oliver's Alphabets* with the class. Have them make a list of other aspects of Oliver's life (or their own) that could be explored. Create an alphabet for one of these worlds. (Examples might be: Oliver's garden; Oliver's kitchen; Oliver's vehicles, etc.) Instead of titling them with Oliver's name, the children can use their own names.

Tongue twisters are ever popular with students. Assign each child a letter of the alphabet and have them find some examples of tongue twisters using words with the featured letter. Then using the activity sheet, each child can write their own tongue twisters. To get them started, have each child choose a letter from their name. Alphabet tongue twister books that are useful include *The Berenstain's B Book* by Stan and Jan Berenstain, *Peter Piper's Alphabet* by Marcia Brown, and *Aster Aardvark's Alphabet Adventures* by Steven Kellogg.

Alliteration is the use of the same letter or sound at the beginning of each word in a sentence or phrase. Have the children create an ABC book of mixed up alliterative animals. Cut out pictures of animals from old magazines or newspapers. Cut apart the animals and rearrange the mixed up animal parts to create a new creature. Name it and describe it in alliterative language.

After sharing *Have You Ever Seen . . . ?* with the children, let them make an alphabetical list of their own "Have you ever seen . . . ?" creatures. Write a description of the creature and then develop a drawing or sketch of it. For preschoolers cut out the basic shapes of creatures, and let the children add details that include the words that they make up.

In *Antics,* the author takes a simple three letter word and shows how three letters are an important part of a larger word. Choose another combination of letters (such as cat) and try to make a list of words from A to Z that contain that combination. Illustrate your list.

Many alphabet books use rhyme, especially rhyming couplets, to introduce the letters of the alphabet. A rhyming couplet is two lines of poetry with words that rhyme at the end. Use any of the rhyming ABC books as examples, and have your students write their own ABC rhyming couplets.

Dahlov Ipcar uses the old phrase, "I love my . . . " as a means of introducing letters and animals for the alphabet. Each of her 26 poems follows a set pattern for each of the five lines. Using the language pattern set up by Ipcar, have your students write their own "I love" poems about animals, things, or people. The pattern includes: Line 1—I love my . . . and why; Line 2—I hate my . . . and why; Line 3—The animal's name and where he is from; Line 4—What he eats (lives on); and Line 5—And his occupation. When they are finished, have the students read their own poem aloud or trade off and read each other's poems.

Since *Alphabet of Girls* deals only with the female gender, have your students write an alphabet of verses using boys names or even one with more girls names. Read selections from Leland Jacobs' collection of humorous verses before working on the poetry project.

Following the style of Edward Lear in *An Edward Lear Alphabet,* have students create their own ABC nonsense verses.

Lecourt's *Abracadabra to Zigzag* is a book about ricochet words. Before reading the book, choose a select word or two from it and have the students write a description of the word or draw a picture of it. The results should be interesting for things like "jeepers creepers" and "nip and tuck." The writing exercise would be particularly useful with upper elementary and high school students. After sharing the book with the class, have them find a curious word or phrase of their own. Create your own description or illustration of the word and then share it with the class.

Based on the popular alphabet story, *Chicka Chicka Boom Boom,* have your students create a "Tropical Alphabet Scene." Bright fluorescent paper can be used as the background. Use other shapes of brightly colored paper and cut out shapes and letters to make your own scene jungle. Glue the cutouts to the background to create a collage scene.

Instead of writing an alliterative phrase or sentences across the page, try writing the sentences in a column as seen in *Nedobeck's Alphabet Book*. Hand out an activity sheet with lines in a column. The children choose a letter of the alphabet and write an alliterative phrase or sentence going down the page.

Discuss the use of American Sign Language and its role in helping hearing-impaired people communicate. Give each child a chart showing how the letters of the alphabet are signed, and have them think of other items that the hand could have held to represent each letter as seen in *Handmade Alphabet*.

Use some of the characters from Richard Scarry's books and create alliterative sentences for them. For example, start with Dan Dog and then add words. Dan Dog drives diesels dangerously downtown and so on. *Richard Scarry's ABC Word Book* is a good title to start with. Alliterative sentences can quickly turn into tongue twisters too.

One Fly's Story

The old black fly spends his day pestering people. Trace the fly's trip through the busy household.

Choose a letter of the alphabet and write a tongue twister using only words that begin with that letter.

Letter I chose: ___

Write a tongue twister using only words beginning with the letter that you selected

_____

_____

_____

_____

_____

_____

_____

Most tongue twisters are written in phrases or sentences across a page. Choose a letter of the alphabet and write your tongue twister in a column down the page. You do not have to use all the lines listed.

For example: *F* at
              F urry
              F rogs
              F rolic
              F uriously

1. _____
2. _____
3. _____
4. _____
5. _____
6. _____
7. _____
8. _____
9. _____
10. _____
11. _____
12. _____

5. MULTICULTURALISM AND ALPHABET BOOKS

Multiculturalism or cultural diversity is a buzzword of the 1990s, and it is a term that is not only difficult to explain but also encompasses a wide variety of topics. In a sense, all of us come from a multicultural background, with ancestors from many countries with different religions, customs, foods, and family rituals. In today's sense of the word, it means that we need to teach children that not everyone comes from the same background and that it is important to learn about other cultures, races, and people in order to be better prepared to deal with the world and to get along with people. While some of the older alphabet books do reflect some cultural diversity, it has been only in the past five years or so that many books have flooded the market with illustrations and text showing a variety of races and cultures including African American, Hispanic, Jewish, Native American, Asian, and European. There are basically two ways in which children's books show cultural diversity. The first is for the entire book, including text and illustrations, to be devoted to explaining the customs and background of a particular region, race, tribe, or culture. The second way in which cultural diversity is shown is through the illustrations. While the text might be general in nature, the illustrations can show children from all kinds of backgrounds (Native American, Asian, Hispanic, etc.) and thus demonstrate in a more subtle way that all peoples have things in common.

African Americans are represented more than any other minority culture in alphabet books. In *The Black BC's* Lucille Clifton assembled an alphabet of famous black Americans and their contributions to the rich heritage of America. Although this alphabet book was published over 20 years ago and is for an older audience, the information is still very valid and useful. One of the few alphabet stories featuring African Americans as the main character is *Amazing Aunt Agatha* by Sheila Samton. Amazing Aunt Agatha works her way through the alphabet with her nephew Andrew. Bright cheerful colors and a simple text make this a good alphabet story for the beginning reader. Although the children in *Adam's ABC* could be any race or culture, there is focus on black-colored objects such as the fire escape, the river at night, and umbrellas in a rainstorm. This story of a day in the life of a city child is an excellent example of everyday things that all children can relate to.

Four alphabet books deal with Africa and African traditions and customs. Leo and Diane Dillon won a Caldecott Award in 1977 for their rich detailed illustrations in *Ashanti to Zulu: African Traditions*. Their paintings show as much detail as possible about the lifestyles and customs of each of the tribes described in the text written by Margaret Musgrove. Musgrove included some customs that were common to many African peoples as well as some that are unique to only one tribe. In *Jambo Means Hello*, Muriel and Tom Feelings give information about East African life through descriptions of the 24 letters of the Swahili alphabet. Ifeoma Onyefulu's *A is for Africa* provides images of family ties and traditional village life from all areas of the continent of Africa. Stunning color photographs are used to show the lives of the people. Another alphabet book, entitled *A is for Africa: "Looking at Africa Through the Alphabet,"* also shows the lifestyles, customs, and history of all kinds of Africans. A small box on each page shows the object for each letter as well as the object as it appears in a larger illustration in the book. One or more sentences of text explain the object and its relationship to Africa.

Malka Drucker's *A Jewish Holiday ABC* introduces some of the customs and traditions followed by Jews on their special holidays. Notes in the back give detailed information on the origins and history of some of the holidays. Not only is this an unusually artistic alphabet book, but it also provides numerous opportunities to discuss how people celebrate holidays other than the commercialized ones in America. There is also a beginner alphabet book that introduces the traditions associated with Hanukkah (*My First Hanukkah*) to the preschooler. The full color photographs in this title show many of the traditional objects associated with the Festival of Lights. A nice complement to these two books is *Alef-bet: A Hebrew Alphabet Book* by Michelle Edwards which shows that the everyday life of Jewish children varies little from that of other cultures.

Native Americans and Hispanics are difficult to find in picture books, but in alphabet books they are virtually nonexistent. Although *Little Indians' ABC* by Faustina Lucero would be considered a Native American alphabet book, the items presented in it, and the tone, might prove to be stereotypical and offensive to some Native Americans. The children shown in the illustrations represent several tribes as noted in the back of the book. A more appropriate alphabet book on Native Americans is *ABC's The American Indian Way* by Richard Red Hawk. Red Hawk offers an alphabet book that not only shows the letters but also provides an alphabetical guide to famous figures, tribes, and other topics that have to do with Native Americans. His book is appropriate for both beginning and older readers. *Idalia's Project ABC: An Urban Alphabet Book in English and Spanish* provides a bilingual alphabet guide to city life. The narrator is a little girl who talks about her family, friend, and life in the city. Both Spanish and English descriptions of the items are given in the book.

Alphabet books dealing with Eastern cultures are almost as scarce as those dealing with Hispanic/Latino cultures. One recent title is an alphabetical exploration of the eastern religion of Zen. *Zen ABC* uses classical haikus, koans, and some contemporary poetry to explore the history and spirtuality of Zen. Full color illustrations with elaborate details enhance the text. *A to Zen: A Book of Japanese Culture* by Ruth Wells is another of the few alphabet books that deal with Asian culture and customs. Not only does it supply a wealth of information about Japanese culture, but it is also printed like a traditional Japanese book with the pages going from back to front, right to left. Only 22 letters are used in the book, because the Japanese language does not have L, Q, V and X. Each letter introduces a Japanese word, showing how it appears in Japanese (reading from the top right corner and reading down the page) as well as the English equivalent (starting at the top left corner and reading right). The illustrations in the book are detailed, using the same techniques that are used to put designs on kimonos. In addition to being exposed to the alphabet, the reader also experiences the writing technique, artistic designs, and customs of the Japanese people.

The Calypso Alphabet by John Agard is an example of a book that shows some of the sights and sounds of another geographic region of the world. Through bright illustrations and rhythmic text, the reader is introduced to the world and calypso sounds of the Caribbean. A glossary in the back of the book explains some of the unfamiliar words. *A is for Aloha* by Stephanie Feeney is a portrait of another island region, Hawaii. Through black and white photographs of people and places, Feeney shows the everyday lives of children on the Hawaiian islands. Many of the things shown in the photographs are also indicative of children from any culture or race.

In Jim Aylesworth's *The Folks in the Valley,* the reader is taken on an alphabetical tour of a Pennsylvania Dutch (German heritage) settlement and the people and activities that take place there. Even the illustrations in this unique alphabet book imitate Pennsylvania Dutch folkways and motifs. Notes in the back give more information about the Pennsylvania Dutch culture. Alice and Martin Provensen offer a look at the Shakers in *A Peaceable Kingdom: The Shaker Abecedarius,* a picture book rendition of the rhyming verse the Shakers used to teach children the alphabet. A foreword in the book explains a bit about the Shakers, but it offers only enough for a taste of history. Use the Provensens' book to encourage students to do further research into the cultures and customs of both the Shakers and the Pennsylvania Dutch. Another look at a special region in the United States can be seen in James Rice's *Cajun Alphabet*. Gaston, the alligator, presents the alphabet in Cajun-style tongue twisters. In the process the reader receives a practical lesson in Cajun French and Cajun customs.

Several alphabet books deal with cultural diversity in the second way, that of using illustrations of people and things from a variety of cultural backgrounds. The Sound Box series (discussed in the story alphabet chapter) by Jane Belk Moncure shows children from diverse cultural backgrounds in the illustrations, but no ethnic customs or information is mentioned in the text. *My First ABC* by Debbie MacKinnon combines photographs of children with ordinary objects to introduce the alphabet. The text is very simple with only a child's name and the name of the object (e.g. Alison's apple; Zachary's zebra), but the children in the photographs represent a variety of cultural backgrounds from Asian and Hispanic to African American and Irish. The use of color photographs of children and simple text make this one of the best examples of cultural diversity in an alphabet book or even in picture books. *The Stephen Cartwright ABC* uses cartoonish pictures to introduce the letters of the alphabet, and the text does not deal with any particular culture. The children, however, in the illustrations in *The Stephen Cartwright ABC* and in Jenny Williams's *Everyday ABC* clearly come from a variety of races and lands. Another example of this type of presentation of cultural diversity can be seen in *The Children's ABC Christmas* by Patricia and Frederick McKissack. Based on a typical Christmas pageant, the 26 children present an event from the Christmas story. The children and the adults helping them prepare for the pageant are clearly from a variety of ethnic backgrounds, but the text is general and does not discuss one culture or another. Although *Alphabet Soup* by Abbie Zabar does not deal with any one ethnic group, it does offer information about foods from a variety of cultures from around the world. This non-fiction book includes a description of 26 unfamiliar but everyday foods from around the world. Foods such as dim sum, matzo, rijsttafel, and zabaglione are all discussed in this illustrated guide. Drawings, anecdotes, and histories, as well as a pronunciation guide, are a part of this unusual informational book.

The books mentioned in this chapter focus on specific ethnic groups and cultures and are valuable resources as alphabet books and as sources of information on the modes of dress, types of shelter, foods, celebrations, and languages of different groups of people. Although they can be used with the preschool group, for the most part they are best suited for upper elementary grades and higher. By using any of them to complement an in-depth study of a culture or ethnic group, teachers can help students develop a greater sensitivity to the similarities and differences among peoples of the world.

Students can examine and explore a particular culture and focus on a unique festival such as Mardi Gras or Hanukkah or even games, dances, and songs associated with a particular ethnic group. They can imitate the writing of a language such as the Japanese, prepare sample ethnic foods such as Cajun, look at the homes and customs of a continent such as Africa or Australia, or study the art techniques of a group like the Pennsylvania Dutch. By looking at alphabet books from a multicultural perspective, teachers and students can develop a new appreciation of other ethnic backgrounds as well as look at the alphabet in a new light.

MULTICULTURALISM AND ALPHABET BOOKS: BIBLIOGRAPHY

Agard, John. *The Calypso Alphabet*. Illustrated by Jennifer Bent. New York: Henry Holt & Co., 1989. ISBN 0-8050-1177-3.
Twenty-six exciting words from the Caribbean islands are used to show the letters of the alphabet
GRADES K–2. Lower case.

Amery, Heather. *The Stephen Cartwright ABC*. London, England: Usborne Pub. Ltd., 1990. ISBN 0-7460-0434-6.
Bright colorful pictures and rhyming text are used to introduce the alphabet letter by letter.
AGES 4 AND UP. Upper and lower case.

Aylesworth, Jim. *The Folks in the Valley: A Pennsylvania Dutch ABC*. Illustrated by Stefano Vitale. New York: Harper/Collins Pub., 1992. ISBN 0-06-021672-7; 0-06-021929-7.
This unique rhyming alphabet book tells about people and activities in a rural valley of a Pennsylvania Dutch settlement.
AGES 3–8. Upper and lower case.

Clifton, Lucille. *The Black BC's*. Illustrated by Don Miller. New York: E.P. Dutton & Co., Inc., 1970. ISBN 0-525-26595-3; 0-525-26596-1 (lib bdg).
Clifton provides an alphabetical celebration from Africa to Zenith of the ways in which African Americans have enriched the American way of life.
AGES 7 AND UP. Upper case.

Drucker, Malka. *A Jewish Holiday ABC*. Illustrated by Rita Pocock. San Diego, California: Harcourt Brace and Jovanovich, Publishers, 1992. ISBN 0-15-200482-3.
In this unusual alphabet book Drucker introduces Jewish holidays and customs.
ALL AGES. Upper and lower case.

Edwards, Michelle. *Alef-bet: A Hebrew Alphabet Book*. New York: Lothrop, Lee and Shepard, 1992. ISBN 0-688-09724-3; 0-688-09725-1 (lib bdg).
Edwards provides a guide to the Hebrew alphabet in a book featuring three children and their parents in their everyday life at home.
AGES 5 AND UP.

Feelings, Muriel. *Jambo Means Hello: Swahili Alphabet Book*. Pictures by Tom Feelings. New York: Dial Press, 1974. ISBN 0-8037-4346-7; 0-8037-4350-5 (lib bdg).
This alphabet book shows the 24 letters of the Swahili alphabet together with a word for each letter and a description of its meaning.
ALL AGES.

Feeney, Stephanie. *A is for Aloha*. Photographs by Hella Hammid. Honolulu, Hawaii: University of Hawaii Press, 1980. ISBN 0-8248-0722-7.
The author uses ABC format to portray the people, places, and experiences that make up the everyday lives of children in Hawaii.
AGES 4 AND UP. Upper and lower case.

Fife, Dale. *Adam's ABC*. Illustrated by Don Robertson. New York: Coward, McCann & Geoghegan, Inc., 1971.
From A to Z, the author guides us through a day in the life of city dweller Adam and his friends Arthur and Albert.
AGES 4 AND UP. Upper case.

Hudson, Cheryl Willis. *Afro-Bets: ABC Book*. Orange, New Jersey: Just Us Productions, 1987. ISBN 0-940975-00-9.
The Afro-Bet Kids form the shapes of the letters of the alphabet together with words and pictures that go with each letter.
AGES 4 AND UP. Upper and lower case.

Kunin, Claudia. *My Hanukkah Alphabet*. Racine, Wisconsin: Western Publishing Co., Inc., 1993. ISBN 0-307-13719-8.
Color photographs are used to introduce traditional objects (dreidels, latkes, etc.) associated with Hanukkah and at the same time introduce the letters of the alphabet.
AGES 2–6.

Lucero, Faustina H. *Little Indians' ABC*. Illustrated by Jeanne Pearson. Fayetteville, Georgia: ODDO Publishing Inc., 1974. ISBN 0-87783-129-7; 0-87783-130-0.
This very simple alphabet book shows items associated with Native Americans.
AGES 3 AND UP. Upper case.

MacKinnon, Debbie. *My First ABC*. Photographs by Anthea Sieveking. Hauppauge, New York: Barron's, 1992. ISBN 0-8120-6331-7.
Photographs of children and objects are used to represent the alphabet from Alison's apple to Zachary's zebra.
AGES 4–8. Upper and lower case.

McKissack, Patricia, and Frederick McKissack. *The Children's ABC Christmas*. Illustrated by Kathy Rogers. Minneapolis, Minnesota: Augsburg Publishing House, 1988. ISBN 0-8066-2356-X.

Based on a typical Christmas pageant, 26 children from many ethnic backgrounds present an event from the Christmas story from Abigail the Angel to Z and Zechariah.

AGES 6 AND UP. Upper case.

Mendoza, George. *The Christmas Tree Alphabet Book.* Illustrated by Bernadette. New York: World Publishing Co., 1971.

Children of all nationalities and races introduce Christmas traditions A to Z from around the world.

ALL AGES. Upper case.

Musgrove, Margaret. *Ashanti to Zulu: African Traditions.* Pictures by Leo and Diane Dillon. New York: The Dial Press, 1976. ISBN 0-8037-0308-2.

This Caldecott award winner provides an introduction to 26 African tribes/peoples with vignettes of their customs and traditions.

ALL AGES. Upper case.

Onyefulu, Ifeoma. *A is for Africa.* New York: Cobblehill Books, 1993. ISBN 0-525-65147-0.

Through color photographs and simple text, the reader is given a view of life on the continent of Africa.

AGES 4 AND UP. Upper and lower case.

Owoo, Ife Nii. *A is for Africa: "Looking at Africa Through the Alphabet."* Trenton, New Jersey: Africa World Press, Inc., 1991. ISBN 0-86543-182-5 (Hardcover); 0-86543-183-3 (soft).

This alphabet book shows the work, culture, history, and everyday lives of all kinds of Africans.

AGES 5 AND UP. Upper and lower case.

Provensen, Alice, and Martin Provensen. *A Peaceable Kingdom: The Shaker Abecedarius.* New York: The Viking Press, 1978. ISBN 0-670-54500-7.

The Shaker way of introducing the alphabet with a 26 line poem is shown in this special alphabet book.

AGES 4 AND UP.

Red Hawk, Richard. *ABC's The American Indian Way.* Newcastle, California: Sierra Oaks Publishing, 1988. ISBN 0-940113-15-5.

Red Hawk gives an alphabetical guide to famous figures, tribes, and other Native American topics.

ALL AGES.

Rice, James. *Cajun Alphabet.* Gretna, Louisiana: Pelican Publishing Co., 1976, 1991. ISBN 0-88289-822-1.

An introduction to the alphabet and a practical but clever lesson in Cajun French is presented by Gaston the alligator.

AGES 6 AND UP. Upper case.

Rosario, Idalia. *Idalia's Project ABC: An Urban Alphabet Book in English and Spanish.* New York: Henry Holt and Co., 1981. ISBN 0-8050-0296-0; 0-8050-0286-3 (Hardcover)

This unique bilingual alphabet book uses both Spanish and English descriptions of city life to introduce the alphabet.

AGES 5 AND UP. Upper and lower case.

Samton, Sheila. *Amazing Aunt Agatha.* Ilustrated by Yvette Banek. Milwaukee, Wisconsin: Raintree Pub., 1990. ISBN 0-8172-3575-2.

Amazing Aunt Agatha and her nephew Andrew work their way through the alphabet with all kinds of accomplishments such as drawing dinosaurs.

AGES 5–8. Upper and lower case.

Wells, Ruth. *A to Zen: A Book of Japanese Culture.* Illustrated by Yoshi. Saxonville, Massachusetts: Picture Book Studio, 1992. ISBN 0-88708-175-4.

Japanese words from A to Z are introduced in the alphabet book printed in traditional Japanese style (back to front.)

ALL AGES.

Williams, Jenny. *Everyday ABC.* New York: Dial Books for Younger Readers, 1991. ISBN 0-8037-1079-8.

This alphabet book is filled with the ordinary objects of a child's universe.

AGES 3–7.

Zabar, Abbie. *Alphabet Soup.* New York: Stewart Tubori and Chang, Inc., 1990. ISBN 1-55670-154-3.

Zabar provides a nonfiction introduction to 26 foods from around the world.

ALL AGES.

Zen ABC. Illustrated by Amy Zerner and Jessie Spicer Zerner. Boston, Massachusetts: Charles E. Tuttle Co., Inc., 1993. ISBN 0-8048-1806-1.

This elaborately illustrated book is an exploration of the history and spirituality of the religion of Zen.

ALL AGES. Upper case.

MULTICULTURALISM AND ALPHABET BOOKS: ACTIVITIES

Read *The Folks in the Valley: A Pennsylvania Dutch ABC* to the class. Discuss the Pennsylvania Dutch area, the peoples, customs, and some of the art techniques attributed to this area. Demonstrate some stenciling techniques to the class. Then have the students create their own stencil pattern based on those used by the Pennsylvania Dutch.

Another activity to use with Jim Aylesworth's book is to have each child research and write a report about one of the activities in the book such as making jam, gathering eggs, building fences, etc. or to write about some activity that their families do (e.g. baking cookies, mowing the yard, etc.)

Discuss some of the Jewish holidays talked about in *A Jewish Holiday ABC* by Malka Drucker. If there are any children in the group from a Jewish family, have them explain some of the customs that their family have for the various holidays. As an extension activity, have each child create a collage of some of the family holiday traditions that they celebrate. Use a variety of materials such as cloth, paper, glitter, etc. to create a collage.

Jambo Means Hello includes a map showing where Swahili is spoken in Africa. Students can research some of the other languages spoken on the continent and create their own maps showing the location of the languages. In connection with this activity, research other languages around the world and where they are spoken.

Musgrove's *Ashanti to Zulu* is an excellent resource to use with children of all ages up to and including high school. Give students an outline map of Africa and have them mark the location of each of the 26 African tribes mentioned in the text. Another activity is to give each student a word puzzle and have them find and circle each of the tribes.

In connection with Musgrove's book, use the same outline map and have the children locate the specific places and countries that are mentioned in *A is for Africa* by Ife Nii Owoo. Discuss some of the differences and similarities in the different parts of the continent.

Following the style introduced in *A to Zen,* and with some prior instruction, have the students imitate Japanese writing.

Choose a holiday unique to a culture other than your own. Research it and write a report about the holiday. When is it? How is it celebrated? Provide other information about the celebration. Include illustrations in your report that explain more about the holiday.

Compare and contrast life on the island state of Hawaii to that in the continental United States.

**Use this outline map and have students mark the location of the 26 tribes mentioned in *Ashanti to Zulu* and/or the specific places and countries mentioned in *A is for Africa*.

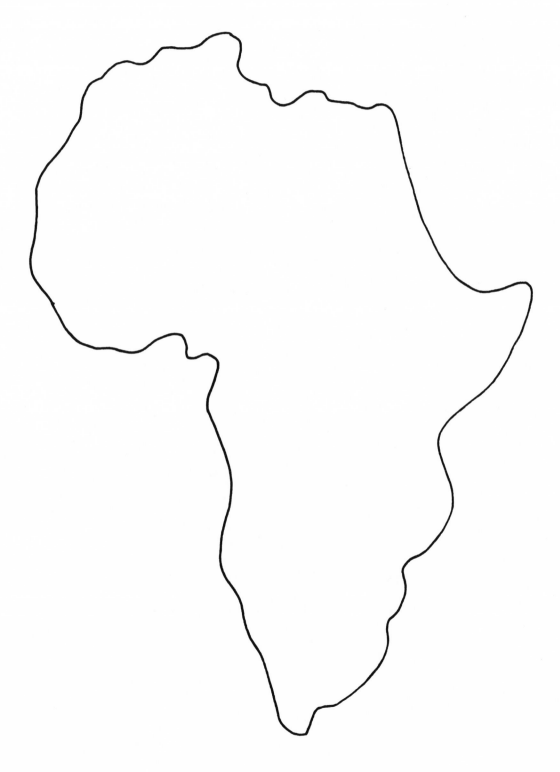

African Tribes

Locate and circle each of the 26 African tribes discussed in *Ashanti to Zulu*. The tribes can be up or down, across or diagonal.

Ashanti	Ga	Ndaka	Uge
Baule	Hausa	Ouadai	Vai
Chagge	Ikoma	Pondo	Wagenia
Dogon	Jie	Quimbande	Xhosa
Ewe	Kung	Rendille	Yoruba
Fanti	Lozi	Sotho	Zulu
	Masai	Tuareg	

```
Q  U  I  M  B  A  N  D  E  U  O

Y  F  N  O  G  O  D  P  Q  W  O

V  A  K  O  T  U  A  R  E  G  E

A  N  U  Y  X  L  K  J  I  E  B

I  T  N  A  H  S  A  N  V  C  A

K  I  G  W  O  O  U  A  D  A  I

O  R  A  U  S  T  M  U  B  V  N

M  E  G  G  A  H  C  L  R  W  E

A  Y  W  E  Y  O  R  U  B  A  G

U  W  A  C  O  U  I  Z  O  L  A

I  R  E  N  D  I  L  L  E  H  W

J  H  L  M  N  W  E  R  T  K  M

M  A  U  N  O  G  M  A  S  A  I

A  D  A  H  V  P  A  S  U  A  H

Q  M  B  U  E  R  T  N  C  V  Z
```

6. STORY ALPHABET BOOKS

One of the most popular formats for alphabet books is the use of the alphabet as a means of telling a story. In some cases the letters of the alphabet are featured prominently in the story, while in other cases the letters are of secondary importance. For example, in *The Alphabet Tree* by Leo Lionni, a tree, filled with leaf-hopping letters, survives strong gale winds that leave the letters clustered together in fear. A word bug and a purple caterpillar suggest that letters form words and words form sentences that "mean something important." While this book does not follow the traditional alphabet format of introducing letters A to Z, it does present the alphabet in a new light, highlighting the talents of artist Leo Lionni. *The Story of Z* by Jeanne Modesitt is another example of a narrative about the alphabet. Tired of always being last, the letter Z runs away to be on her own. Throughout the story, people try to make do without using the letter Z in any words, and the reader learns that each letter including Z is important in language. Again, in this book the letters of the alphabet are not presented in the traditional A to Z format, but they are presented as a unit that when combined provides words and sentences that are essential to communication.

Alphabet Soup by Kate Banks would not be considered a true picture alphabet book, but it is a story that emphasizes the importance of letters used to create words. A little boy uses the letters in his alphabet soup to create words to help him and his imaginery bear friend as they go on a series of interesting adventures. One of the more recent additions to the alphabet book story genre, *The Alphabet Soup* by Mirko Gabler, introduces the letters of the alphabet in a rather wacky but humorous way. Zack follows the witch twins, Gurgla and Blog, home from school only to discover that he may become a part of their homework assignment of making alphabet soup. The witch twins and their mother add some unusual ingredients to the soup including **A**nts, **B**agworms, **C**runchy **C**rabs, pickled **S**nakes, a **T**arantula, and **V**ampire Teeth. Not only are the letters of the alphabet introduced through the wacky ingredients for witch's alphabet soup, but the reader is also entertained with a humorous story. The text in this book is not for the beginning reader. It is, however, an excellent read-aloud story for the classroom teacher, a library storytime, or an individual student.

The Rebellious Alphabet does not resemble the traditional alphabet story in any way, but it emphasizes the importance of words and reading. An illiterate dictator bans all reading and writing in his country, but an old man defies the dictator and trains his birds to print words and messages. The illustrations are modernistic with bright colors and sharp corners, while the text is complex and not designed for the beginning reader. The alphabet is not shown in a traditional manner, but letters are shown on pages as the birds print messages. This modern day fable on censorship and resistance is an excellent title to use as a discussion topic for upper elementary and high school students. In fact it could prove to be a good title to use as a basis of a unit on censorship. Another alphabet story that would be useful with middle or high school students is *The Great Alphabet Fight and How Peace Was Made*. In this book, a boy dreams about going through a secret door and entering a school room where the letters C and E are at odds with one another. Throughout the course of the story, the other letters tell about words that they are a part of. Finally the letter D manages to make peace between C and E and all ends well. Although the tone of the story is a bit moralistic, it does make the point that peace can be achieved if all sides begin to communicate with one another. This alphabet book can act as a discussion starter with older students on the state of the world and how peace might be achieved in the various troubled areas around the world. In addition to discussing the issue of peace, it would also be thought-provoking to discuss the artist, Joni Eareckson Tada. Joni was permanently paralyzed from the neck down in a diving accident several years ago. Just as her letters are quarrelsome in the book, so was Joni when she discovered that her condition was permanent. As time passed, Joni made peace with herself and now leads an active life painting, writing books and music, and enjoying herself. She serves as an example of how a physically challenged person can lead a productive, happy life and how making peace with oneself is the first step to this goal. All of these titles are very useful in helping students understand the importance of letters in language skills, as well as providing entertaining stories and topics for discussion.

Just as picture book stories follow a variety of plot lines, including the adventure story and the cumulative tale, so do alphabet story books. One recently published series, *Read Around Alphabet Town,* uses the adventure plot line to familiarize the reader with a letter of the alphabet. Several authors contributed to the writing of this series. The main character in each adventure book lives in a house shaped like the first letter identifying him (e.g., Dinosaur lives in a "D" shaped house, Squirrel lives in a "S" shaped house, etc.). As the character walks around the town or goes on some kind of adventure, young readers discover many words that begin with that particular letter. Another series, entitled *Sound Box Books,* written by Jane Belk Moncure uses a main character on an adventure as a means for introducing the letter of the alphabet. Each character has a sound box that he is trying to fill with objects beginning with a letter of the alphabet. In the series *ABC Adventures* by Patricia Whitehead, each of the individual titles combines a traditional upper and lower case letter and a word with a brief story. The letter of the alphabet appears on the page accompanied by an appropriate word from the text. The words do not follow any thematic approach but are simply lifted from the text of the story. All three of these series are valuable for use with preschoolers and young readers as a means of expanding vocabularies, introducing sound/symbol relationships, nurturing beginning reader skills, and building an appreciation for a good story.

In addition to these series of adventure books, there are some excellent examples of alphabet books where the characters have interesting and unusual adventures. *Miss Hindy's Cats* is a superb title for a read-aloud storytime for a classroom or library or for a parent's nighttime story. Miss Hindy takes in a stray cat who mysteriously appears on her doorstep one day and names it Agnes. Before she has time to think, she has a houseful of cats from A to Z and more companions than she ever dreamed about. *The Pigs' Alphabet* by Leah Palmer Preiss is truly an adventure for anyone who likes pigs. Pinkerton and Prue are two pigs who never seem to stop eating (or arguing). Finally the maitre d' proposes an eating competition to end the argument of who is the hungriest. Prue and Pinkerton eat their way through the alphabet and end up with an unbelievable prize for the winner. The characters are true to their "eat anything" pig nature, and the pink cover and pink borders reinforce the image of piggies at play.

In *The ABC Mystery,* Doug Cushman has written a simple story involving the search for stolen art. The characters and the search are reminiscent of the old slapstick comedies involving a "cops and robbers" chase. The text consists of a simple sentence that offers an alphabet of people, objects, and clues that lead to the art thieves. Bright cheerful colors and comical animal characters make this alphabetical mystery a delight for both the beginning and advanced reader.

Proper names figure prominently in the adventures of several alphabet books. In *Flannery Row* by Karen Ackerman, Commander Ahab Flannery bids farewell to his 26 children before going off to sea. Patricia Lillie's book, *One Very, Very Quiet Afternoon* also deals with an alphabet of names, but with a different twist. Annabelle Barbara Cavendish decides to have a quiet tea party, only to have her quiet disturbed by Daniel Ezra Fiddleston and his friends. All of the children in this book have first, middle, and last names that follow the sequence of the alphabet. A different type of adventure awaits the residents of *Hurricane City,* where hurricane season never ends. Names feature prominently in this story—as the names of the hurricanes that pass through. One family relates the story of what happens in their town when hurricanes from A to Z blow their way through. Although no one seems to get hurt during the windy times, things do get blown around and mixed up helter skelter. A litany of proper names parades before the reader in *Hooper Humperdink . . . ? Not Him!* by Theo LeSieg (LeSieg is a pseudonym of Theodore Seuss Geisel. LeSieg is Geisel backwards). A young child decides to throw an elaborate party and invite all his friends but Hooper Humperdink. He names all the people from A to Z that he intends to invite, but not Hooper. The colorful, comic illustrations and the rhyming verse in this easy-to-read story make it both inviting and entertaining for readers of all ages.

The cumulative tale is a very popular means of introducing the alphabet. In *This Is the Ambulance Leaving the Zoo* by Norma Farber, the young reader is on a merry chase to find out what is in the ambulance leaving the zoo. The ambulance encounters all kinds of alphabetical sights on its way to its destination. Two pages in the back recount the key words and actions that take place. *Crazy Alphabet* by Lynne Cox is a cumulative tale of the events that occur after a bird eats an apple. Cox uses crazy-quilt designs to illustrate all the objects and creatures in her zany story. Janet Wolf's *Adelaide to Zeke* is an excellent example of a cumulative story interwoven with the traditional A to Z presentation. Each of the inhabitants completes an activity that leads to the next letter of the alphabet (e.g., Q is for Quentin, who quacked at Ron; R is for Ron, who read to Sally, etc.). The letter is clearly identified, but at the same time it is interdependent upon the rest of the text. By presenting the letters of the alphabet in a story format, the author is able to provide an interesting twist to a traditional topic. Although *Once Upon A to Z: An Alphabet Odyssey* by Jody Linscott is not a traditional cumulative tale, each action in the story is dependent upon the lines which come before and after it. Andy's appetite is so enormous that he eats all his food before the dawdling Daisy can make her deliveries. Andy goes off to find her, and somehow they manage to form a musical group, the Worthy Wonders. The alliterative language and some unfamiliar words make *Once Upon A to Z* a story more appropriate for older middle school children. The collage illustrations are very unusual and were created by applying layers of colored paper in cut-out shapes and sizes.

While simple identification alphabet books are best for introducing the letters to very young children and beginning readers, story alphabet books are useful for continuing reinforcement of letter recognition, increasing word knowledge and contextual understanding, and entertaining the reader as he or she learns. Alphabet books range from the traditional A to Z introduction to letters to humorous cumulative stories and adventure tales. Some of the more unusual tales can be used with children as a discussion-starter on topics that are in the news or that figure prominently in their own lives. Such books can be used to encourage creativity and inventiveness as well as serve as instruments of pure entertainment. In any case, story alphabet books are a welcome addition to the alphabet genre and will continue to contribute some unusual titles to this traditional topic.

Ackerman, Karen. *Flannery Row: An Alphabet Rhyme*. Illustrated by Karen Ann Weinhaus. Boston, Massachusetts: The Atlantic Monthly Press, 1986. ISBN 0-87113-054-8.

Before Commander Ahab Flannery sets off to sea, he has to say goodbye to each of his 26 children.

AGES 3–7. Upper case.

Berger, Terry. *Ben's ABC Day*. Photographs by Alice Kandell. New York: Lothrop, Lee and Shepard Books, 1982. ISBN 0-688-00881-X; 0-688-00882-8 (lib bdg).

Through a series of photographs, Ben shows an ordinary day and all the activities that he does.

AGES 3–7. Upper case.

Budd, Lillian. *The Pie Wagon*. Illustrated by Marilyn Milter. New York: Lothrop, Lee and Shepard, Inc., 1960.

When the tall thin Pie Man comes around with his pie wagon, Tilly has trouble choosing a pie from the A–Z assortment of Apple to Zig-Zag Cranberry until she looks at the X-tra special shelf.

AGES 5–8. Lower case.

Burton, Marilee Robin. *Aaron Awoke: An Alphabet Story*. New York: Harper and Row, Publishers, 1982. ISBN 0-06-020891-0; 0-06-020892-9.

Aaron's alphabet actions are followed on a day on the farm.

AGES 3–6. Upper case.

Chardiet, Bernice. *C is for Circus*. Illustrated by Brinton Turkle. New York: Walker and Company, 1971. ISBN 0-8027-6083-X.

In a unique approach, the entire panorama of a circus performance is revealed in alphabetical, rhythmic style.

AGES 3–8. Upper case.

Cox, Lynne. *Crazy Alphabet*. Illustrated by Rodney McRae. New York: Orchard Books, 1990. ISBN 0-531-05966-9; 0-531-08566-X (lib bdg).

This cumulative tale recounts the events that occur after a bird eats an apple.

AGES 3 AND UP. Upper and lower case.

Cushman, Doug. *The ABC Mystery*. New York: HarperCollins Publishers, 1993. ISBN 0-06-021226-8; 0-06-021227-6 (lib bdg).

Inspector McGroom uses an alphabetical list of people, objects, and clues to find a gang of art thieves.

AGES 4–9. Upper case.

DeLage, Ida. *ABC Easter Bunny*. Drawings by Ellen Sloan. Champaign, Illinois: Garrard Publishing. Co., 1979. ISBN 0-8116-4356-5.

As the Easter bunny makes his deliveries far and wide, he enlists the help of his friends with all kind of activities from A to Z.

AGES 3–7. Upper case.

———. *ABC Halloween Witch*. Drawings by Lou Cunette. Champaign, Illinois: Garrard Publishing Co., 1977. ISBN 0-8116-4353-0.

A witch introduces the reader to Halloween things from A to Z.

AGES 3–7. Upper case.

———. *ABC Triplets at the Zoo*. Drawings by Lori Pierson. Champaign, Illinois: Garrard Publishing Co., 1977. ISBN 0-8116-4357-3.

The triplets take a walk through the zoo and meet all kinds of animals and zoo things.

AGES 3–7. Upper case.

Diaz, Jorge. *The Rebellious Alphabet*. Illustrated by Oivind S. Jorfald. Translated by Geoffrey Fox. New York: Henry Holt and Co., 1983. ISBN 0-8050-2765-3.

After an illiterate dictator bans all reading and writing, an old man trains his birds to continue to print words and messages.

AGES 6 AND UP.

Farber, Norma. *This Is the Ambulance Leaving the Zoo*. Illustrated by Tomie de Paola. New York: E.P. Dutton & Co., Inc., 1975. ISBN 0-525-41125-9.

In this cumulative tale an ambulance leaves the zoo and encounters all kinds of alphabetical landmarks on the way to its destination.

AGES 5–8.

Gabler, Mirko. *The Alphabet Soup*. New York: Henry Holt & Co., 1992. ISBN 0-8050-2049-7.

When Zack follows the witch twins home from school, he finds himself among the possible ingredients for their homework, making ABC soup.

AGES 6 AND UP. Upper case.

LeSieg, Theo. *Hooper Humperdink . . . ? Not Him!* New York: Random House, 1976. ISBN 0-394-83286-8; 0-394-93286-2 (lib bdg).

When he throws a sensational party, a young child decides to invite all his friends but not Hooper Humperdink.
ALL AGES.

Lillie, Patricia. *One Very, Very Quiet Afternoon*. New York: Greenwillow Books, 1986. ISBN 0-688-04322-4.

When Annabelle Barbara Cavendish has a quiet tea party, she doesn't think that Daniel Ezra Fiddleston and friends would disrupt it.
AGES 3–7.

Linscott, Judy. *Once Upon A to Z: An Alphabet Odyssey*. Illustrated by Claudia Porges Holland. New York: Doubleday, 1991. ISBN 0-385-41893-0; 0-385-41907-4 (lib bdg).

The amazing appetite of Andy leads him to Daisy the delivery girl, and they form a musical group, the Worthy Wonders.
AGES 5 AND UP. Upper and lower case.

Lionni, Leo. *The Alphabet Tree*. New York: Pantheon, 1968. ISBN 0-679-80835-3.

A tree, full of leaf hopping letters, survives gale force winds that leave the letters all scattered.
AGES 4–8.

Mack, Stan. *The King's Cat is Coming*. New York: Pantheon Books, 1976. ISBN 0-394-83302-3; 0-394-93302-8.

When the people hear about the imminent arrival of the king's cat, they speculate about the characteristics that he might possess.
ALL AGES. Upper case.

Mendoza, George. *A Beastly Alphabet*. Pictures by Joseph Low. New York: Grosset & Dunlap, 1969.

Mendoza based his cumulative tale of some very unusual creatures on the bestiaries (animal books) of the Middle Ages.
AGES 5–10. Upper case.

Miller, Roberta. *Richard Scarry's Chipmunk ABC*. Illustrated by Richard Scarry. Racine, Wisconsin: Western Publishing Company, 1963. ISBN 0-307-02024-X; 0-307-68024-X (lib bdg).

In this easy-to-read story book, Chipmunk and his friends encounter all kinds of A to Z things.
AGES 3–8. Upper case.

Modesitt, Jeanne, and Lonni Sue Johnson. *The Story of Z*. Saxonville, Massachusetts: Picture Book Studio, 1990. ISBN 0-88708-105-3.

Tired of always being last, Z walks away from the alphabet only to discover that she is needed after all.
AGES 6–9.

Moncure, Jane Belk. Series: *Sound Box Books*. Elgin, Illinois: The Child's World. 24 titles.

This series features children from many cultures.

Individual titles include:

My "a" Sound Box.	1984.	ISBN 0-89565-296-X.
My "b" Sound Box.	1977.	ISBN 0-89565-182-3
My "c" Sound Box.	1979.	ISBN 0-89565-052-5.
My "d" Sound Box.	1978.	ISBN 0-89565-044-4.
My "e" Sound Box.	1984.	ISBN 0-89565-297-8.
My "f" Sound Box.	1977.	ISBN 0-89565-185-8.
My "g" Sound Box.	1977.	ISBN 0-89565-053-3
My "h" Sound Box.	1977.	ISBN 0-89565-184-X.
My "i" Sound Box.	1984.	ISBN 0-89565-298-6.
My "j" Sound Box.	1979.	ISBN 0-89565-049-5.
My "k" Sound Box.	1979.	ISBN 0-89565-050-9.
My "l" Sound Box.	1978.	ISBN 0-89565-045-2.
My "m" Sound Box.	1979.	ISBN 0-89565-051-7.
My "n" Sound Box.	1979.	ISBN 0-89565-054-1.
My "o" Sound Box.	1984.	ISBN 0-89565-299-4.
My "p" Sound Box.	1978.	ISBN 0-89565-047-9.
My "q" Sound Box.	1979.	ISBN 0-89565-100-9.
My "r" Sound Box.	1978.	ISBN 0-89565-048-7.
My "s" Sound Box.	1977.	ISBN 0-89565-181-5.
My "t" Sound Box.	1977.	ISBN 0-89565-183-1.
My "u" Sound Box.	1984.	ISBN 0-89565-300-1.
My "v" Sound Box.	1979.	ISBN 0-89565-101-7.
My "w" Sound Box.	1978.	ISBN 0-89565-046-0.
My "x, y, z" Sound Box.	1979.	ISBN 0-89565-102-5.

AGES 3–9.

Pittman, Helena Clare. *Miss Hindy's Cats*. Minneapolis, Minnesota: Carolrhoda Books, 1990. ISBN 0-87614-368-0.

    On the day that a stray cat appears on her doorstep, little does Miss Hindy know that she will soon have 26 cats, a new home, and a surprise guest.

AGES 4–9. Upper and lower case.

Polette, Nancy. *The Hole by the Apple Tree: An A–Z Discovery Tale*. Pictures by Nishan Akgulian. New York: Greenwillow Books, 1992. ISBN 0-688-10557-2; 0-688-10558-0 (lib bdg).

    As Harold digs a hole by the apple tree, his friends happen by, and his imagination leads them through the alphabet with many familiar characters.

AGES 5–8. Upper case.

Preiss, Leah Palmer. *The Pigs' Alphabet*. Boston, Massachusetts: David R. Godine, Publisher, 1990. ISBN 0-87923-781-3.

    When Pinkerton and Prue argue about who is the hungriest, the maitre d' proposes a twenty-six course alphabetical feast to settle the argument.

AGES 4–8. Upper case.

Read Around Alphabet Town. Series of 24 titles. Chicago, Illinois: Childrens Press, 1992.

    Individual titles include:

Ape's Adventure in Alphabet Town. by Janet McDonnell; Illustrated by Linda Hohag. ISBN 0-516-05405-5.

Bear's Adventure in Alphabet Town. by Janet McDonnell; Illustrated by Linda Hohag. ISBN 0-516-05402-3.

Cat's Adventure in Alphabet Town. by Laura Alden; Illustrated by Jodie McCallum. ISBN 0-516-05403-1.

Dinosaur's Adventure in Alphabet Town. by Doris Cook; Illustrated by Russ Rigo. ISBN 0-516-05404-X.

Elfin's Adventure in Alphabet Town. by Laura Alden; Illustrated by Linda Hohag. ISBN 0-516-05405-8.

Fox's Adventure in Alphabet Town. by Janet McDonnell; Illustrated by Jodie McCallum. ISBN 0-516-05406-6.

Goat's Adventure in Alphabet Town. by Janet McDonnell; Illustrated by Tom Dunnington. ISBN 0-516-15407-4.

Hippo's Adventure in Alphabet Town. Written & Illustrated by Janet McDonnell. ISBN 0-516-05408-2.

Ichabod's Adventure in Alphabet Town. by Janet McDonnell; Illustrated by Pam Peltier. ISBN 0-516-05409-0.

Jack and Jill's Adventure in Alphabet Town. by Janet Riehecky; Illustrated by Linda Hohag. ISBN 516-05410-4.

Kangaroo's Adventure in Alphabet Town. by Janet McDonnell; Illustrated by Jodie McCallum. ISBN 0-516-05411-2.

Little Lady's Adventure in Alphabet Town. by Janet Riehecky; Illustrated by Jodie McCallum. ISBN 0-516-05412-0.

Mouse's Adventure in Alphabet Town. by Janet McDonnell; Illustrated by Jenny Williams. ISBN 0-516-05413-9.

Nightingale's Adventure in Alphabet Town. by Laura Alden; Illustrated by Jodie McCallum. ISBN 0-516-05414-7.

Owl's Adventure in Alphabet Town. by Laura Alden; Illustrated by Jodie McCallum. ISBN 0-516-05415-5.

Penguin's Adventure in Alphabet Town. by Laura Alden; Illustrated by Jenny Williams. ISBN 0-516-05416-3.

Quarterback's Adventure in Alphabet Town. by Janet McDonnell; Illustrated by Jodie McCallum. ISBN 0-516-05417-1.

Raccoon's Adventure in Alphabet Town. by Janet McDonnell; Illustrated by Helen Endres. ISBN 0-516-05418-X.

Squirrel's Adventure in Alphabet Town. by Laura Alden; Illustrated by Judi Collins. ISBN 0-516-05419-8.

Turtle's Adventure in Alphabet Town. Written and Illustrated by Janet McDonnell. ISBN 0-516-05420-1.

Umpire's Adventure in Alphabet Town. by Laura Alden; Illustrated by Linda Hohag. ISBN 0-516-05421-X.

Victor's Adventure in Alphabet Town. by Janet McDonnell; Illustrated by Pam Peltier. ISBN 0-516-05422-8.

Walrus's Adventure in Alphabet Town. by Janet Riehecky; Illustrated by Diana Magnuson. ISBN 0-516-05423-6.

X Y Z Adventure in Alphabet Town. by Janet McDonnell; Illustrated by Linda Hogag. ISBN 0-516-05424-4.

AGES 5–9.

Reese, Bob. *ABC*. Chicago, Illinois: Childrens Press, 1992. ISBN 0-516-05577-1.

    A teacher shows her class how to put letters of the alphabet together to make words.

AGES 4–6.

Rey, H.A. *Curious George Learns the Alphabet*. Boston, Masschusetts: Houghton Mifflin Co., 1963. ISBN 0-395-16031-6; 0-395-1718-7 (soft).

    The man in the yellow hat teaches George, the curious monkey, all about the letters of the alphabet.

AGES 6–10.

Sedgwick, Paulita. *Circus ABC*. New York: Holt, Rinehart & Winston, 1978. ISBN 0-03-042391-0.

    When the Alphabet Man opens his bag, he introduces the circus as well as the letters of the alphabet.

AGES 4 AND UP. Upper and lower case.

Stock, Catherine. *Alexander's Midnight Snack: A Little Elephant's ABC*. New York: Clarion Books, 1988. ISBN 0-89919-512-1.

    When Alexander decides to eat a midnight snack, it soon turns into an A to Z feast (and mess).

AGES 3–6. Upper case.

Tada, Joni Eareckson, and Steve Jensen. *The Great Alphabet Fight and How Peace Was Made*. Sisters, Oregon: Gold 'n' Honey Books; Questar Publishers, Inc., 1993. ISBN 0-88070-572-8.

    A small boy dreams about the day the letters C and E began to quarrel and how peace was finally achieved.

AGES 7 AND UP. Upper case.

Travers, Mary. *Mary Poppins from A to Z*. Illustrated by Mary Shepard. New York: Harcourt Brace & World, Inc., 1962. ISBN 0-15-252590-4.

This alphabet story tells all about Mary Poppins and the Banks family.

AGES 6–12.

Warren, Cathy. *Victoria's ABC Adventure*. Illustrated by Patience Brewster. New York: Lothrop, Lee and Shepard Books, 1984. ISBN 0-688-02021-6; 0-688-02023-2 (lib bdg).

Victoria, the little brown snake, saves the lives of her family when trouble at a cookout threatens their lives.

AGES 4–8.

Watson, Clyde. *Applebet: An ABC*. Pictures by Wendy Watson. New York: Farrar, Straus & Giroux, 1992. ISBN 0-374-30384-3.

This book follows the alphabetical adventures of a farmer and his daughter when they go the country fair with a cartful of apples.

AGES 4–8. Upper case.

Weeks, Sarah. *Hurricane City*. Illustrations by James Warhola. New York: Harper/Collins, 1993. ISBN 0-06-021572-0; 0-06-02173-9 (lib bdg)

Weeks presents an alphabetical romp through a mythical city where things are blown around, but no one gets hurt, and hurricane season never ends.

AGES 3–8. Upper case.

Whitehead, Patricia. Series: ABC Adventures. Mahwah, New Jersey: Troll Associates, 1985.

Arnold Plays Baseball. Illustrated by G. Brian Karas. ISBN 0-8167-0367-1 (lib bdg); 0-8167-0368-X (soft).

Best Halloween Book. Illustrated by Stephanie Britt. ISBN 0-8167-0373-6 (lib bdg); 0-8167-0374-4 (soft).

Best Thanksgiving Book. Illustrated by Susan T. Hall. ISBN 08167-0371-X (lib bdg); 0-8167-0372-6 (soft).

Best Valentine Book. Illustrated by Paul Harvey. ISBN 0-8167-0369-8 (lib bdg); 0-8167-0370-1 (soft).

Christmas Alphabet Book. Illustrated by Deborah Colvin Borgo. ISBN 0-8167-0365-5.

Dinosaur Alphabet Book. Illustrated by Joel Snyder. ISBN 0-8167-0363-9 (lib bdg); 0-8167-0364-7 (soft).

Here Comes Hungry Albert. Illustrated by G. Brian Karas. ISBN 0-8167-0379-5 (lib bdg); 0-8167-0380-9 (soft).

Let's Go to the Farm. Illustrated by Ethel Gold. ISBN 0-8167-0377-9.

Let's Go to the Zoo. Illustrated by Patti Boyd. ISBN 0-8167-0375-2 (lib bdg); 0-8167-0376-0 (soft).

What a Funny Bunny. Illustrated by Don Page. ISBN 0-8167-0361-2 (lib bdg); 0-8167-0362-0 (soft).

AGES 3–9. Upper and lower case.

Wolf, Janet. *Adelaide to Zeke*. New York: Harper and Row, Publishers, 1987. ISBN 0-06-026597-3.

The inhabitants of a small town relate an A to Z story.

AGES 4–8. Upper case.

Wylie, Joanne, and David Wylie. *A Fishy Alphabet Story*. Chicago, Illinois: Childrens Press, 1983. ISBN 0-516-02981-9.

A young boy tells how to catch fish, from the A-B-C fish to the X-Y-Z fish, in this beginning reader.

AGES 3–7. Upper case.

STORY ALPHABET BOOKS: ACTIVITIES

Both *Flannery Row* and *One Very, Very Quiet Afternoon* use proper names for the letters of the alphabet. Have the class make an ABC list of other names that could have been part of either or both of the stories. Just as Annabelle uses three letters of the alphabet for her three names, make a list of other groups of three letter names.

After sharing *Ben's ABC Day* with the class, have each student make up a list of A to Z activities for a typical day. Use personal photographs, sketches, or pictures from magazines to create a book of your own. Write a word or phrase underneath each picture to explain it.

Share *The Pie Wagon* with the children. Have the children make a list of other kinds of pies that the pie man might have carried on his wagon. Bring in several different kinds of pie, cherry, strawberry, lemon meringue, key lime, ice cream, apple, peach, banana cream, chocolate, etc., and let the children taste them. As a take home activity, give each child an activity sheet, "Bake Your Own Pie," to complete on their own.

The illustrations in *C is for Circus* are reminiscent of old-time circus posters. Have each child select a letter of the alphabet and a circus-related activity or character to use in creating a circus bill. Use the circus bills as part of a display in the classroom or library together with books and other materials about the circus.

Have the students try to identify as many items as possible in each of the pictures in *Circus ABC* as well as trying to find the clown jester that appears in the pictures. He makes at least 19 appearances. Use this book together with *C is for Circus* as part of a circus day theme.

This Is the Ambulance Leaving the Zoo by Norma Farber is a perfect story to use as a flannelboard/participation story. Before reading it aloud, make flannelboard figures for each of the 26 alphabetical items mentioned in the story. Then make cue cards for sounds for several of the items. Pass out the sound cue cards and explain to the children that they are going to help tell this ABC story by making the sounds on their cue cards. Sounds might include: swishing for the launderette, barking dogs in the kennel, horns for the traffic jam, screeching brakes for the bus stopping, and others that you can make up. After the story, have the children help create more sounds that would enhance the story.

After reading aloud *The Alphabet Soup* by Mirko Gabler have the students create their own "Witches Alphabet Soup." Make a list of ingredients that they might have added to the soup, not including the ones mentioned in the text of the story. Draw or find pictures of the ingredients. Use the student drawings and pictures to create a bulletin board or display. Use a large black kettle (drawn in center of bulletin board, or a real one for a display) as the focal point and place the ingredients around the kettle. Second, third, and fourth graders will like this story and activity because at this age they are very much interested in gory, disgusting things.

The Story of Z by Jeanne Modesitt and Lonni Sue Johnson is a good book to use in teaching children the importance of each and every letter in the alphabet. After reading the story, have the children choose a letter (other than Z) to remove from the alphabet. Experiment with words without using that letter. Make up a story or adventure for the AWOL letter to have after leaving the alphabet. High school students could also try this activity and discuss the ease or difficulty of language and words without a certain letter.

Miss Hindy's Cats is an excellent story for a read-aloud session based on the theme of cats. After the story, have the children make a list of other names that Miss Hindy might have named her stray cats. Give each child an activity sheet to take home to help them remember the story.

Animals and food are a popular topic for any storytime or classroom and *The Pigs' Alphabet* and *Alexander's Midnight Snack: A Little Elephant's ABC* are perfect stories that combine both topics. Two activities that are useful with the stories are: 1. Give the children precut pig or elephant shapes and have them create their own versions of Pinkerton and Prue or Alexander; and 2. Give each child an activity sheet filled with pictures of food items. The children are to circle the items that Pinkerton and Prue or Alexander ate in the story as well as drawing pictures A to Z of other foods that they might have eaten.

Ask the class to identify the fairy tale/storybook characters named in the story, *The Hole by the Apple Tree*. Make an alphabetical list of other fairy tale and storybook characters that might have been woven into the story.

After using the series *Read Around Alphabet Town*, have each child select a letter of the alphabet and write a story about an animal, person, or object and their adventure in alphabet town. Have the children illustrate their stories. Using one of the titles in the series, have the children create a list of other favorite words that the main character in the text might have encountered. For example, make a list of "D" words that Dinosaur might like.

Another activity to use with the series, *Read Around Alphabet Town,* is to have children draw a map of an imaginary town. Include streets and locations for each letter of the alphabet such as Dino District, Quail Quarter, Hippo Hollow, Elephant Esplanade, Alligator Alley, Cardinal Corner, Platypus Plaza, Walrus Ward, and Vole Village. Children can include artwork and drawings to illustrate the 26 areas.

After reading the story *The Great Alphabet Fight,* share with the students a little about Joni Eareckson Tada's life and the diving accident that left her permanently paralyzed. Her personal story of fighting back and turning her life into a productive one as an artist and author can serve as an example for overcoming obstacles that are set forth in our life paths. You might share the movie based on her life with the students and then discuss overcoming personal obstacles and disabilites that affect people. This discussion is definitely one that would be best suited for high school students and adults. An additional topic to discuss with this book is the issue of peace, not only on a personal level, but in troubled lands around the world.

Victoria the snake saves her family in *Victoria's ABC Adventure.* After sharing the story, give the children model clay to fashion their own snakes. Tell the children to name their snake and mold it into the shape of the letter beginning with its name. Paint the snakes, let dry, and take them home for a souvenir.

An excellent follow-up activity for *Adelaide to Zeke* by Janet Wolf is to have the children write their own story about the inhabitants of a town. For a starter, make a list of all the names of the inhabitants. Use as many of the names of the students in the class as possible. Then assign each child a name to write a sentence about for the class story.

In *Hurricane City,* one family tells the story of their town where hurricane season never ends. In humorous rhyming verse, hurricanes from A to Z create all kinds of funny situations. Discuss how real hurricanes are named, and have each child think of a name for a hurricane and write a verse about its visit to Hurricane City. For a science related tie-in, have the students find information about hurricanes, tornadoes, and other types of wind storms. Divide them into small groups and have each group present an oral report about their findings. This would be a good time to discuss the impact of hurricanes such as Hurricanes Andrew and Hugo that hit heavily populated areas.

A Fishy Alphabet Story is a good story to use with a group of toddlers and preschoolers. Give each child a precut fish shape and have them decorate the fish with fabric, markers, crayons, or other types of media. Have each child choose one or more letters of the alphabet to write on their fish. Make a mural/bulletin board collage of the ABC fish. You can also play a type of "Go Fish" game. Use different colored paper to create a series of 26 fish shapes with a letter of the alphabet written in large print on each shape. Punch large holes at the top of the fish. Make fishing lines from pieces of string with a bent paper clip tied to the end of the line. Divide the children into groups of four to five and have them try to catch a fish from the bowl. After catching a paper fish, the children hold their fish in front of them and place themselves into ABC order. If working with a large group, you may need to make more than one set of the 26 fish.

After reading aloud some alphabet stories, have students create their own yarns with "(K)not-a-Story" times. Beforehand take a large skein of yarn or strong string and wind it into a ball. As you wind the ball make knots in it at irregular intervals. Be sure to make at least 26 knots, one for each letter of the alphabet. Place the ball of yarn in a jar or small box. The children take turns pulling yarn from the ball, and as they pull they make up an ABC story. The first child uses the letter A as the basis for the beginning of the story and stops when he reaches a knot. The next child continues the story with the letter B until reaching a knot. The story continues in alphabetical sequence until all 26 letters have been exhausted. As an alternative, have each child tell a letter story until they can't think of anything else. The child then makes a knot in the string, and the next child goes on with the story. Continue until all 26 letters have been discussed.

Choose a letter of the alphabet and bake your own pie for *The Pie Wagon*. Answer the following questions to construct your pie.

Name of Pie: _____

Ingredients:

_____

_____

_____   _____

                                         _____

                                         _____

How long does it take to bake? _____

At what temperature? _____

How many people does it serve? _____

Other comments:

Circle and color the cats below that belong to Miss Hindy.

Find eight foods that Pinkerton and Prue ate in *The Pigs' Alphabet*. Circle and color them.

eggs

cherries

toast and tea

cheddar cheese and crackers

Rice

cake

olive

kale

milk

yogurt

peas

sorrel soup

watermelon

pickled peppers

ice cream

pumpkin

celery

Ketchup

lollipop

Find 10 foods that Alexander ate on his trek to the kitchen for a midnight snack. Circle and color them.

ice cream

cinnamon cookies

mushroom

eggs

quarter of cheese

banana

sandwich

jam

jam

Ketchup

Ket...

Honey

carrot

Strawberries

lettuce

pumpkin

Milk

glass of water

watermelon

soup

nuts

7. SCIENCE, TECHNOLOGY, AND THE ALPHABET

Nothing stimulates a child's imagination more than the opportunity to examine, explore, and experiment with the world around them. Many of the alphabet books produced today provide children with opportunities to view the world around them, to learn more about animals, plants, and the earth, and to discover how things work. These ABC books are useful not only with the younger children as a means of introducing letters and sounds, but also with older readers as valuable sources of information for research and for pleasure reading. One trend in science ABC books is the inclusion of full color photographs and detailed drawings that provide readers with a sense of being on-site. Animal alphabet books were discussed earlier in this book, and while many of the animal ABC books are also useful as introductory and supplementary science resources, the books described in this section are directly applicable to the science curriculum and useful as reference resources for students.

One of the most prolific authors of science alphabet books is Jerry Pallotta. While the beautiful color illustrations in his books are wonderful for introducing the letters of the alphabet to the youngest reader, Pallotta's books are excellent reference tools for those seeking information about animals, birds, and plants. Not only are the drawings accurate, but the text also provides descriptions of the animal and its food, habitat, means of reproduction, in addition to other valuable data. Pallotta's alphabet books provide a unique way to explore both the alphabet and special areas of nature. His books can inspire teachers to initiate units of study on science topics and students to search for information about science and nature.

On the River ABC is a recent addition to the alphabet genre that offers a look at wildlife along a Western United States waterway. During a summer thunderstorm, an ant on a leaf is swept downstream. Along the way she encounters a plethora of wildlife from A to Z that lives on or near the water. A colorful painting of the creature in its natural habitat and a small pen and ink sketch provide an accurate portrait of nature. Simple rhyming text is used throughout the book while explanatory notes in the back tell more about the wildlife found along the Western and Southwestern waterways in the United States.

Marcia Brown's *All Butterflies: An ABC Cut* not only uses unusual word combinations, but also includes many varieties of butterflies that students can identify and study. Two recent books from Crown Publishers, *Under the Sea from A to Z* by Anne Doubilet and *Astronaut to Zodiac: A Young Stargazer's Alphabet* by Roger Ressmeyer, provide a wealth of information about marine life and space. Each book includes full color photographs and a simple sentence about each item so that younger children can easily identify the object shown on the page. In addition to the brief text, there is a sidebar on the same page that offers more detailed information about the object. A glossary in the back and explanatory notes make both volumes valuable science resources. The detailed information the sidebar notes presents is better suited for use with junior high and high school students.

Gardening is a popular topic in alphabet books, and there are several titles that deal with flowers, fruits, and vegetables as well as the creatures found in gardens. Anita Lobel has two titles that fit into the gardening field, *Pierrot's ABC Garden* and *Alison's Zinnia*. The first title is found in a "Golden Book," and it is the story of Pierrot who decides to visit his friend and takes a basket of goodies from his garden. The illustrations are colorful, easily identifiable fruits, vegetables, and garden items. The text consists of upper and lower case letters and a one-word identification of the item in the picture. The second book by Anita Lobel, *Alison's Zinnia,* is one of the best picture alphabet books published in the past few years. Not only is it a superb read-aloud story for young children, but it is also an excellent book to use as a tie-in to a unit on flowers and plants. Each letter in the text is dependent upon the next letter ("Alison acquired an Amaryllis for Beryl"), but at the same time each sentence can be viewed as a single unit. Jerry Pallotta's *The Flower Alphabet Book, A Flower Fairy Alphabet Book* by Cecily Barker, and *Alphabet Garden* by Laura Jane Coats are other resources that could be used with Anita Lobel's book.

Vegetable gardening is the topic of *The Victory Garden Alphabet Book* by Pallotta. By combining Pallotta's book with Lois Ehlert's *Eating the Alphabet* the entire field of fruits and vegetables is covered. Jerry Pallotta worked with victory gardener Bob Thomson in creating an alphabetical list of vegetables to grow. The illustrations are so realistic that you can almost step into the garden and touch the vegetables. Lois Ehlert provides a different type of illustration in her book *Eating the Alphabet*. She uses bright bold colors and dozens of fruits and vegetables to dot the pages of her book. While the illustrations are not as realistic, the bright colors and simple labelling make this book a natural to use with young children.

A Garden Alphabet by Isabel Wilner is not a literal guide to gardening from A to Z, but it does offer a narration of one garden from the early April rains to the Fall harvest. Wilner provides a humorous look at gardening for the young child. A frog and a border collie preside over a garden throughout the growing season and describe all the things that happen in the garden from the early rains and selecting seeds from a catalog in April to the excitement of harvesting and the bees falling asleep in the fall. All of these alphabet books are helpful in providing children with information on how to prepare a garden for flowers, fruits, and vegetables as well as information about growing seasons, types of soil, fertilizers, heights of the plants, and more. This information would also be useful as part of a study unit on plants and gardens. While most of the garden, flower, and plant ABC books are best used with the preschool and primary age crowd, the information in them is still relevant to older students.

It seems only natural after talking about fruits, vegetables, and gardens that the topic of food and alphabet books would follow. Food is a popular topic in alphabet books, and the titles range from simple stories of alphabet feasts to nonfiction descriptions of unfamiliar foods and cookbooks. Alphabet stories where food is a prominent feature are discussed in the section on story alphabet books. Some of the best include: *Alligator Arrived with Apples* by Crescent Dragonwagon, *Alphabet Soup: A Feast of Letters* by Scott Gustafson, *Potluck* by Anne Shelby, *The Pigs' Alphabet* by Leah Palmer Preiss, and *Alexander's Midnight Snack* by Catherine Stock. Although the first three stories differ somewhat in the food items named in the text, they deal with a party where the guests bring food to eat. Crescent Dragonwagon writes about a Thanksgiving feast where all the guests bring a unique dish to share. In *Potluck* Alpha and Betty have a potluck dinner and invite their friends to bring their favorite dishes, while in *Alphabet Soup,* the occasion is a housewarming party where the guests supply ingredients for a special pot of soup. Both *The Pigs' Alphabet* and *Alexander's Midnight Snack* are adventure stories where the main characters are involved in eating a variety of foods. All of these titles offer a plethora of foods from A to Z, and just reading them aloud is guaranteed to bring on a snack attack.

General Mills has produced a small paperback cookbook (*Alpha-Bakery Children's Cookbook*) that uses the A to Z format to present recipes for all kinds of foods that kids can make by themselves. Comic illustrations and easy-to-read recipes for each letter of the alphabet, from D for Delicious Drumsticks to T for Turtle Bread, make this a delightful book for the beginning reader. *Alphabet Soup* by Abbie Zabar is one alphabet book that is best used by the older reader. It includes a description of 26 unfamiliar foods from different cultures around the world. The book is an alphabetical guide to exotic food, including drawings, a pronunciation guide, and anecdotes and histories of the foods. *Alphabet Soup* would make a nice supplemental resource for Home Economics or adult cooking classes.

After studying flowers, vegetables, and plants, George Ella Lyon's *ABCedar: An Alphabet of Trees* makes a smooth transition to a broader look at nature. Twenty-six different leaves are shown in this easy-to-read alphabet book of trees native to North America. In *A Walk in the Rainforest* Kristin Joy Pratt presents the reader with a picture of the world of the tropical rainforest and its role in the earth's environment. Pratt wrote this book when she was only 15, and she presents information about a timely topic in alphabet format. The style is similar to Anne Doubilet's and Roger Ressmeyer's books, with a large simple sentence about a single object representing the letter of the alphabet as well as a sidebar giving more detailed information. Pratt includes some fascinating facts about the rainforest and the unusual vegetation and animals found there. The book also includes a map showing the locations of rainforests around the world.

When studying rainforests, you could also use *Marie Angel's Exotic Alphabet*. Although the title was discussed in an earlier chapter on beginner books, it is also a valuable resource for a science unit on jungles. The book unfolds into a 9-foot frieze of scenes from jungles around the world, including an African coastal jungle, a South American jungle, and an Asian jungle. The background scenes include the vegetation and creatures who reside in these regions along with "lift the flap" squares that reveal an alphabet of exotic jungle creatures. Both Pratt's and Angel's books complement a study of trees, jungles, and wildlife.

The different components of an object and how they work are the subject of two books on transportation by Doug Magee and Robert Newman. In *All Aboard ABC* and *Let's Fly from A to Z,* the authors use candid photographs to provide a behind-the-scenes view of the world of air and rail transportation. Each book uses an ABC format to introduce letters and various aspects of trains or planes. A sentence or two is used to further explain the term and inform the reader about trains or planes. Florence Cassen Mayers offers an alphabet book that would be useful to students wanting more information about airplanes and the history of aviation. In *ABC: The National Air and Space Museum* each letter of the alphabet is represented with items from the National Air and Space Museum. Over 30 color photographs of airplanes, spaceships, and other aviation items are shown in this book, together with brief text explaining the significance of each object. Angela Royston and Terry Pastor provide a unique look at classic and modern cars in *The A to Z Book of Cars.* Full color photographs are used for each featured car along with color drawings for more cars. They include cars as old as a 1924 Bugatti 35 and models from the 1990 line. The variety of makes and models of cars as well as paragraphs of background information on the featured autos guarantees that this ABC book will please car lovers of all ages. Alphabetical guides to other modes of transportation can be found in Adelaide Holl's *The ABC's of Cars, Trucks and Machines,* Seymour Reit's *Things That Go,* and Dorothy Shuttlesworth's *ABC of Buses.* Shuttlesworth's book is filled with old-fashioned illustrations and brief text about buses and their features. A humorous approach to transportation is offered by Richard Scarry in his *Richard Scarry's Cars and Trucks from A to Z,* a board book for the very young reader.

Construction, buildings, and how things are made is a topic found in several alphabet books. *Architects Make Zigzags* by Diane Maddex is an alphabetical guide to architectural concepts. The detailed black and white drawings illustrate 26 of the most common features of buildings, as well as providing detailed information about the names and locations of the buildings and information about their construction. Maddex includes everyday terms such as roof and column as well as less familiar terms such as quoin, newel post, and jigsaw work. A bibliography and more detailed information are found in the back of this guide to the alphabet through architecture. *Archabet* by Korab is also an architectural guide to the alphabet. Unlike Maddex's book, however, Korab's shows how letter forms can be found in, on, and around the features of buildings. It too is illustrated in black and white, but with photographs instead of drawings. The text is comprised of quotations from famous architects and observers of buildings. Included in the back of the book is an identification of the piece of architecture with the name and type of building where it is found. A third book, edited by Diane Maddex, *Built in the U.S.A.: American Buildings from Airports to Zoos,* provides a look at why buildings look the way they do.

Although *Albert's Alphabet* by Leslie Tryon does not concern architecture in the formal sense, it does deal with the construction of an alphabet for the school playground. In this wordless book, Albert, the duck, uses the supplies in his workshop to construct an alphabet. Wood, metal, wire, and all kinds of miscellaneous supplies are used to create the letters. The very detailed drawings of Albert carefully constructing his letters challenge the reader to see how parts can be used to create a whole object. As a complement to the constructed letters that Albert makes, use *Anno's Alphabet* to demonstrate how wood blocks can be carefully arranged to create letters. In *Albert's Alphabet* the letters are shown in their entirety, while in *Anno's Alphabet* some of the letters are distorted or not always perfectly fitted.

Many of the alphabet books currently available can be used to supplement parts of the science curriculum in schools, both on the primary and the middle and high school levels. Primary students look at these books as a means of becoming acquainted with some interesting areas of science and nature and as an introduction to the alphabet and how it can be interwoven with science issues. Older students can use ABC science books for a number of different purposes including as reference sources of information about birds, fish, flowers and other aspects of nature; as examples of materials to examine for scientific accuracy; as models to describe relationships in nature; and as a means of investigating a scientific topic in an alphabetical sequence.

SCIENCE, TECHNOLOGY, AND THE ALPHABET: BIBLIOGRAPHY

Alpha-Bakery Children's Cookbook. Minneapolis, Minnesota: General Mills, Inc., 1991.
   This A to Z cookbook for kids includes comic illustrations and easy-to-make recipes for each letter of the alphabet.
ALL AGES. Upper and lower case.
Angel, Marie. *Marie Angel's Exotic Alphabet*. New York: Dial Books for Young Readers, 1992. ISBN 0-80737-1247-2.
   An alphabet of exotic creatures from jungles of the world are revealed in this combination lift-the-flap and frieze board book.
ALL AGES. Upper case.
Anno, Mitsumasa. *Anno's Alphabet: An Adventure in Imagination*. New York: Thomas Y. Crowell Co., 1975. ISBN 0-690-00540-7; 0-690-00541-5 (lib bdg)
   In this wordless book, wooden letters and intricate borders introduce the letters of the alphabet.
ALL AGES. Upper case.
Asimov, Isaac. *ABC's of the Earth*. New York: Walker and Co., 1971. ISBN 0-8027-6091-0; 0-8027-6092-9 (lib bdg).
   A science dictionary of earth terms using an alphabetical format.
AGES 6–12. Upper case.
———. *ABC's of the Ocean*. New York: Walker and Co., 1970. ISBN 0-8027-6086-4; 0-8027-6087-2 (lib bdg).
   Two oceanographic terms are given for each letter of the alphabet.
AGES 6–12. Upper case.
Barker, Cicely. *A Flower Fairy Alphabet*. New York: Bedrick Books, 1985. ISBN 0-87226-023-2.
   In illustrated poems, fairies introduce the alphabet by describing the flowers where they live, using English and botanical names.
ALL AGES.
Coats, Laura Jane. *Alphabet Garden*. New York: Macmillan, 1993. ISBN 0-02-719042-0.
   A little boy takes an alphabetical tour of the animals and plants that live in his garden.
AGES 4 AND UP. Upper and lower case.
Doubilet, Anne. *Under the Sea from A to Z*. Photographs by David Doubilet.   New York: Crown Publishers, Inc., 1991. ISBN 0-517-57836-0; 0-517-57837-9 (lib bdg).
   An alphabetical look at all kinds of exotic marine life.
ALL AGES. Upper case.
Dragonwagon, Crescent. *Alligator Arrived with Apples: A Potluck Alphabet Feast*. Pictures by Jose Aruego and Ariane Dewey. New York: Macmillan Publishing Co., 1987. ISBN 0-689-71613-3.
   All of the animals get together and bring food for a potluck Thanksgiving feast.
ALL AGES. Upper case.
Ehlert, Lois. *Eating the Alphabet: Fruits and Vegetables from A to Z*. San Diego, California; Harcourt Brace Jovanovich, 1989. ISBN 0-15-224435-2.
   The reader is taken on an alphabetical tour of the world of fruits and vegetables, from apricot to zucchini.
ALL AGES. Upper and lower case.
Gustafson, Scott. *Alphabet Soup: A Feast of Letters*. Chicago, Illinois: Calico Books, 1990. ISBN 0-8092-4299-0.
   When Otter has a housewarming party, 26 of his friends bring a variety of foods for the alphabet soup.
AGES 4–10. Upper case.
Holl, Adelaide. *The ABC of Cars, Trucks and Machines*. New York: American Heritage Press, 1970. ISBN 0-8281-5019-2; 0-8291-8017-2 (lib bdg).
   From A to Z, all kinds of cars, trucks, and other machines, including dump trucks, taxicabs, and jeeps, are shown.
AGES 3 AND UP. Upper case.
Incredible Animals A to Z. Washington, D.C.: National Wildlife Federation, 1985. ISBN 0-912186-66-6.
   From A to Z, the reader goes on a global tour of the world's most unusual and bizarre animals.
ALL AGES. Upper case.
Kingdon, Jill. *The ABC Dinosaur Book*. Illustrated by Seymour Fleishman. Chicago, Illinois: Childrens Press, 1982.
   For each letter of the alphabet, there is a dinosaur word, pronunciation guide, and descriptive paragraph.
AGES 4–12.
Korab, Balthazar. *Archabet: An Architectural Alphabet*. Washington, D.C.: Preservation Press, 1985. ISBN 0-89133-117-4.
   By looking in, on, and around buildings, the reader can find letters of the alphabet.
ALL AGES. Upper case.
Kurz, Ann. *Cranberries from A to Z*. Port Edwards, Wisconsin: Cranberry Original Press, 1989. ISBN 0-962278-40-8.
   From A to Z, the reader learns all about cranberries, from growing to harvesting to the final product.
ALL AGES.

Lobel, Anita. *Alison's Zinnia*. New York: Greenwillow Books, 1990. ISBN 0-688-08865-1; 0-688-08866-X (lib bdg).

The alphabet is introduced through a combination of girls' names, verbs, and flowers.

ALL AGES.

———. *Pierrot's ABC Garden*. Racine, Wisconsin: Western Publishing Company Inc., 1992. ISBN 0-307-17551-0.

When Pierrot decides to visit his friend Pierette, he gathers a basket of goodies from his garden including asparagus, beets, pineapple, quince, and a zebra.

AGES 2–8. Upper and lower case.

Lyon, George Ella. *ABCedar: An Alphabet of Trees*. Designed and illustrated by Tom Parker. New York: Orchard Books, 1989. ISBN 0-531-05795-X; 0-531-08395-0 (lib bdg).

The leaves from 26 kinds of trees are presented in an unusual ABC book.

ALL AGES. Upper case.

Maddex, Diane. *Architects Make Zigzags: Looking at Architecture from A to Z*. Drawings by Roxie Munro. Washington, D.C.: The Preservation Press, 1986. ISBN 0-89133-121-2.

Twenty-six architectural concepts, together with detailed drawings and brief definitions, are presented.

ALL AGES. Upper case.

Maddex, Diane, editor. *Built in the U.S.A.: American Buildings from Airports to Zoos*. Washington, D.C.: The Preservation Press, 1985.

Maddex offers the reader a look at why buildings look the way they do.

ALL AGES. Upper case.

Magee, Doug, and Robert Newman. *All Aboard ABC*. New York: Cobblehill Books, 1990. ISBN 0-525-65036-9.

The authors present a close-up look at the world of rail transportation.

ALL AGES. Upper and lower case.

———. *Let's Fly from A to Z*. New York: Cobblehill Books, 1992. ISBN 0-525-65105-5.

With candid photographs and brief text, the reader is taken on an alphabetical tour of the world of aviation.

ALL AGES. Upper and lower case.

Marolda, Maria Rizzo. *Cuisenaire Alphabet Book*. Graphics by Diane Phillips. White Plains, New York: Cuisenaire Co. of America, Inc., 1979. 1980.

Using a workbook format, Cuisenaire rods are used to recreate the letters of the alphabet.

ALL AGES. Upper case.

Mayers, Florence Cassen. *ABC: The National Air and Space Museum*. New York: Harry N. Abrams, 1987. ISBN 0-8109-1859-5.

From early aviation to the latest in space technology, this book is an alphabetical guide to the world of flight.

ALL AGES. Upper and lower case.

Pallotta, Jerry. *The Bird Alphabet Book*. Illustrated by Edgar Stewart. Watertown, Massachusetts: Charlesbridge Publishing, 1986. ISBN 0-88106-451-3 (soft); 0-88106-457-2.

Pallotta offers a guide to all kinds of birds from A to Z.

ALL AGES. Upper and lower case.

———. *The Dinosaur Alphabet Book*. Illustrated by Ralph Masiello. Watertown, Massachusetts: Charlesbridge Publishing, 1991. ISBN 0-88106-466-1 (soft); 0-88106-467-X (hardcover).

From A to Z, the reader is introduced to some familiar and not so familiar dinosaurs.

ALL AGES. Upper and lower case.

———. *The Extinct Alphabet Book*. Illustrated by Ralph Masiello. Watertown, Massachusetts: Charlesbridge Publishing, 1993. ISBN 0-88106-686-9 (hardcover); 0-88106-470-X (soft).

The letters of the alphabet are introduced along with some interesting facts about creatures that are now extinct.

ALL AGES. Upper and lower case.

———. *The Flower Alphabet Book*. Illustrated by Leslie Evans. Watertown, Massachusetts: Charlesbridge Publishing, 1989. ISBN 0-88106-453-X (soft); 0-88106-459-9 (hardcover).

This A to Z guide includes a description of a garden of flowers, including colorful borders around each flower.

ALL AGES. Upper and lower case.

———. *The Frog Alphabet . . . and Other Awesome Amphibians*. Illustrated by Ralph Masiello. Watertown, Massachusetts: Charlesbridge Publishing, 1990. ISBN 0-88106-462-9 (soft); 0-88106-463-7 (hardcover).

This title offers a fascinating, informative look at frogs and other amphibians from A to Z.

ALL AGES. Upper and lower case.

———. *The Furry Alphabet Book*. Illustrated by Edgar Stewart. Watertown, Massachusetts: Charlesbridge Publishing, 1990. ISBN 0-88106-464-5 (soft); 0-88106-465-3 (hardcover).

In this alphabet book, some very unusual mammals of the world are introduced.

ALL AGES. Upper and lower case.

————. *The Icky Bug Alphabet Book*. Illustrated by Ralph Masiello. Watertown, Massachusetts: Charlesbridge Publishing,
    1986. ISBN 0-88106-450-5 (soft); 0-88106-456-4 (hardcover).
    From ant to zebra butterflies, this is a guide to some very interesting, but icky, bugs.
ALL AGES. Upper and lower case.
————. *The Ocean Alphabet Book*. Illustrated by Frank Mazzola, Jr. Watertown, Massachusetts: Charlesbridge Publishing,
    1989. ISBN 0-88106-452-1 (soft); 0-88106458-0 (hardcover).
    This A–Z book describes fish and other creatures in the North Atlantic Ocean.
ALL AGES. Upper and lower case.
————. *The Underwater Alphabet Book*. Illustrated by Edgar Stewart. Watertown, Massachusetts: Charlesbridge Publishing,
    1991. ISBN 0-88106-461-0 (hardcover); 0-88106-455-6 (soft)
    Pallotta provides an alphabetical look at fishes, sharks, and other underwater inhabitants of the coral reefs.
ALL AGES. Upper and lower case.
————. *The Victory Garden Alphabet Book*. Illustrated by Edgar Stewart. Watertown, Massachusetts: Charlesbridge Publish-
    ing, 1992. ISBN 0-88106-468-8 (soft).
    Pallotta teams up with the victory gardener, Bob Thomson to present an alphabetical guide to vegetable gardening.
ALL AGES. Upper and lower case.
————. *The Yucky Reptile Alphabet Book*. Illustrated by Ralph Masiello. Watertown, Massachusetts: Charlesbridge Publish-
    ing, 1989. ISBN 0-88106-454-8 (soft); 0-88106-460-2 (hardcover).
    Some unusual and rather grotesque reptiles are presented.
ALL AGES. Upper and lower case.
Pratt, Kristin Joy. *A Walk in the Rainforest*. Nevada City, California: Dawn Publications, 1992. ISBN 1-878265-53-9 (soft); 1-
    878265-99-7 (hardcover).
    An ant, named XYZ, goes for a walk in the rainforest and encounters a variety of animals, plants, and other vegetation.
ALL AGES. Upper case.
Preiss, Leah Palmer. *The Pigs' Alphabet*. Boston, Massachusetts: David R. Godine Publishing, 1990. ISBN 0-87923-781-3.
    An alphabetical feast is used to settle a dispute between two very hungry pigs.
AGES 4–8. Upper case.
Reit, Seymour. *Things That Go: A Traveling Alphabet*. Illustrated by Fulvio Testa. New York: Bantam Books, 1990. ISBN 0-
    553-05856-8; 0-553-3489-3.
    From ambulance to zeppelin, Reit has created a guide to vehicles that go.
AGE 4 AND UP. Upper and lower case.
Ressmeyer, Roger. *Astronaut to Zodiac: A Young Stargazer's Alphabet*. New York: Crown Publishing, Inc., 1992. ISBN 0-
    517-58805-6; 0-517-58816-4 (lib).
    Through colorful illustrations and text, the reader is introduced to astronomy and related topics.
ALL AGES. Upper case.
Royston, Angela, and Terry Pastor. *The A to Z Book of Cars*. New York: Barron's, 1991. ISBN 0-8120-6209-4.
    This unique book provides an alphabetical drive through the 20th century, with both modern and classic cars.
ALL AGES. Upper case.
Scarry, Richard. *Richard Scarry's Cars and Trucks from A to Z*. New York: Random House, 1990. ISBN 0-679-80663-6.
    Scarry offers a humorous look at motor vehicles in this ABC book.
AGES 1–3. Upper and lower case.
Shelby, Anne. *Potluck*. Pictures by Irene Trivas. New York: Orchard Books, 1991. ISBN 0-531-05919-7; 0-531-08519-8 (lib
    bdg).
    Alpha and Betty invite all their friends to a potluck dinner with foods from A to Z.
AGES 4–9.
Shuttlesworth, Dorothy. *ABC of Buses*. Illustrated by Leonard Shortall. New York: Doubleday & Co., Inc., 1965.
    This unique ABC book tells all about buses and their parts and different features.
AGES 5 AND UP. Upper case.
Simon, Seymour. *Space Words: A Dictionary*. Illustrated by Randy Chewning. New York: HarperCollins Pub., 1991. ISBN 0-
    06-022532-7; 0-06-022533-5 (lib bdg).
    In this A to Z picture dictionary, Simon presents 70 space-related words from Apollo Program to zero gravity.
ALL AGES.
Stock, Catherine. *Alexander's Midnight Snack: A Little Elephant's ABC*. New York: Clarion Books, 1988. ISBN 0-89919-512-
    1.
    Alexander decides to eat a midnight snack that turns into an alphabetical feast.
AGES 3–6.

Stutson, Caroline. *On the River ABC*. Illustrated by Anna-Maria L. Crum. Nivot, Colorado: Roberts Rinehart Pub., 1993. ISBN 1-879373-4.

When a sudden summer storm sweeps an ant down the river, she encounters the beautiful and varied wildlife found near Western waterways in the United States.

ALL AGES. Upper case.

Tryon, Leslie. *Albert's Alphabet*. New York: Atheneum, 1991. ISBN 0-689-31642-9.

Albert cleverly uses all the supplies in his workshop to build an alphabet for the school playground.

ALL AGES. Upper case.

Wilner, Isabel. *A Garden Alphabet*. Pictures by Ashley Wolff. New York: Dutton Children's Books, 1991. ISBN 0-525-44731-8.

Comic characters and rhyming verses are used to introduce the alphabet and describe how a garden is planned.

AGES 4 AND UP. Upper and lower case.

Wilson, Ron. *100 Dinosaurs from A to Z*. Illustrated by Cecilia Fitzsimons. New York: Grosset & Dunlap/Putnam Publishing Group.

Dinosaurs and detailed information about them are presented in ABC sequence.

ALL AGES.

Zabar, Abbie. *Alphabet Soup*. New York: Stewart, Tabori & Chang, Inc., 1990. ISBN 1-55670-154-3.

Zabar presents a nonfictional guide to 26 (A to Z) unfamiliar but everyday foods from around the world.

ALL AGES.

Zacks, Irene. *Space Alphabet*. Pictures by Peter P. Plasencia. New Jersey: Prentice-Hall, Inc., 1964.

Although somewhat dated, this alphabet book presents things related to space and flying.

AGES 4–7. Upper case.

Zimmer, Velma E. *Come with Me from A to Z*. Minneapolis, Minnesota: T. S. Denison & Co., Inc., 1968.

Rhyming text is used to present an alphabetical guide to common foods including apple, bread and butter, and watermelon.

AGES 5–8. Upper case.

SCIENCE, TECHNOLOGY, AND THE ALPHABET: ACTIVITIES

Share *Alpha-Bakery Children's Cookbook* with the class. Divide the class into several groups and have them experiment with some of recipes. Afterwards have a food tasting party to sample the results. Have the students bring in recipes of their own to create a class alphabet cookbook. Brainstorm new titles for the recipes so that you will have one for each of the 26 letters. Each child should handwrite their recipe and illustrate it before it is placed into a cookbook format.

Organize an Alphabet Food Feast. Prior to the day of the feast, share some of the alphabet food stories with the children. Good choices for titles to share include: *Alligator Arrived with Apples* by Crescent Dragonwagon, *Alphabet Soup* by Scott Gustafson, *The Pigs' Alphabet* by Leah Palmer Preiss, *Alexander's Midnight Snack* by Catherine Stock, and *Potluck* by Ann Shelby. Let the children make an A to Z list of all the possible foods that they might bring. Have each child select at least one food item to bring to the feast. Be sure that all 26 letters are represented at the feast. Make a menu for the feast. On the day of the alphabet feast, gather together all the food items and take them outside for a feast beyond belief. Take pictures of the children enjoying their feast and make a bulletin board display to remember the day. Give each child a photograph for a memento.

Use *All Butterflies: An ABC Cut* by Marcia Brown as an initial introduction to a unit on butterflies. Have the students study the butterflies in the book and use identification guides to try to name the species shown. You can use an opaque projector to project the illustrations on the wall so that everyone can see them at the same time. Discuss the eating habits, location, life span, and other basic information about butterflies. As a follow-up activity, give each child an activity sheet with the outline of a butterfly. Each child can fill in details on the butterfly (colors, size, eating habits, etc.) either using information from their studies or creating an imaginary butterfly. Collect the sheets and use as a display in the classroom or library.

Alison's Zinnia provides an interesting lead-up to a unit on flowers and plants. Prior to reading the story, have your students plant zinnia seeds in paper cups. They can watch the flowers grow and then later take them home. Everytime they look at zinnias, they will remember the story.

Share *The Flower Alphabet Book* and *The Fairy Flower Book* with the children before having them make a class alphabet flower book. On the blackboard, write the names of all the children in the class. Have the students place the names in alphabetical order and explain that they are going to create a sheet for a class flower page. Provide seed catalogs and magazines that have pictures of all kinds of flowers. Each child is to find a flower that they like that begins with the first letter in their name. Cut out and glue pictures of the flower on the activity sheet. Underneath the picture(s) the child can write a description of the flower, as well as a sentence using the child's name and the flower name in it.

Other activities that can be used in connection with the garden alphabet books include: 1. Grow fast-sprouting seeds such as radishes, carrots, and mustard in different kinds of soil such as clay and sand. Compare the results from the experiment and discuss why some things grow better than others; 2. Draw a plan for a flower garden in front of the school. Consider such factors as height, color, growing conditions, climate, season lengths, etc. when planning the garden; and 3. Show the children how to create tissue paper flowers. Make a vase of paper flowers of all colors, shapes, and sizes.

Vegetables and fruits are topics that are popular with children. You can use both *Eating the Alphabet* by Ehlert and *The Victory Garden Alphabet* by Pallotta as an introduction to fruits and vegetables. Talk about some of the vegetables and fruits that are not as familiar to the children. Bring in samples of unusual ones. Bring in seed catalogs and seed packets for as many different kinds of vegetables and fruits as you can possibly find. Have the children go through the packets and catalogs to find information about the growing season, soil types, height and color, ways to prepare to eat, etc. Give each child an activity sheet to use to map out their own garden and orchard. Discuss some of the things to consider in planning their gardens such as what to grow, where to place it, when to harvest, etc. Have each child select a vegetable to plant in a pot and watch grow over a period of weeks. Study the backs of the seed packets. What kind of information did you find? Compare this information with that in gardening books, encyclopedias, or a dictionary.

ABCedar shows the leaves of twenty-six trees of North America. Have students find leaves from trees indigenous to the area and identify them. Another activity might be to find pictures of trees unique to certain areas of the world, such as the cypress of the Monterey pensinula and the ginkgo of China. In the spring students can also sprout tree seeds or twigs in water to transplant later.

Use any of the science alphabet books by Jerry Pallotta to create word searches or crossword puzzles based on the alphabetical list of creatures in the book. A sample word scramble based on *The Furry Alphabet Book* is included at the end of this chapter.

Even the youngest child is environmentally aware in today's day and age, and Kristen Joy Pratt's *A Week in the Rainforest* is an excellent book to use to continue awareness of the need to preserve the remaining tropical rainforests. Some of the activities that might be useful as follow-up to this book include:

1. Choose one of the animals mentioned in the alphabet book. Write an adventure story about the animal.
2. Build your own rainforest by making a terrarium. Research how a terrarium imitates the atmosphere of a rainforest.
3. Make rainforest pictures. Cut out many shapes and sizes of leaves from different shades of green and brown paper. Cover a piece of cardboard with the leaves. Add a combination of flowers, insects, and animals found in a rainforest while using the greenery as a background.
4. Write a letter to the World Wildlife Fund and Conservation Foundation (1250 24th St., NW, Suite 500, Washington DC 20037). Tell them about your interest in saving the rainforest.

After sharing *Marie Angel's Exotic Alphabet,* have students research different jungle regions around the world. Divide them into groups and assign a different region to each group. Find information on the weather and climate, plant life and vegetation, animals, birds, insects, and other information about the assigned jungle region. Create a decorative frieze of several panels to share the information with the class.

Extinct creatures is the topic of *The Extinct Alphabet Book* by Jerry Pallotta. Prior to reading the book, discuss with the class the difference between extinct and endangered species. Afterwards, have your students find out more about some of the extinct creatures named in the book. What are some other species that are no longer in existence? Discuss endangered species. Make a list of some of the ones in your area that are considered endangered. What can you do to help save these creatures? Have students do reports on an extinct or endangered species. Write a letter to a wildlife organization such as World Wildlife Fund and Conservation Foundation expressing interest in saving endangered creatures.

After sharing several alphabet books about vehicles and transportation, have the children choose a vehicle to write a story about. Draw an outline of the vehicle and write the story on the outline form. Some of the things the children might write include a description of the vehicle, the driver, things to see along the way, and the destination.

Alphabet Feast

Using all 26 letters of the alphabet, make a list of foods that you could bring to an alphabet feast. Create a menu for your feast.

Foods to bring:

Menu:

Select a butterfly species to research. Find out some information about your butterfly and write a fact story about it. If you cannot find a real butterfly to write about, create an imaginary one.

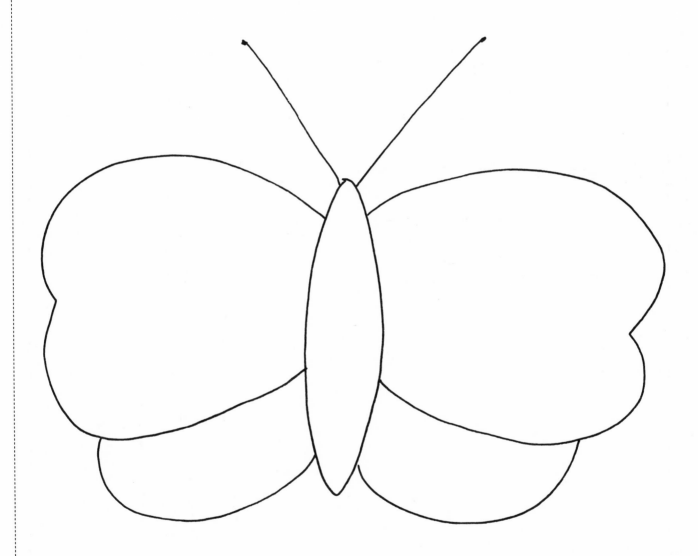

Garden Plot

Use this map to plan your garden and/or orchard. Include the names and locations of your fruits and vegetables.

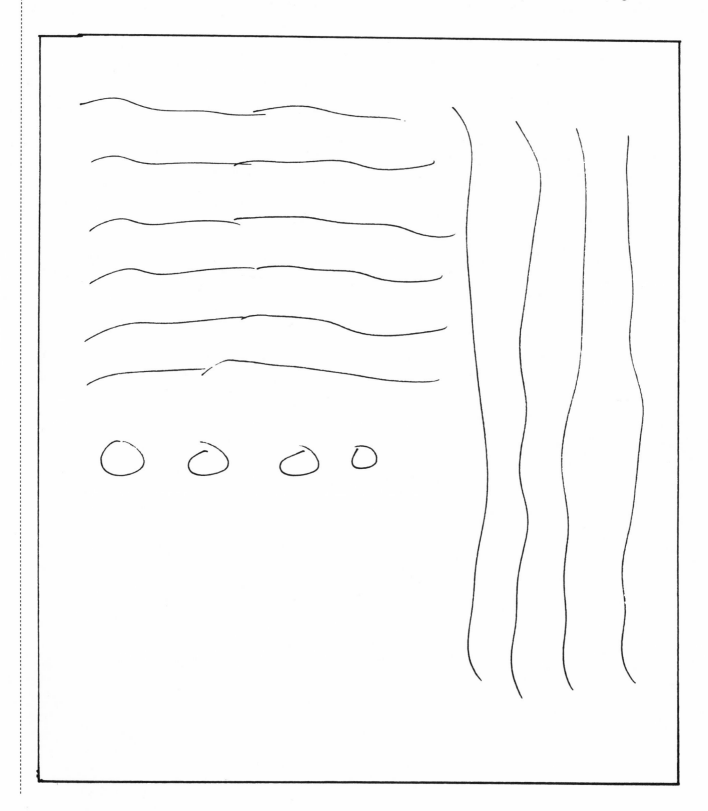

Mammal Scramble

Find the 26 unusual mammals discussed in *The Furry Alphabet Book* by Jerry Pallotta. The names can be found up, down, across or diagonally. Circle each name as you find it.

aye-aye
beaver
cheetah
dingo
ermine
flying squirrel
golden lion marmoset
hydrax

ibex
jack rabbit
kangaroo
llama
musk ox
numbat
okapi
proboscis monkey
quokka

reindeer
springbok
rat tarsier
unau
vizcacha
wallaroo
xukazi
yapok
zorilla

```
P R O B O S C I S M O N K E Y
U E I O K M D L R T J M A R T
P I V C A B I T A B M U N P E
U N A U P M N T E R W Q G F S
Y D U N U B G C H E E T A H O
B E A V E R O M N B H G R Z M
A E R M I N E K L I N B O S R
Y R L M E M U S K O X P O P A
E G H V I Z C A C H A Y R R M
A R W A L L A R O O M I A I N
Y E C X L Q U O K K A Z T N O
E I M F A M S E O N J A R G I
U S M B M E W A P X C K M B L
Z R T Y A M C F A B H U E O N
O A B J L P O H Y R A X I K E
R T N E R W L Z I M N A K I D
L E R R I U Q S G N I Y L F L
L M J A C K R A B B I T C F O
A M N G U T R E L X C O A M G
```

8. SOCIAL STUDIES AND ALPHABET BOOKS

While science is one area where ABC books are useful as information sources, social studies is another area where they can provide vital resources. Social studies involves exploring the historical backgrounds of people, places, and things, as well as looking at the various elements that affect society as a whole, such as transportation, careers, communication, and homes. Many ABC books are useful to share historical information, point out important events and facts about the past, and trace the history and culture of a particular country, culture, lifestyle, or region.

Depictions of rural life and scenes from early America are the subject of Mary Azarian's *A Farmer's Alphabet* and Eric Sloane's *ABC Book of Early Americana*. These two books make nice companion volumes for any study of American history by children of all ages. Azarian's book was originally black and white posters commissioned by the Vermont Department of Education for elementary schools in the state. Each letter and object in the book is placed on a page with a blank back so that they can be used as posters. Black and white woodcuts are used for the objects depicting each letter of the alphabet, while red ink is used for the letter and the word identifying the object. Azarian included some familiar scenes and some that might not be easily identified by children in today's fast moving world (e.g., S for stove, M for maple sugar). As a companion to Azarian's look at farm life, use Jane Miller's light-hearted look at people, places, and things found on a farm, *Farm Alphabet Book*. The color photographs and simple text about common farm life such as chickens, pigs, and crops are useful with the very young as a means of introduction to rural life and with older students as a starting point to write about even more A to Z items on the farm. Eric Sloane's *ABC Book of Early Americana* uses black and white ink sketches to depict places and things from the American past. While Azarian has only one item per letter, Sloane includes four to seven items. In addition to the drawing and word identification, Sloane adds a paragraph of background information on the object. Azarian's book is useful with very young children, while Sloane's book serves more as a reference work on early America.

A Prairie Alphabet presents a different view of farming and rural life by concentrating on life on the prairies. The detailed paintings are of prairie life in Canada, but the scenes could have been taken from any prairie in the United States or around the world. The paintings are so realistic that they look like photographs that one can step into. Many objects beginning with the featured letter are found in the paintings, with a complete list in the back of the book. This title would provide a unique look at the sights and sounds of the prairie for any student who is studying prairie life. As companion volumes to a study of Canada, use *A Prairie Alphabet* and *A Canadian ABC* by Lyn Cook. Cook's volume was orginally published in 1931, but the latest edition includes new illustrations that give the reader a rich look at Canada. Cook combines the alphabet with poetry to show the reader the beauty and wonder of our northern neighbor. In *A Northern Alphabet*, Ted Harrison presents a look at life in the colder regions of North America. The book covers people, places, and things as far south as the 55th parallel. Around the edge of each page are the names of places that begin with the featured letter of the alphabet. In another look at life in the northern regions, Betsy Bowen takes the reader through the changing seasons in the northern woods of Minnesota with *Antler, Bear, Canoe*. The woodcut illustrations show some of the beauty of the country and the lifestyles of the people who live there. Bowen combines a tour of the alphabet with information about seasons, geography, and social studies in her book about life in this very special area of the United States.

As a contrast to the northern regions, James Rice presents an interesting look at the South Central region of Louisiana, Texas, and cowboy country in his three alphabet books, *Cajun Alphabet, Texas Alphabet,* and *Cowboy Alphabet*. The tone in *Cajun Alphabet* is humorous, but the reader is treated to a practical lesson in Cajun French and an alphabetical look at the Cajun lifestyles. *Texas Alphabet* takes a look at a nearby neighbor of the Cajuns, with an alphabetical look at words and people that are an important part of Texas history. It presents some background information about each of the items and serves as an introduction to Texan history. *Cowboy Alphabet* gives a view of cowboys, ranch life, and things that are a part of their everyday lives. Lots of western words, such as armadillo and jerky, are used as well as words specifically related to cowboy life, such as drag, greenhorn, and javelina. Rice includes brief explanations and color illustrations of all the terms in his alphabet books.

There are also several titles dealing with other states and areas of the country. Each of these books takes an alphabetical look at the people, places, and events that are important to a particular state. Most of the authors of these "ABCs of a state" books employ alliterative text and/or rhyme to relate some interesting facts about their state. Natural history, geography, and history are taught through an alphabetical tour of the state. The ABC state books include *M is for Montana, The California Alphabet Book, ABC's of Maine, The Alaska ABC Book, C is for Colorado, The Arizona Alphabet Book,* and others that are listed in the annotated bibliography at the end of this chapter. All of these titles are useful in a middle school or high school class that is studying the geography and history of a particular area. They can also be used as simple ABC books.

While alphabet books about life on the farm and rural areas of the country are one means of studying people, life in the city offers a different perspective. Rachel Isadora uses black and white sketches and one-word text to show the sights and sounds of the city in *City Seen from A to Z;* Patricia Ruben also chooses to use black and white photographs to portray scenes of the city in *Apple to Zippers.* Francine Grossbart also uses black as a predominant color in *A Big City,* but the black is used in silhouettes of city objects (e.g., antennas, hydrant, ice cream wagon) shown on brightly colored backgrounds. Despite being almost 30 years old, Grossbart's book is still practical to use with children today. While Isadora, Ruben, and Grossbart write about life in any city, Phyllis McGinley's *All Around the Town* deals specifically with New York City. Her brown and white sketches dotted with spot color won a Caldecott Honor Award in 1949. James Stevenson also writes about city life—but with a humorous tone. In his wordless alphabet book, *Grandpa's Great City Tour,* Grandpa takes his grandchildren on an aerial tour of the city. The illustrations are hilarious, and the objects representing the letters of the alphabet are numerous and funny. Marguerite Walters shows not only the hustle and bustle of city life, but also the quiet beauty of country life in her turnaround dual story book, *The City-Country ABC.*

Purviance, Carle, and Bayer use alliterative sentences and rhyme to provide a look at cities and other places around the world. *A My Name Is Alice* by Jane Bayer is based on an old jump rope rhyme that introduces the alphabet by using names, places, and things beginning with the same letter. The places in this ABC book are scattered around the world. On the other hand, *Alphabet Annie Announces an All-American Album* concentrates strictly on American cities. The upper case letters on each double page are designed to look like the flag with stars on one half and stripes on the other. All kinds of interesting characters from Alice Allosaurus to Zany Zelda Zebra are shown performing activities in cities across the nation. The text is composed of tongue twisting sentences accompanied by illustrations filled with bright, vibrant colors created by using acrylic paints. Eric Carle also concentrates on American cities in *All About Arthur.* Arthur is a lonely ape who travels around the country making friends in many cities. Many of his new friends play some kind of interesting instrument. Carle combines linoleum cuts of Arthur and the other animals with photographs of the letters of the alphabet. The photographs are from letters on signs, brick walls, sweaters, billboards, and other natural settings from around the country. All three of these titles use alliterative text and humorous, colorful illustrations to introduce the letters of the alphabet, cities, and other places. The rhyme and pictures make all three titles guaranteed winners for both the beginning reader, as an alphabet book, and for the older reader, as a guide to geography locations.

In conjunction with stories of life in the city or rural communities, several alphabet books deal with occupations and careers found in these areas. Both Ruth Kahn's *My Daddy's ABC's* and Clare Bowman's *Busy Bodies* present occupations from A to Z. The problem with both titles is their stereotypical presentation of male and female roles. On the other hand, Jean Johnson's community helpers series (from A to Z) shows all kinds of people performing the tasks required of the job. The black and white photographs and brief text show the workers and equipment in various settings. The series includes firefighters, police officers, postal workers, teachers, sanitation workers, and librarians.

For a broader look at American history, see *Oscar de Mejo's ABC.* It features facts as well as myths and legends from American history on topics like the Boston Tea Party, jazz music, the Statue of Liberty, and the Wild West. Paintings are used to illustrate the text, with one or more words used to identify the piece of Americana depicted. Although some of the words do not seem to have much to do with Americana, the reader is able to detect exactly De Mejo's meaning upon closer examination of the painting. For example, K for Kites is used, and in the painting Ben Franklin is seen flying a kite during an electrical storm. De Mejo's book could serve as a good starting point for students wishing to create their own alphabetical list of Americana. Two other books that can be used in conjunction with De Mejo's are Maud and Miska Petersham's *An American ABC* and *Norman Rockwell's Americana ABC*. The illustrations in *An American ABC* are old-fashioned, and the text does not include things from the past 50 years, but the information about people and events is valid. Norman Rockwell is best known for his paintings on the covers of the *Saturday Evening Post*. In *Norman Rockwell's Americana ABC* some of his paintings depicting American life and events are used to celebrate history in an ABC format. Published on the eve of the Bicentennial, this ABC book includes holiday scenes and historical events, such as the landing on the moon.

Three other alphabet books offer a different but unique perspective on American history. In *A Garland of Games and Other Diversions,* Barbara Cooney uses scenes and activities from Colonial America to present the alphabet. The people in the illustrations are dressed in authentic colonial clothing, and the activities expressed for each letter were a part of everyday life in Colonial America. They include shooting arrows, embroidery, hunting for turtles and possums, and playing marbles. The Shakers were one of the first to use rhyme and music as a means of teaching the letters of the alphabet. *A Peaceable Kingdom* by Alice and Martin Provensen is a new illustrated version of the Shaker abecedarius, which was orginally published in the Shaker Manifesto of July 1882. The abecedarius is a 26-line rhymed verse that uses successive letters of the alphabet at the beginning of each line. A menagerie of over 100 animals is listed in the rhymed verse. Not only does this title provide a rhyming alphabet, but its illustrations are also reminiscent of early Colonial American history. The people in the illustrations are shown in colonial costume and in typical Shaker occupations, providing a link to the past. *A Peaceable Kingdom* is a good book to use as an introduction to the Shaker culture and its influence on American life. The Shakers led strictly disciplined lives, yet their use of music and dance provides a interesting contrast to this lifestyle. The abecedarius illustrates one of these contrasts. *Eight Hands Round* by Ann Whitford Paul also offers a view of early American history using the quilts and handiwork of the times. Paul presents an alphabetical guide to early American patchwork quilt patterns as well as a glance at the history, origin, description, and illustration of the patterns. She offers more than an ABC guide to quilt patterns in this historical tome.

Alphabet books are not limited to the culture, history, and geography of North America. There are titles available for all parts of the world and many different time periods. Peter Der Manuelian has written an alphabet book on ancient Egypt. *Hieroglyphs from A To Z: A Rhyming Book With Ancient Egyptian Stencils for Kids* shows the relationship between the English and the Egyptian alphabet. It includes a stencil kit with the letters of the Egyptian alphabet so that children can try their hand at writing words. A brief history and a chart in the back makes this a valuable resource on an ancient topic. The drawings are based on actual hieroglyphs carved or painted on Egyptian tombs. The text in the book includes the English letter as well as the ancient Egyptian hieroglyph that is representative of the sound, and a rhyme describes the item that begins with the featured letter.

Although alphabet books dealing with the history and culture of Africa and African Americans were dealt with in the chapter on multiculturalism, it is worth mentioning here that there are several excellent resources on this topic that would be useful for any study of the continent of Africa or African Americans. They include: *The Black BC's* by Lucille Clifton, *Jambo Means Hello* by Muriel Feelings, *Ashanti to Zulu* by Margaret Musgrove, *A is for Africa* by Ifeoa Onyefulu, and *A is for Africa* by Ife Nii Owoo.

Illuminated manuscripts and life in the Middle Ages is the subject of Jonathan Hunt's *Illuminations*. Illustrated in the style of a medieval manuscript, it is an alphabetical guide to life in the Middle Ages. While this is an alphabet book, the text is more appropriate and useful for older students. The information includes alchemist, excalibur, joust, quintain, troubadour, and zither. Even the letters of the alphabet are written in medieval style. Mayer's *The Unicorn Alphabet* provides another look at medieval life. From A to Z, stories and symbols associated with the mythical unicorn are presented in this complex alphabet book. The elaborate illustrations include detailed borders around the text and pictures. In addition to the borders, Mayer includes illustrations of complex medieval tapestries with decorative motifs. These tapestries often contain messages and symbols that explain the meanings of the stories and legends surrounding the unicorn. Both of these titles are certainly useful as alphabet books, but the information in them is even more vital as a resource on life in medieval times. The illustrations are also indicative of the type of elaborately detailed artwork that was used in the Middle Ages.

Social studies involves more than a look at history. It also includes an examination of the customs of a community, the people and events that shaped the area, lifestyles, and geography. While alphabet books can be used solely for examining letter and sound relationships, many ABC books can be used to fill the gaps in a social studies unit.

SOCIAL STUDIES AND ALPHABET BOOKS: BIBLIOGRAPHY

Azarian, Mary. *A Farmer's Alphabet*. Boston, Massachusetts: David R. Godine, Publishers, 1981. ISBN 0-87923-394-X (Hardcover); 0-87923-397-4 (Soft).
The 26 letters of the alphabet present scenes from rural America in woodcut illustrations.
ALL AGES. Upper and lower case.
Bannatyne-Cugnet, Jo. *A Prairie Alphabet*. Art by Yvette Moore. Montreal, Quebec: Tundra Books, 1992. ISBN 0-88776-292-1.
From A to Z the sights and sounds of the prairie are seen through the eyes of children.
ALL AGES. Upper and lower case.
Bayer, Jane. *A My Name Is Alice*. Illustrated by Steven Kellogg. New York: Dial Books, 1984. ISBN 0-8037-0123-3; 0-8037-0124-1 (lib bdg).
People, places, and things from A to Z are introduced in this picture book rendition of a jump rope rhyme.
ALL AGES. Upper case.
Bowen, Betsy. *Antler, Bear, Canoe: A Northwoods Alphabet Year*. Boston, Massachusetts: Little, Brown & Co., 1991. ISBN 0-316-10376-4.
Through woodcut illustrations and brief text, the reader is treated to an alphabetical look at the changing seasons of the northern woods in Minnesota.
AGES 3–9. Upper and lower case.
Bowman, Clare. *Busy Bodies: The Busy ABC's*. Illustrated by Virginia Carten. Chicago, Illinois: Rand McNally & Co., 1959.
This somewhat dated alphabet book is a guide to busy bodies, from daddies and mommies to lifeguards, zookeepers, and more.
AGES 4–8.
Carle, Eric. *All About Arthur (An Absolutely Absurd Ape)*. New York: Franklin Watts, 1974. ISBN 0-531-02662-0.
Arthur, the lonely ape, travels from Atlanta to Yonkers and meets all kinds of friends who play different instruments.
AGES 4–9. Upper case.
Cleary, Beverly. *The Hullabaloo ABC*. Illustrated by Earl Thollander. Berkeley, California: Parnassus Press, 1960.
A young boy and girl wander around their farm and encounter all kinds of things and sounds.
AGES 4–8. Upper case.
Clifton, Lucille. *The Black BC's*. Illustrated by Don Miller. New York: E.P. Dutton & Co., Inc., 1970. ISBN 0-525-26595-3; 0-525-26596-1 (lib bdg.)
Clifton provides an alphabetical presentation of African Americans and their impact on this country.
AGES 7 AND UP. Upper case.
Cook, Lyn. *A Canadian ABC: An Alphabet Book for Kids*. Illustrated by Thoreau MacDonald. Waterloo, Ontario: Penumbra Press, 1990. ISBN 0-921-25424-5.
Originally published in 1931, this ABC book combines the alphabet with poetry to introduce the reader to the wonders of Canada.
ALL AGES.
Cooney, Barbara. *A Garland of Games and Other Diversions*. Williamsburg, Virginia: Colonial Williamsburg, Inc., 1969. ISBN 0-910412-01-4; 0-910412-02-2 (lib bdg).
Scenes and activities of Colonial America are used to introduce the alphabet.
ALL AGES. Upper case.
Deasy, Michael. *City ABC's*. Illustrated by Robert Peron. New York: Walker and Co., 1974.
Black and white photographs of people, places, and things in the city are combined with the alphabet.
AGES 5–8.
De Mejo, Oscar. *Oscar de Mejo's ABC*. New York: HarperCollins, 1992. ISBN 0-06-020516-4; 0-06-020517-2.
From A for American to Z for Zoo, De Mejo uses paintings to illustrate American myths and legends for each letter of the alphabet.
ALL AGES. Upper case.
Der Manuelian, Peter. *Hieroglyphs From A to Z: A Rhyming Book with Ancient Egyptian Stencils for Kids*. Boston, Massachusetts: Museum of Fine Arts, 1991. ISBN 0-87846-329-1.
Each page in this alphabet book shows the relationship between an English letter and an Egyptian hieroglyph and gives background information.
ALL AGES. Upper case.
Feelings, Muriel. *Jambo Means Hello: Swahili Alphabet Book*. Pictures by Tom Feelings. New York: Dial Press, 1974. ISBN 0-8037-4346-7.

The Feelings provide a close look at the 24 letters of the Swahili alphabet and their English counterparts.
ALL AGES.
Grossbart, Francine. *A Big City*. New York: Harper and Row, 1966.
   Grossbart uses silhouettes on brightly colored backgrounds to present an alphabetical guide to all the things she loves about the city.
AGES 4–9.
Harrison, Ted. *A Northern Alphabet*. Montreal, Canada: Tundra Books, 1982. ISBN 0-88776-209-3 (Hardcover); 0-88776-233-6 (soft).
   The reader is treated to a sampling of places and things from the north for each letter of the alphabet.
ALL AGES. Upper and lower case.
Hunt, Jonathan. *Illuminations*. New York: Macmillan Publishing, 1989. ISBN 0-689-71700-8 (soft).
   Illustrated in the style of illuminated manuscripts, this medieval alphabet book tells about life in the Middle Ages, from alchemist to zither.
ALL AGES. Upper case.
Isadora, Rachel. *City Seen from A to Z*. New York: Greenwillow Books, 1983. ISBN 0-688-01803-3.
   Isadora provides a simple A to Z introduction to the city life.
AGES 3 AND UP. Upper case.
Jeffares, Jeanne. *An Around-the-World Alphabet*. New York: Peter Bedrick Books, 1989. ISBN 0-87226-324-X.
   Using both common words and those from different world cultures, the reader is introduced to the alphabet.
ALL AGES. Upper case.
Johnson, Jean. *Firefighters A to Z*. New York: Walker & Co., 1985. ISBN 0-8027-6590-4.
   Firefighters, their jobs, and equipment from A to Z are shown in this volume in the series.
ALL AGES. Upper case.
———. *Librarians A to Z*. New York: Walker & Co., 1988. ISBN 0-8027-6841-5; 0-8027-6842-3 (lib bdg).
   Through photos and brief text, the reader is introduced to the alphabet and to many libraries and librarians.
ALL AGES. Upper case.
———. *Police Officers A to Z*. New York: Walker and Co., 1986. ISBN 0-8027-6614-5; 0-8027-6615-3 (lib bdg).
   This title is an alphabetical introduction to the equipment and work that police officers encounter on their daily jobs.
ALL AGES. Upper case.
———. *Postal Workers A to Z*. New York: Walker & Co., 1987. ISBN 0-8027-6663-3; 0-8027-6664-1 (lib bdg).
   Black and white photographs provide an alphabetical guide to postal workers and the jobs they do.
ALL AGES. Upper case.
———. *Sanitation Workers A to Z*. New York: Walker and Co., 1988. ISBN 0-8027-6772-9; 0-8027-6773-7 (lib bdg).
   From A to Z, sanitation workers, their jobs, equipment, and working conditions.
ALL AGES. Upper case.
———. *Teachers from A to Z*. New York: Walker and Co., 1988. ISBN 0-8027-6676-5; 0-80276677-3 (lib bdg).
   From alphabet to zipper, the reader learns all about teachers and the work they do.
ALL AGES. Upper case.
Kahn, Ruth E. *My Daddy's ABC's*. Illustrations by Celeste K. Foster. Minneapolis, Minnesota: T.S. Denison & Co., 1969.
   In verse and rhyme, Kahn provides an ABC guide to fathers and their jobs.
AGES 4–8. Upper case.
Kreeger, Charlene, and Shannon Cartwright. *The Alaska ABC Book*. Paws Four Publishing, 1978. ISBN 0-933914-01-6.
   Kreeger offers an alphabetical look at the animals, environment, and culture of our northernmost state, Alaska.
AGES 5–9.
McGinley, Phyllis. *All Around the Town*. Illustrated by Helen Stone. Philadelphia, Pennsylvania: J.B. Lippincott Co., 1948.
   In this A to Z story, children and the sights and sounds of New York City are presented.
AGES 3–8. Upper case.
Martin, Cyd. *A Yellowstone ABC*. Niwot, Colorado: Roberts Rinehart Publishers, 1992. ISBN 1-879373-12-2.
   Through rhyming verse and hand-drawn color scenes, this is an alphabetical tour of the natural history of Yellowstone National Park.
ALL AGES. Upper case.
Mayer, Marianna. *The Unicorn Alphabet*. Pictures by Michael Hague. New York: Dial Books, 1989. ISBN 0-8037-0373-2.
   Legend and lore surrounding the mythical unicorn are revealed in this complex alphabet book.
ALL AGES.
Miller, Jane. *Farm Alphabet Book*. New York: Scholastic, 1981. ISBN 0-590-31991-4 (soft).
   The letters of the alphabet are used to introduce people, places, and things on the farm.
AGES 3–8. Upper and lower case.

Musgrove, Margaret. *Ashanti to Zulu: African Traditions*. Pictures by Leo and Diane Dillon. New York: The Dial Press, 1976. ISBN 0-8037-0308-2.

Twenty-six African tribes and their customs and traditions are introduced in this award-winning alphabet book.

ALL AGES. Upper case.

Onyefulu, Ifeoma. *A is for Africa*. New York: Cobblehill Books, 1993. ISBN 0-525-65147-0.

A view of the continent of Africa is displayed in lavish color photographs.

AGES 4 AND UP. Upper and lower case.

Owoo, Ife Nii. *A is for Africa: "Looking at Africa Through the Alphabet."* Trenton, New Jersey: Africa World Press, Inc., 1991. ISBN 0-86543-182-5 (Hardcover); 0-86543-183-3 (soft).

This is an alphabetical guide to the history and everyday lives of Africans.

AGES 5 AND UP. Upper and lower case.

Paul, Ann Whitford. *Eight Hands Round: A Patchwork Alphabet*. Illustrated by Jeanette Winter. New York: HarperCollins, Pub., 1991. ISBN 0-06-024689-8; 0-06-024704-5.

By using the names of early American patchwork quilt patterns and explaining their origins, the author introduces the alphabet.

ALL AGES. Upper case.

Petersham, Maud, and Miska Petersham. *An American ABC*. New York: Macmillan, 1941.

From A to Z, each letter tells a story about important people and events from America's past.

ALL AGES. Upper case.

Porter, Gail A. *Hugo Hippo's ABC Fun Book in Africa*. Illustrated by James Okello. 1992. ISBN 9966-884-24-6

Using alphabetical structure and alliterative language, loveable Hugo Hippo presents all kinds of information about the geography of Africa.

AGES 5–10.

Provensen, Alice, and Martin Provensen. *A Peaceable Kingdom: The Shaker Abecedarius*. New York: The Viking Press, 1978. ISBN 0-670-54500-7.

An alphabetical menagerie of 100 real and fanciful animals march across the pages of this unique alphabet book.

AGES 4 AND UP.

Purviance, Susan, and Marcia O'Shell. *Alphabet Annie Announces an All-American Album*. Illustrated by Ruth Brunner-Strosser. Boston, Massachusetts: Houghton Mifflin Co., 1988. ISBN 0-395-48070-1.

From Alice Allosaurus to Zany Zelda Zebra, a host of characters crisscross America performing all kinds of alphabetical activities.

ALL AGES. Upper case.

Rice, James. *Cajun Alphabet*. Gretna, Louisiana: Pelican Publishing Co., 1976, 1991. ISBN 0-88289-822-1.

Gaston the alligator leads the way through the alphabet, Cajun French style.

ALL AGES. Upper case.

———. *Cowboy Alphabet*. Gretna, Louisana: Pelican Publishing Co., 1990 (rev ed.) Austin, Texas: Shoal Creek Publishing, 1977. ISBN 0-88289-726-8.

Rice presents an alphabetical view of cowboy and ranch life from armadillo to quirt.

ALL AGES. Upper and lower case.

———. *Texas Alphabet*. Gretna, Louisiana: Pelican Publishing Co. 1992. ISBN 0-88289-692-X.

From Austin to Lorenzo De Zavala, the reader is introduced to words and names that are important parts of Texas history.

ALL AGES. Upper case.

Rockwell, Norman. *Norman Rockwell's Americana ABC*. New York: Dell Publishing Co., Inc.; Harry N. Abrams, Inc., Pub., 1975. ISBN 0-440-05944-5.

Published on the eve of the Bicentennial, this collection of Norman Rockwell paintings and poetry celebrates America in ABC format.

ALL AGES. Lower case.

Ruben, Patricia. *Apples to Zippers: An Alphabet Book*. Garden City, New York: Doubleday & Co., Inc., 1976. ISBN 0-385-11442-7; 0-385-11443-5.

Through black and white photographs, people, places, and things found in the city are shown.

AGES 3 AND UP. Upper and lower case.

Rubin, Cynthia Elyce. *ABC Americana from the National Gallery of Art*. New York: Harcourt Brace Jovanovich, Inc., 1989. ISBN 0-15-200660-5.

Rubin selected watercolor paintings of objects that were once a part of daily life to present her version of the alphabet.

ALL AGES. Upper case.

Schmid-Belk, Donna D. *The Arizona Alphabet Book*. Ilustrated by Michael Ives. Donna Dee Books, 1989. ISBN 0-685-28841-2.

This unique ABC book tells the reader all about the state of Arizona.

ALL AGES.

Shirley, Gayle. *C is for Colorado*. Illustrated by Constance Bergum. Helena, Montana: Falcon Press, 1989. ISBN 0-937959-85-5; 0-937959-81-2 (soft).

The natural history and geography of Colorado are combined with lessons in the alphabet in this unique book.

ALL AGES. Upper and lower case.

———. *M is for Montana*. Illustrated by Constance Bergum. Helena, Montana: Falcon Press, 1988. ISBN 0-937959-32-4.

Full color illustrations and fanciful rhyme are used to combine the ABC's with the natural history and geography of Montana.

ALL AGES. Upper and lower case.

Sloane, Eric. *ABC Book of Early America: A Sketchbook of Antiquities and American Firsts*. Garden City, New York: Doubleday & Co., Inc., 1963.

Black and white sketches and brief descriptions of antiquities and American firsts are used.

ALL AGES. Upper case.

Smith, Harry W. *ABC's Of Maine*. Camden, Maine: Down East Books, 1980. ISBN 0-89272-070-0.

In this unusual alphabet book the reader is shown the simple beauty and wilderness of Maine.

ALL AGES.

Somes, Laurie. *ABC's of Washington State*. Arlington, Washington: Timberberry Products, 1984.

From A to Z, Somes discusses the unique features of Washington state.

ALL AGES.

Stevenson, James. *Grandpa's Great City Tour: An Alphabet Book*. New York: Greenwillow Books, 1983. ISBN 0-688-02323-1; 0-688-02324-X (lib bdg).

Grandpa takes Mary Ann and Louis on an aerial tour of the city where anything can and does happen.

AGES 2 AND UP. Upper and lower case.

Torrence, Susan, and Leslie Polansky. *The California Alphabet Book*. Illustrated by Susan Torrence. Eugene, Oregon: T.P. Publishing, 1987. ISBN 0-914281-48-8.

Using short episodic text, the authors provide an alphabetic guide to California and the things that make it special.

ALL AGES. Upper and lower case.

———. *The Oregon Alphabet Book*. Illustrated by Susan Torrence. Eugene, Oregon: T.P. Publishing, 1983. ISBN 0-914281-00-3.

Alliterative alphabetical sentences are used to tell all about names, places and activities that are synonymous with the state of Oregon.

ALL AGES. Upper and lower case.

———. *The Washington Alphabet Book*. Illustrated by Susan Torrence. Eugene, Oregon: T.P. Publishing, 1983.

Tongue twisting text is used to present an alphabetical tour of the people, places, and things that are important about the state of Washington.

ALL AGES. Upper and lower case.

Walters, Marguerite. *The City-Country ABC*. Illustrated by Ib Ohlsson. Garden City, New York: Doubleday & Co., Inc., 1966.

This unusual turnabout alphabet book presents both the quiet beauty of a walk in the country and the hustle and bustle of the people and places in a busy city.

AGES 4 AND UP. Upper case.

SOCIAL STUDIES AND ALPHABET BOOKS: ACTIVITIES

Share *A Farmer's Alphabet* and *Farm Alphabet Book* with the class. Think of more farm animals and sights and sounds that might have been a part of these books. Explain that the illustrations in Azarian's book were originally designed as posters and that they are black and white woodcuts. Discuss woodcuts and how they are constructed. Let the children design and make their own simple woodcut designs. Be sure to tell them that on a woodcut everything is reversed: right is left and left is right. After cutting styrofoam meat containers into squares, use a pencil point to make a design in the styrofoam. Paint over the design with tempera paint and press the design onto a sheet of paper. You can make your own invitations, announcements, and more with these simple woodcut-type designs.

A Farmer's Alphabet and Eric Sloane's *ABC Book of Early Americana* both have a nostalgic spirit from an earlier and simpler time in American history. Compare some of the things mentioned in both books to today's lifestyles (e.g., popcorn popper, toaster, egg beater, butter churn, candle making, and others). Have some of these older items for children to see and to touch. If that is not possible, use pictures. Have some old-fashioned foods for the children to taste, such as apple butter and maple toast.

Antler, Bear, Canoe shows the changes that occur as the seasons pass in the northern Minnesota woods. Discuss how the seasons change in your area. As a group, make an A to Z list of words that describe the seasonal changes and events that mark the passing of the year.

Other activities to use with your students along with farm ABC books include:

—Select a farm or country animal and pretend to interview the animal about its life. Include questions about food, homes, entertainment, friends, and more. Have the children write about their interviews and make an alphabet book collection of the interviews.

—Examine a *Farmer's Almanac*. Look up information about weather predictions, crop forecasts, phases of the moon, etc. What did you find out about your region and local area? Use the data from the almanac and your own creativity to create your own mini-almanac. Use an ABC format to present facts about your area.

Using a map of the United States, trace the American cities mentioned in the text in both *All About Arthur* and *Alphabet Annie Announces an All-American Album*. Make an A to Z list of other American cities not mentioned in the text of either book. Write your own American city odyssey using alliterative alphabet text, or use an A to Z list of cities in your state to create an odyssey across your state.

After sharing *A My Name is Alice*, give each child a map of the world and have them locate and mark each of the 26 locations mentioned in the book. Then choose one of the locations, find five to seven facts about it, and write a paragraph. Using the same letter, find another location in the world and write your own rhyming verse to match the rhyming pattern established in the book.

Use *Oscar de Mejo's ABC* and *An American ABC* as introductory materials for information on American history. Students can create their own A to Z guide to American history using people, places, and events from the past and present to make a class alphabet book. Have students write a sentence or two about each object and compile the information into an ABC American history guide.

In conjunction with the book *Hieroglyphs from A to Z*, show the film *Pyramid* based on David Maccaulay's book. Discuss how hieroglyphs adorn the pyramids, their significance, and their importance in ancient Egyptian history. Duplicate the stencil or chart in the book and give a copy to the students. Have them write their name and a sentence using hieroglyphs. Do research on some of the terms mentioned in the text and share it with the class.

Have the students locate the places mentioned in *A Northern Alphabet* on maps and label them. Give each child a copy of a map to use. Discuss life in the colder regions of America and the people, places, and things (e.g. Inuit, kayak, husky, Yukon River, moose, etc.) that are presented in the book. Let students look up more information and pictures about these topics.

After sharing *Illuminations* by Jonathan Hunt, assign each of your students a letter and topic to research. Have the student recreate the letter in medieval style and illustrate their report in the style of illuminated manuscripts.

Use Marianna Mayer's *The Unicorn Alphabet* as an accompaniment to Hunt's book. Make a collage of symbols and items that are related to the legend and lore of unicorns. Include shapes of unicorns cut from different types and textures of paper and materials.

Based on the black and white sketches in Isadora's *City Seen from A to Z*, Grossbart's *A Big City,* and Ruben's *Apples to Zippers,* have students make silhouettes of city objects. Choose either one of the A to Z objects depicted in the books or make up one of your own. Draw an outline of the object on black construction paper and cut it out.

Mount the silhouette on white or colored cardboard to provide a contrast. After the students complete their silhouettes, display them one by one and ask them to identify these sights of city life. Use the silhouettes to create a bulletin board or display on "City Life from A to Z."

Share Walker's *The City-Country ABC* and compare some of the differences and similarities between city and country life. Make an ABC list of city words and country words, city sounds and country sounds. Discuss the advantages and disadvantages of living in each setting. Find pictures of city and country things and sounds. Use these pictures to create a bulletin board contrasting these two different living areas.

Have each student choose one letter of the alphabet and use the items shown and named in Jeffares' *An Around-the-World Alphabet*. Write a definition and description of each of the items under the letter in the book, including information about the location of these items. Make your own around-the-world list of four to six items for that letter. For example, under O Jeffares listed Orion, ostrich, octopus, obelisk, and olive branch. A student might add oranges, Oakland, and obsidian to the list.

After sharing the Johnson series on community workers, Ruth Kahn's *My Daddy's ABC's,* and Bowman's *Busy Bodies,* have the children make their own list of A to Z of jobs and occupations. Have each child choose one or two jobs from the list and find out more about them (education needed, job requirements, salaries, working conditions, etc.). The children can then report their findings.

A Yellowstone ABC deals with only one of the national park sites in the United States. Make a list of other national parks and historical sites around the country. Using a map, have the students mark the location of these parks and sites. Have older children locate information about one and present their findings to the class. What historical sites and/or parks are located in your area? Find out more about them.

Using any of the alphabet books about Africa, locate the people and places mentioned in the book.

Eight Hands Round by Paul offers a unique combination of history and patchwork quilt patterns. After sharing the book with your students, you can have them make their own patchwork quilt blocks using a variety of methods varying with the age of the students. For very young children, use nine precut triangular shapes and have them try to arrange the triangles into a pattern that forms a square. You can also create a paper quilt block by giving each child a cardboard square and having them cut colored shapes to arrange and glue into a quilt block pattern. Take all the cardboard quilt blocks and place them on the wall or a bulletin board to make a class quilt. A third method is to have children take scraps of fabric, cut them into shapes, and sew together a quilt block just as a craftsman would. You could also give each child a white or light colored plain block and have them draw and paint a design on the block. Sew the individual pieces together to make a class quilt. Have a raffle or contest at the end of the school year to choose a winner to take the quilt home.

Do some background research on the Shakers and their religion, culture, and lifestyles. What lasting effects have they had on American history and life? Find pictures of some of the things that are associated with the Shaker culture. Write a brief report about the Shakers. Make a map showing the location of Shaker colonies in the United States.

Sponsor a cowboy day for your students after sharing *Cowboy Alphabet* by James Rice. Let students choose a cowboy term such as Texas longhorn, wrangler, whirlwind, quirt, lariat, or other word and do a little more research on it. Have them dress up for cowboy day to present their findings to the class. For a food treat, have some typical cowboy fare such as beef jerky for the students to taste.

Use *Texas Alphabet* as a basis for reports on famous Texans or even famous Americans. Choose a person, event or thing that was mentioned in the book (or one of your own) and write a brief report about it.

Provide students ready access to the alphabet books on particular states and/or geographic regions. Create an alphabetical list of historical events, places, and people from your own state or one of the other 50 states.

Trace the path that Arthur took in his alphabetical trip around the United States.

Where Did Alphabet Annie Go?

Alphabet Annie talked about all kinds of American cities in *Alphabet Annie Announces an All-American Album*. Locate these cities on the map and trace her trip through the alphabet.

In *A My Name is Alice,* the author establishes a set language pattern for each letter of the alphabet. Using this pattern, write your own alphabet verse.

_____ my name is _____
And my husband's name is _____
We come from _____
And we sell _____
(_____ is _____ .
_____ is _____ .)

Make a list of all the places mentioned in *A My Name is Alice*. Then find and mark these geographic locations of the outline map of the world.

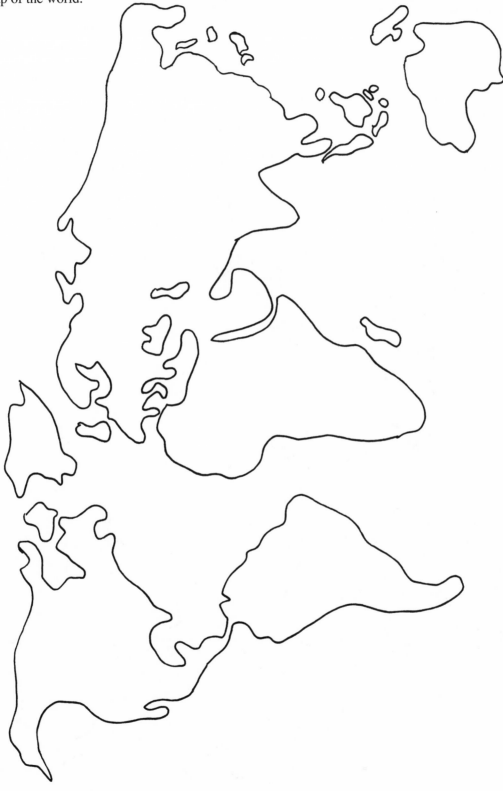

All kinds of places in the northern section of North America are mentioned in *A Northern Alphabet* by Ted Harrison. Choose one letter of the alphabet. Make a list of the places for that letter mentioned in the book, then locate these places on the map.

9. PUZZLES, GAMES, AND RIDDLES IN ALPHABET BOOKS

Many alphabet books are intended for more than letter recognition and identification of objects representing letters. They challenge the reader to look beyond the literal content of the page and to solve a puzzle, answer a question, or do a visual search. They force the reader to think and see relationships between a letter and an object, understand the significance of letters and words, and go beyond exact interpretation. These challenging alphabet books are, in most cases, best used with older children.

Several different types of puzzle, riddle, or game alphabet books exist. One type is letter transformations, where letter shapes change into the objects or animals that begin with them such as those in Suse MacDonald's *Alphabetics*. In MacDonald's book, the letter is shown in its original form, but as you look across the page, the letter is shrunk, expanded, manipulated, and shaped into an object that begins with that letter. An A turns into an ark, a C turns into a clown's grin, an F turns into a fish, and an S turns into a swan. As you look at the page, there is almost a feeling of movement as if water or sand were shifting and propelling the letter into motion. Letter transformation is also used in the black and white illustrations in *A is Anything: An ABC Book of Pictures and Rhymes* by Katharina Barry. Rhyming verse introduces each letter of the alphabet, while the letter in the picture turns into the object named. The letter C turns on its side and becomes the canoe a little boy uses for fishing. *A Folding Alphabet* by Monica Beisner combines changing letters with a book that unfolds as the reader goes through it. The objects representing each letter turn into the letter itself before the reader's eyes. The elephant's trunk winds and twists itself into the letter E, while flags flying from poles form the shape of an F. As the reader goes from letter to letter, the book unfolds into a long alphabet frieze. One side of the unfolding book is in color, while the reverse is in black and white. The combination of black and white and full color pictures with rhyming text makes Beisner's book popular with the very young. Both Dorothy Schmidered in *The Alphabeast Book* and Don Freeman in *Add-A-Line Alphabet* use letter transformations to introduce the alphabet and animals. In Schmidered's book the letters are presented in a four-panel sequence where the reader watches the letter evolve into an animal (e.g., B turns into a butterfly, E turns into an elephant). Freeman employs a different approach by taking large red capital letters and turning them into outlines of all kinds of animals. The capital letter A turns into an anteater, while C becomes a cat. All five of these titles use letter transformation techniques, each with special twists.

Although *Action Alphabet* by Neumeier and Glaser does not really involve letters transforming into objects, the letters in the alphabet come to life and act out the words that they represent. For some words such as those beginning with V and K, the letter becomes a part of the picture. In this case the V forms the fangs for a vampire, while the K turns into a kite with a string. For others, the letter becomes the word such as J for jump with J's jumping across the page; M for mistake with part of the M being erased; and G for Gone with nothing on the page to represent gone. *We Read: A to Z* by Donald Crews presents a similar unusual treatment of letters. A double page spread presents each letter and a visual depiction of a concept such as color, position, size, shape, or quantity. On one side of the page is a word, while on the other side is a brightly colored illustration for a concept that is easily understood. For example, L is for left with the illustration on the left side of the page, while Z for zigzag shows splashes of blue and green zigging and zagging across the page. Both *Action Alphabet* and *We Read* present easily understood concepts and letters in a unique manner.

Visual searches are the most common type of puzzle alphabet book. They ask the reader to solve a mystery without words, to identify something from a rhymed verse, to look for hidden objects, letters, or animals in a picture, or to predict what is behind the literal image. *Humbug Potion* by Lorna Balian encourages children to decipher the mystery of the missing words by using the ABC code in the book. Not only do children have the fun of being able to solve a puzzle on their own, but they are also practicing their alphabet and honing letter recognition skills. Pam Adams' *Mr. Lion's I-Spy ABC* invites the reader to find the answer to "I Spy . . . " for each letter of the alphabet. Die cuts on each page give clues to the possible answers. A small version of the answer, together with many other items, is shown on the facing page of die cuts. An illustrated list in the back shows the answers to the questions as well as more items for each letter of the alphabet.

On the surface, *"M" is for Mirror* by Duncan Birmingham appears to be a simple alphabet book. Upon closer examination, the reader learns that to solve the real mystery in the text, a mirror is required. A mirror is provided in the front of the book. On a similar note, *The Magic Moving Alphabet Book* also requires the reader to use a special piece of material (in this case, an acetate sheet) to find the hidden picture on each page. By moving the sheet slowly across and up and down the page, the hidden drawing is uncovered and appears to move. For example on the A page, airplanes are hidden in the patterned design. When the acetate sheet is moved up and down the page, the airplanes appear to be flying in the sky.

Anno uses complicated wood block arrangements to form the letters of the alphabet in *Anno's Alphabet*. On the opposite page is a full-size illustration of objects beginning with that letter. Hidden in the border around both pages are more objects that the reader is challenged to identify. A guide in the back names the objects. Another alphabet book by Anno, *Anno's Magical ABC,* uses optical illusions to capture the reader's interest. By placing a silver cylinder in the center of the page, one can turn a distorted image into a full color picture of animals and objects for a letter of the alphabet. All kinds of different images can be seen on the pages, depending on how and where the viewer looks. In addition to showing the letters of the alphabet with traditional words and circular sketches, Japanese characters are added. A child could spend endless hours poring over the fascinating pictures in this book. *Alpha-Blocks* by Kat Anderson offers another unconventional visual search. Each double page spread offers a large white letter on a black background with the facing page filled with 24 small blocks containing a wide array of people, places, and things, all beginnng with the featured letter. The reader is invited to try to identify all of the objects in the small blocks. For those who have difficulty, an answer key is found in the back of the book. Other visual search books include *The Great ABC Search* by Johannson, *Alphabeasts* by Bernhard, *Demi's Find the Animal ABC,* and *Animalia* by Base (the last two have been discussed in the animal alphabet section).

Two books, *Dr. Moggle's Alphabet Challenge* and *The Annotated Ultimate Alphabet Book,* offer an alphabetical challenge for children (and adults) of all ages. Each of these titles have complex, detailed illustrations for each letter of the alphabet, and the authors challenge the reader to identify hundreds of objects in each of the illustrations. It would take many hours of poring over the pictures to locate all of these objects.

Although *It Begins with an A* involves visual identification, it also combines a word riddle with the pictures as a clue to finding the answer to a question. Four pictures and four written clues are given for each alphabetical object. The children have four tries to guess what the object is. Answers are given in the back. Another interesting riddle alphabet book is *Q is for Duck: An Alphabet Guessing Game.* On one page the letter is greeted with a rather ambiguous statement. The reader then must discover why the statement is true. For example, "G is for Horse. Why? Because a horse Gallops." The answers are given on the next page. With its colorful, funny illustrations and unusual approach to the alphabet, *Q is for Duck* is a good title to use with young children. Satoshi Kitamura's *What's Inside* offers a whimsical game of hide-and-seek that is sure to capture imaginations. Two boxes are shown side by side, and the book asks the title question "What's Inside?" Visual clues about the contents of each box are given on the page. By turning the page the reader finds the answer to the question. Kitamura's densely-packed pictures and unusual word combinations (snow and tiger; octopus and piano) offer the reader hours of imaginative play. A memory game is an important component of *I Unpacked My Grandmother's Trunk.* As a little girl searches the trunk, she discovers all kinds of items from A to Z. Each time that she finds another item, the entire litany of objects is repeated.

Rebus puzzles, which challenge the reader to use clues in pictures to find an answer, are another method used in alphabet books. *Owl and Other Scrambles* by Lisl Weil uses one type of rebus puzzle. The letters of a word are used to form a picture. The letters are not necessarily in the correct order and, in some cases, not all the letters in the word are used. The reader must discover what word is used by studying the letters and pictures. The picture puzzles are in alphabetical order and the entire alphabet is seen across the bottom of the page. In *From A to Z* by Coletta, limericks are told through rebus puzzles. Each rhyme is rimmed by a border filled with pictures of objects beginning with the letter of the alphabet featured on the page. Some of the rebuses are hard, but most are fairly easy to solve. This book is definitely for use with older children. *The Ark in the Attic* by Eileen Doolittle is another alphabet book that uses rebus riddles, along with photo collages, for each letter of the alphabet. The complex collage designs in the photographs make it a book that is also more appropriate for use with older children.

Simple text, hidden letters, and little piggies make *Pigs from A to Z* by Arthur Geisert an alphabet book for all ages. On the surface it is the story of seven little pigs who are building a tree house. The letters are shown on each page as we watch the construction of the house. A more complex hidden puzzle awaits the older child. In each picture are five forms of the featured letter, as well as one of the previous and one of the next letter. It is not always easy to locate the letters. Miska Miles's *Apricot ABC* offers a hidden letter puzzle for the younger reader. It is a simple story of a ripe apricot that falls to the ground and all the woodland creatures from A to Z that come to investigate it. Upper case letters are hidden in the leaves in the illustrations, and they are very easy to locate.

Puzzles and games appeal to children of all ages, and they are effective devices to use for introducing the alphabet. The books described in this chapter, as well as those listed in the bibliography, can be used with a wide age range. Some of the simple riddle puzzles and visual searches are easily solved by preschoolers and primary students, while the more complex ones are best used with middle graders or even adult readers. Titles such as *Dr. Moggle's Alphabet Challenge* and *The Annotated Ultimate Alphabet Book* would challenge even the most sophisticated reader. In any case, puzzles, games, and riddles are unique means of introducing letters and alphabetical objects to readers.

Adams, Pam. *Mr. Lion's I-Spy ABC*. Child's Play (International) Ltd., 1976, 1989. ISBN 0-85953-06-5.
   Die cuts on each page invite the reader to guess the answer to the question, "I Spy . . . " for each letter of the alphabet.
ALL AGES. Lower case.

Anderson, Kat. *Alpha-Blocks*. Atlanta, Georgia: Longstreet Press, 1993. ISBN 1-56352-083-4.
   Twenty-four blocks filled with all kinds of people, places, and things are shown for each letter of the alphabet.
ALL AGES. Upper and lower case.

Anno, Mitsumasa. *Anno's Alphabet: An Adventure in Imagination*. New York: Thomas Y. Crowell Co., 1975. ISBN 0-690-00540-7; 0-690-00541-5 (lib bdg)**.**
   In this wordless book, wooden letters and intricate borders introduce the alphabet.
ALL AGES. Upper case.

———. *Anno's Magical ABC: An Anamorphic Alphabet*. Illustrated by Mitsumasa and Masaichino Anno. New York: Philomel, 1980.
   Optical illusions and magic make this an alphabet book beyond compare.
AGES 8 AND UP. Upper and lower case.

Balian, Lorna. *Humbug Potion: An A-B-C Cipher*. Nashville, Tennessee: Abingdon Press, 1984. ISBN 0-687-18021-X.
   When a homely witch discovers a magic beauty potion, she has to decipher it before making it for herself.
AGES 4–9. Upper and lower case.

Barry, Katharina. *A is Anything: An ABC Book of Pictures and Rhymes*. New York: Harcourt, Brace & World, Inc., 1961.
   As a small boy and his dog make their way through the alphabet, the letters become a part of the picture and the text.
AGES 3–7. Upper case.

Base, Graeme. *Animalia*. New York: Harry N. Abrams, Inc., 1986. ISBN 0-8109-1868-4.
   Intricately detailed illustrations, all kinds of animals, and a small hidden boy are used to present the letters of the alphabet.
ALL AGES. Upper case.

Beisner, Monica. *A Folding Alphabet Book*. New York: Farrar, Straus & Giroux, 1979, 1993. ISBN 0-374-32420-4.
   As each letter of the alphabet is unveiled, the book unfolds to reveal pictures of the objects.
AGES 3–7. Upper and lower case.

Bernhard, Durga. *Alphabeasts: A Hide and Seek Alphabet Book*. New York: Holiday House, 1993. ISBN 0-8234-0993-7.
   From ape to zebra fish, camouflaged animals are found in jungles, ponds, and other natural settings.
AGES 2–7. Upper case.

Birmingham, Duncan. *"M" is for Mirror*. Norfolk, England: Tarquin Publication, 1988. ISBN 0-906212-66-9.
   In this seemingly simple alphabet book, a mirror is needed to reveal secrets.
AGES 3–9. Upper and lower case.

Bishop, Ann. *Riddle-iculous-Rid Alphabet Book*. Illustrated by Jerry Warshaw. Chicago, Illinois: Albert Whitman, 1979.
   Riddles, silly questions, and word tricks are used for each letter of the alphabet.
AGES 5 AND UP.

Calmenson, Stephanie. *It Begins with an A*. Illustrations by Marisabina Russo. New York: Hyperion Books for Children, 1993. ISBN 1-5628-122-9; 1-56282-123-7 (lib bdg).
   Twenty-six catchy, rhyming riddles are used to challenge the reader to guess objects from A to Z.
ALL AGES. Upper case.

Coletta, Irene, and Hallie Colletta. *From A to Z*. Englewood Cliffs, New Jersey: Prentice Hall, Inc., 1979. ISBN 0-13-331678-5.
   In this unusual alphabet book, rhyming verse presents a rebus puzzle.
AGES 6–10. Upper and lower case.

Crews, Donald. *We Read: A to Z*. New York: Greenwillow Books, 1967. ISBN 0-688-03843-3; 0-688-03844-1 (lib bdg).
   Each letter of the alphabet introduces a brightly-colored concept such as color, position, size, shape, or quantity. Reprint of an earlier edition.
AGES 3–7. Upper and lower case.

Demi. *Demi's Find the Animal ABC*. New York: Putnam, 1985. ISBN 0-448-18970-4
   Demi uses a simple seek and find animal guessing game to introduce the alphabet.
ALL AGES. Upper and lower case.

Doolittle, Eileen. *The Ark in the Attic: An Alphabet Adventure*. Text and painted background by Eileen Doolittle; photographs by Starr Ockenga. New York: Godine, 1987. ISBN 0-87923-648-1.
   Complex photo collages and rebuses are used in this full color guide to the alphabet.
ALL AGES.

Downie, Jill. *Alphabet Puzzle*. New York: Lothrop, Lee and Shepard Books, 1988. ISBN 0-688-08044-8.
The reader tries to discover the letters of the alphabet and guess the secrets beyond the window on the page.
AGES 3–8. Upper and lower case.

Elting, Mary, and Michael Folsom. *Q is for Duck: An Alphabet Guessing Game*. Pictures by Jack Kent. Boston, Massachusetts: Houghton Mifflin Co., 1980. ISBN 0-395-29437-1; 0-395-30062-2 (soft).
The reader is invited to guess why A is for Zoo and more in this alphabet riddle book.
AGES 3–7. Upper case.

Folsom, Marcia, and Michael Folsom. *Easy as Pie: A Guessing Game of Sayings*. Pictures by Jack Kent. New York: Clarion Books, 1985. ISBN 0-89919-303-X.
This guessing game version of the alphabet invites the reader to solve 26 hilarious riddles.
AGES 4–8.

Freeman, Don. *Add-A-Line Alphabet*. San Carlos, California: Golden Gate Junior Books, 1968.
Freeman turns bright red capital letters into alphabetical animals.
AGES 7 AND UP. Upper case.

Garten, Jan. *The Alphabet Tale*. Illustrated by Muriel Batherman. New York: Random House, 1964.
Rhymes are used to warn the reader to beware of the tail of . . . (some kind of animal on the next page).
AGES 4 AND UP.

Geisert, Arthur. *Pigs from A to Z*. Boston, Massachusetts: Houghton Mifflin Co., 1986. ISBN 0-395-38509-1.
Seven little piggies cavort through a landscape of hidden letters as they build a tree house.
AGES 4 AND UP. Upper case.

Hayward, Linda. *Alphabet School*. Illustrated by Ann Schweninger. New York: Random House, 1989. ISBN 0-394-82226-9; 0-394-92226-3.
The reader tries to match the letters on the page with the letters on the shirts of twenty-six kittens.
AGES 3–7.

Hoguet, Susan Ramsey. *I Unpacked My Grandmother's Trunk*. New York: E.P. Dutton, Inc., 1983. ISBN 0-525-44069-0.
As a little girl unpacks her grandmother's trunk, she discovers all kinds of objects from A to Z.
ALL AGES. Upper case.

Johannson, Anna T. *The Great ABC Search*. Illustrated by Dave Lowe. Los Angeles, California: Lowell House, 1991, 1993. ISBN 1-56565-059-X.
Animals and objects fill the pages inviting the reader to go on an alphabet hunt.
AGES 7 AND UP. Upper and lower case.

Kitamura, Satoshi. *From Acorn to Zoo and Everything in between in Alphabetical Order*. New York: Farrar, Straus & Giroux, 1992. ISBN 0-374-32470-0.
In this quirky, stylistic alphabet book over 400 words and a series of questions are posed to the reader.
ALL AGES. Upper and lower case.

Kitamura, Satoshi. *What's Inside? The Alphabet Book*. New York: Farrar, Straus & Giroux, 1985. ISBN 0-374-38306-5.
In this unique ABC book, the reader is invited through pictures to discover "What's Inside?" the boxes.
AGES 4 AND UP. Lower case.

Lopshire, Robert. *ABC Games*. New York: Thomas Y. Crowell, 1986. ISBN 0-690-04443-7; 0-690-04444-5 (lib bdg).
In this ABC game book, the reader has to choose a person, animal, or thing that goes with the facing page.
AGES 4 AND UP. Upper and lower case.

MacDonald, Suse. *Alphabetics*. New York: Bradbury Press, 1986. ISBN 0-02-761520-0.
The letters of the alphabet are magically transformed into 26 objects.
ALL AGES. Upper and lower case.

Magel, John. *Dr. Moggle's Alphabet Challenge: A Quest for All Ages*. Illustrated by Claudia Del Col. Chicago, Illinois: Childrens Press, 1985. ISBN 0-516-09772-5.
Rhyming text and complex illustrations introduce the alphabet and challenge the reader to find over 1000 words in the A to Z pictures.
ALL AGES. Upper case.

Miles, Miska. *Apricot ABC*. Illustrated by Peter Parnall. Boston, Massachusetts: Little, Brown & Co., 1969.
A yellow, ripe apricot falls to the ground, and all the creatures in the woods come to investigate it.
AGES 3–9.

Moore, Frank J. *The Magic Moving Alphabet Book*. New York: Dover Publications, Inc., 1978. ISBN 0-486-23593-9.
In order to discover the hidden alphabet pictures, the reader must use a special acetate screen.
ALL AGES. Upper case.

Neumeier, Marty, and Byron Glaser. *Action Alphabet*. New York: Greenwillow Books, 1984, 1985. ISBN 0-688-05703-9; 0-688-05704-7 (lib bdg).

In this imaginative book, the letters of the alphabet come to life by becoming parts of the pictures of the items they represent.

AGES 3 AND UP. Upper case.

Rockwell, Anne. *Albert B. Cub and Zebra: An Alphabet Storybook*. New York: Thomas Y. Crowell, 1977. ISBN 0-690-01350-7; 0-690-01351-5 (lib bdg)

In this wordless alphabet story, Albert B. Cub tries to find who took his friend Zebra.

AGES 2–7. Upper and lower case.

Rourke, Linda. *Eye Spy: A Mysterious Alphabet*. San Francisco, California: Chronicle Books, 1991. ISBN 0-87701-805-7.

Although this wordless book looks like a simple alphabet book, the reader needs to find the answer to the picture puzzle and what follows on the next page.

AGES 3–7. Upper case.

Schmidered, Dorothy. *The Alphabeast Book: An Abecedarium*. New York: Holt, 1971.

In this unusual alphabet book, the letters evolve into alphabetical creatures.

AGES 5 AND UP.

Weil, Lisl. *Owl and Other Scrambles*. New York: Dutton, 1980. ISBN 0-525-36527-3.

The letters of the alphabet are illustrated with picture words to unscramble.

ALL AGES. Upper case.

Wilks, Mike. *The Annotated Ultimate Alphabet*. New York: Henry Holt & Co., 1986. ISBN 0-8050-0918-3.

In this intricate alphabet book 7,825 items are portrayed in 26 complex paintings. An updated version of *The Ultimate Alphabet*.

ALL AGES.

PUZZLES, GAMES, & RIDDLES IN ALPHABET BOOKS: ACTIVITIES

After sharing *Mr. Lion's I-Spy ABC*, it is only natural to play the age-old game of "I Spy" using items around the room. Let the children take turns asking the question and try to use as many letters of the alphabet as possible.

Anno uses wooden blocks to show the letters of the alphabet. Across the top of the activity sheet, write your name in block style. Then find a picture of or draw an object that begins with each letter in your name.

Secret codes and messages are always popular with children. After reading *Humbug Potion* by Balian, have the students invent their own ingredients for a witch's brew using the code that was in the book. As a guideline, give each child an activity sheet. Discuss how codes can be created, and show the children a simple way to make up their own codes. Encourage them to try their hand at writing codes and ciphers.

Although the riddles in *It Begins with An A* are easy to discover, this is a good alphabet book to use as a story-time read-aloud. As you read each clue, let the children try to guess the answer. Afterwards, let the children create their own alpha-riddle rhymes.

True rebus puzzles (combinations of words, letters, and numbers) are used in *From A to Z* by Irene and Hallie Coletta. As you go through the book, let the students try to identify all the objects shown in the borders around the puzzles. After sharing the book, have your students compose their own rebuses. Use a name and do rebus illustrations for it as a starting point.

A flannelboard presentation for *Q is for Duck* is a perfect way to let the children participate in this alphabet riddle game. As you make the statement, place the object on the board and pose the question: Why? Children will have a lot of fun trying to guess the answer and in the process will be more apt to remember the letter presented. When you are finished, let the children make up their own Why? riddles, create a flannelboard figure, and ask the other children to answer the question.

Share Hoguet's *I Unpacked My Grandmother's Trunk* with the children. Assign each child a letter of the alphabet and give them a 4″ × 6″ index card. The child is to think of an object beginning with the letter, write the name of the object on one side of the card, and then either draw a picture or find one in a magazine to place on the other side of the card. Play the memory game with the class after everyone finishes their card.

Share *What's Inside?* by Satoshi Kitamura with the children. After they have tried guessing what's inside of the boxes in the book, have them make their own surprise boxes. Choose a letter and label the outside of the box with the letter and the child's name. Place items beginning with a letter in the box. Students can share their surprise boxes with the group and pose the question, "What's Inside?" With preschoolers and early primary students, you can make up a set of your own surprise boxes.

Letter transformations are always fun to do with children. Show them examples from Suse MacDonald's *Alphabetics*. Ask each child to choose a letter of the alphabet and transform it into an object that begins with that letter.

Action Alphabet presents letters that become a part of the picture of the word they represent. V becomes the fangs of a vampire, while K is a kite with a string. Children can let their imaginations run wild while taking letters of the alphabet and turning them into parts of a picture of a word beginning with that letter.

After sharing *Albert B. Cub and Zebra*, ask the children to make up an imaginary story about what Bear and Zebra could do in your town. Write it as a group story, and make sure that each child has a chance to make a contribution. What would they do? see? wear? stay? eat? Brainstorm a list of other places "around the world and through the alphabet" where Albert B. Cub might go (U.S. cities, counties in your state, English-speaking countries, and more).

Try creating your own word scrambles based on *Owl and Other Scrambles*. Ask each child to select a letter of the alphabet and to think of an animal or object beginning with that letter. Use the letters of the word to create a picture puzzle.

Puzzles, games, and riddles appeal to people of all ages. You can use the ABC format to adapt a variety of popular game shows, board games, and other games to use with students of all ages. Alphabet versions of *Jeopardy*, *Win, Lose or Draw*, Bingo, Scattergories, or any board game can be created and adapted according to the age level. For example, you could base a game on the popular TV show, *Win, Lose or Draw*. In this game, one person draws a version of the word or phrase on paper, while the other members of his team try to guess it. You could choose a letter of the alphabet, make up a phrase, and have one student draw it while others on his team try to guess. Before starting the game, divide the class into teams, explain the rules, and choose a letter to feature. An example might include a phrase using the letter, B, such as "big brown bear bounces baseballs badly." Many popular games can be adapted to the ABC format.

Just as Anno uses wooden blocks in *Anno's Alphabet* to show the letters of the alphabet, try your hand at writing your name in block style. Then find a picture or draw one of an item beginning with each letter of your name.

For example: Ann

The witch in *Humbug Potion* must decipher the code of the secret potion before she could make it. Create your own recipe for a magic potion. Then try to create a secret code for it.

MAGIC POTION RECIPE

Recipe for _____

By _____

Start with _____

Add _____

Mix _____

Sift in _____

Flavor with _____

Stir and mix in _____

Blend carefully and strain through a white cloth. Drink every drop.

Now create a secret code for your ingredients.

10. ART AND ILLUSTRATION IN ALPHABET BOOKS

The illustrations in alphabet books are often as important, or even more important, than the text itself. While one of the primary purposes of an alphabet book is to provide letter/sound/word recognition, the illustrations in the book may be the deciding factor in a child's ability to remember and to recognize letters. Illustrators and artists of alphabet books have the many things in common with other types of artists and illustrators. They use their talents to create unique pieces of art and imaginative ways to present the letters of the language. Illustrators use different techniques including color overlays, fine details, and bold poster style as well as different kinds of media (gouache, tempera, pen and ink, collage, etc.) to send their messages to the reader. The pictures and print combine to create a rich collection of letters and objects for the letters of the alphabet. Artists are able to see letters all around them, and through various types of media, they are able to convey their visions to the reader.

Using photographs of real objects is one technique that is used frequently by authors of alphabet books. Photographs bring a sense of reality and immediacy to the viewer. The real trick to a photographic alphabet book is using materials that provide clearly identifiable images and do not become dated. Both black and white and color photographs can be used to present the letters of the alphabet in a clear and concise manner.

Perhaps the best known author/photographer is Tana Hoban. She has created dozens of photograph books to demonstrate concepts to children through real objects. Two of the titles, *A, B, See!* and *26 Letters and 99 Cents,* use real objects to show the alphabet. The first title uses black and white photograms of familiar objects from A to Z, while the second title is filled with full color photographs of the soft touch letters found in toy stores and objects for each letter.

Both Arlene Alda (*Arlene Alda's ABC*) and Balthazar Korab (*Archabet*) use photographs of letters found in objects around us to illustrate their alphabet books. Arlene Alda chose to use color photographs of natural objects that bear a resemblance to the letters on the page. C is a photograph of shrimp frying in a pan; J is a clothes hanger upside down; O is a headlight; and U is a necklace around someone's neck. Korab uses black and white photographs of letter forms found in, on, and around buildings. By carefully examining the photographs, the reader can see letter forms in all parts of buildings including under the eaves, on the front, or even under foot. Korab combines quotes from famous people with photographs of buildings. Both Korab and Alda have a unique talent of being able to see beyond the obvious and to communicate their perceptions to the reader. Children in action are the subject of Janet Beller's *A-B-C-ing: An Action Alphabet.* She uses black and white photographs of children doing what comes naturally to present the alphabet, from acting and blowing bubbles to yawning and zipping up coats.

Unusual illustrations are an important aspect of several different alphabet books including *The Ark in the Attic, An Alphabet in Five Acts, Once Upon A to Z,* and *All About Arthur.* In each of these alphabet books, the illustrators chose to mix art media by combining two or more types to create collage illustrations. Both *The Ark in the Attic* by Eileen Doolittle and *An Alphabet in Five Acts* by Karen Born Andersen use photo collages with different backgrounds to showcase the letters of the alphabet and the objects that represent them. In *The Ark in the Attic,* Doolittle combines rebus riddles and photo collages for each letter. The complex collage designs are shown in full color photographs, and each illustration has literally dozens of items for each letter. For example, on the page for the letter P, the background is a wood design with all kinds of "P" objects overlayed on top of it. Cut-out pictures of the items include Pinocchio, a pretzel, a pig, a pair of pliers, a puzzle piece, a pumpkin, a peanut, a package, and many more for the reader to seek and identify. Andersen uses a similar technique in *An Alphabet in Five Acts,* with the exception that her photo collages combine morticed pictures with cut paper designs applied to background materials. The text consists of one word for each letter of the alphabet on each page with the words combined into five sets to make zany sentences. For example in one act, the letters F, G, H, I, and J are combined to make the sentence, "Friendly Gwen Has Icky Juice." In both of these books three-dimensional photo collages are created by using an unusual color or material for the background. Photographs of people, places, and things as well as paper shapes and designs are cut out and applied or morticed onto the background. The insertion of faces, shapes, and things gives the illustrations an illusion of reality with a three-dimensional effect.

The alphabet story lines of both *Once Upon A to Z* and *All About Arthur* have been discussed in other chapters, but it is important to mention the artistic elements of each of these books. The illustrations in *Once Upon A to Z* are paper collages created by layering different colors, shapes, and sizes of paper onto solid backgrounds. Eric Carle combines linoleum cuts interspersed with full color photographs for the illustrations in *All About Arthur*. The black ink linoleum cuts form the figures of the animals and things that Arthur encounters in his travels. Photographs of letters of the alphabet as shown on signs, brick walls, billboards, sweaters, and other natural settings are mixed in and around.

Woodcuts and ink are also used to create designs for alphabet books. William Nicholson, C. B. Falls, and Mary Azarian use woodcuts to create their orignal poster art alphabet designs. Nicholson's artwork was originally published in 1898 as posters, but it was later adapted as an alphabet book, entitled *An Alphabet*. The detailed figures of people are used to represent all kinds of jobs and occupations such as an artist, a huntsman, a nobleman, and a trumpeter. Earth tones and black backgrounds are predominant. In the early part of the 20th century, C. B. Falls created an animal alphabet book *ABC Book,* using the same style as Nicholson's earlier work. Falls used the same meticulous craftsmanship to create woodcuts of familiar animals. He used blue, green, orange and yellow backgrounds to enhance his black inked woodcuts, a decided departure from the earth tones and black used in other picture books of the time. Azarian's *A Farmer's Alphabet* was originally commissioned as a series of alphabet posters, but it was later produced as an alphabet book presenting scenes and objects from rural life. Red ink is used for the letters while black ink is used on the rest of the woodcut design.

In *Erni Cabat's Magical ABCs,* familiar farm animals (cow, pig, rooster) as well as some surprising ones (katydid, weasel, vole) present unusual drawings. The paintings are of single animals on an uncluttered background. The animals are outlined in black, with a multitude of colors, patterns, and designs used to fill in the details of the creature. One part of the body may be filled with purple and yellow swirls, while another part may have green and blue paisley designs. Only a single uppercase letter and one word identification are found on the page facing the colorful painting. A glossary in the back presents basic facts and curiosities about animals named in the text.

In *The Accidental Zucchini,* Max Grover uses brightly colored paintings to present visual interpretations of some ordinary objects and phrases for each letter of the alphabet. Grover combines rather ordinary words to present some extraordinary visual images such as apple autos, bathtub boat, cupcake canyon, hotel hop, and junk jungle. The hotel has shoes on and is seen hopping down the street, while the green jungle is filled with all sorts of junk. The bold primary colors and interesting perspectives make Grover's book an interesting addition to the alphabet genre.

Although pictures created through artistic media and photographs are techniques to illustrate an alphabet book, there are pictures of paintings, sculptures, or other artifacts used to represent the letters of the alphabet. Florence Cassen Mayers designed a series of ABC books that uses art from museums around the world to represent the letters of the alphabet. Full color photographs of the art works are used together with information concerning artists, types of media, locations, dates, and other pertinent data about the piece of art. The collections are theme-based and include musical instruments, Egyptian art, the Wild West, and fine arts.

In *Alphabet Animals,* Charles Sullivan combines poetry with illustrations of paintings, sculpture, and photographs from museum collections from all around the world. Along with the lighthearted rhyming verse, Sullivan includes information about the artist, date of the work, and other pertinent data. Gretchen Simpson uses paintings of ordinary objects as a means of introducing the alphabet in *Gretchen's ABC*. Instead of painting the entire object, however, she uses only parts of the object, close-up views, or unusual angles to capture the essence of the object. For example, for G, a close-up view of blades of grass is used, while I is a painting of a petal of an iris. Both of these books are useful with a wide range of ages, but they are especially effective with high school students and adults in studying perspective and technique.

I Spy: An Alphabet in Art by Lucy Micklethwait uses 26 paintings from museums around the world to represent the letters of the alphabet. The text used the old rhyme "I spy . . ." and the reader is invited to find the object in the painting. Information about the title of the painting and artist are given in the text of this ABC book designed for children of all ages.

The ABCs of Origami by Claude Sarasas takes an unusual approach to demonstrating the ancient Japanese art of paper folding. Illustrated directives for creating 26 paper objects from A to Z are shown in the book. The initial introduction to the origami object is a color photograph of a collage with the origami figure overlayed. A trilingual caption identifies the object in Japanese, French, and English. On the flip side of the photograph the author provides step-by-step directions for creating the paper figure. Under the collage photograph, Japanese writing naming the object is shown. Although labelled for children, this ABC guide is better suited for middle school students and older.

In addition to looking at the art media and techniques, alphabet books can also be used to introduce a particular author or illustrator. Many artists have and will continue to be intrigued by the possibilities of using a solitary letter to create a dramatic impact on a page. By looking at the pictures in the alphabet book and comparing them to other books by a particular illustrator, students can see patterns in the techniques and media preferred. One artist may prefer pastel watercolors, another may use only bright primary colors, while a third might use only cartoon sketches for the illustrations. Although it is important to consider the illustrations in each and every alphabet book, there are some illustrators that are particularly outstanding and worth taking a second or even third look at. *Brian Wildsmith's ABC* combines a simple one-word text with illustrations that offer a rainbow of subtle hues and tints. Rich bright shades of purple, green, and blue are interspersed with softer shades in abstract artwork. The objects are simple and clearly recognizable. Like Brian Wildsmith, Bruno Munari uses watercolors, but with a distinctive look for *Bruno Munari's ABC*. Munari provides some interesting associations between words and letters such as an ant sitting on the stem of a large apple. His illustrations provide a strong visual message through the use of color and white space. In *Eating the Alphabet* Lois Ehlert also sends a strong visual message, but she uses bright, vibrant primary colors to convey her alphabetical message. The pages are filled with all kinds of fruits and vegetables in dazzling intense colors that draw the reader into the pages.

In *From Letter to Letter* by Teri Sloat and *On Market Street* by Arnold and Anita Lobel, the artists use some unusual illustrations to feature objects for the 26 letters of the alphabet. In Sloat's book, each double page spread includes an upper case letter connecting across the page to the lower case letter with all kinds of objects and animals intermingled. For example, on the R page, rainbows, robins, rats, and other things fill up the upper case R while a ribbon connects the upper case letter with the ends of the lower case R holding flags to signal the end of the rat race. Across the bottom of the page are words identifying some of the objects that fill up the outlined letter and are scattered all around the page. A list of items found on the pages is included in the back of the book. The reader could literally spend hours looking at the pictures and clever details in this book, trying to identify everything that fits with the featured letter. Anita Lobel also fills her illustrations with dozens of details, but they all feature one item for each of the 26 letters. A young child goes shopping *On Market Street* and buys all kinds of items from A to Z. Instead of filling the pages with the items, Lobel concocted an ingenious decorative stick person who is dressed in the featured object. For example, on the L page the figure is covered in a costume of lollipops, for the letter O the character wears oranges, and for Z the figure is clothed in zippers. A rhyme at the beginning and end of the book and a one word identification of the objects completes this Caldecott Honor Book.

Using humorous cartoonish figures is one technique used by illustrators of picture books, and James Stevenson and Dr. Seuss are two of the most profilic proponents of this technique. Stevenson has done an entire series of books using the character of Grandpa and his two grandchildren, Mary Ann and Louie. In his alphabet book addition to the series, *Grandpa's Great City Tour,* Grandpa takes the children on an aerial tour of the city where all kinds of things from A to Z can be seen. Usually Stevenson uses cartoon balloons to enclose his text, but the alphabet book does not include text identifying all the objects in the pictures. Stevenson does use his usual technique of cartoonish figures and soft pastel colors for the illustrations. Dr. Seuss is probably the most popular author and illustrator of children's books in the past 50 years. He is best known for his humorous characters and rhyming tongue twisting text. If no word existed to fit a situation, then Dr. Seuss created his own. In *Dr. Seuss's ABC,* he sticks to his standard formula of bright colorful pictures of some fanciful creatures coupled with familiar and newly created words. Seuss presents all kinds of things from A to Z in a book that is a surefire pleaser for all ages.

Chris Van Allsburg has been heralded as one of the best author/illustrators of children's books in the past decade, and he certainly outdid himself in his contribution to alphabet books with *The Z Was Zapped*. Van Allsburg is best known for his realistic three dimensional drawings that invite the reader to become a part of the book. In *The Z Was Zapped,* the 26 letters of the alphabet are on stage, one at a time, but all 26 suffer a series of mishaps that are first shown in the black and white drawing followed by a sentence on the back of the page describing what happened to the letter. For example, the picture of the letter F shows a shoe that is smashing the letter, while the text on the back states, "The F was firmly flattened." All of the letter-by-letter destruction is described in words beginning with that letter.

Although only a few illustrators and their alphabet books have been discussed, there are dozens of others that would be appropriate to use in the study of art and alphabet books, media and techniques, or as introduction to more titles by the same authors. Illustrators like Leo and Diane Dillon, Ed Emberley, Anita Lobel, Anno, Mercer Mayer, Roger Duvoisin, and Wanda Gag are only a few of those who merit study. Alphabet books are a superb genre to use with children as a means of discussing art techniques and media. Young children can enjoy the pictures for the sheer pleasure of the colors and designs of the page, while older students can look at the artists and the effect that illustration has on the text and the reader. In any case, pictures are "worth a thousand words" in alphabet books as in all kinds of children's books.

Alda, Arlene. *Arlene Alda's ABC: A New Way of Seeing.* Millbrae, California: Celestial Arts, 1981. ISBN 0-89742-042-X (soft)
Alda has created a collection of photographs of natural objects that resemble the letters of the alphabet.
ALL AGES. Upper and lower case.

Andersen, Karen Born. *An Alphabet in Five Acts.* Pictures by Flint Born. New York: Dial Books, 1993. ISBN 0-8037-1440-8.
The letters of the alphabet are presented in five acts with the words used to form zany sentences.
ALL AGES. Upper case.

Azarian, Mary. *A Farmer's Alphabet.* Boston, Massachusetts: David R. Godine, Publishing, 1981. ISBN 0-87923-394-X; 0-87923-397-4 (soft).
Scenes from rural life are used in this woodcut alphabet book.
ALL AGES. Upper and lower case.

Beller, Janet. *A-B-C-ing: An Action Alphabet.* New York: Crown Publishers, Inc., 1984. ISBN 0-517-55208-6.
Photographs and an action word are combined to present the letters of the alphabet.
AGES 5 AND UP.

Cabat, Erni. *Erni Cabat's Magical ABCs: Animals Around the Farm.* Paintings by Erni Cabat; verse and notes by Michael J. Rule. Tucson, Arizona: Harbinger House, Inc., 1992. ISBN 0-943173-73-6.
Familiar old letters and some unusual paintings present domestic animals in a tantalizing look at the alphabet.
ALL AGES. Upper case.

Carle, Eric. *All About Arthur (An Absolutely Absurd Ape).* New York: Franklin Watts, 1974. ISBN 531-02662-0.
Arthur crisscrosses the country in search of new friends.
ALL AGES. Upper case.

Doolittle, Eileen. *The Ark in the Attic: An Alphabet Adventure.* Text and painted background by Eileen Doolittle; photographs by Starr Ockenga. New York: Godine, 1987. ISBN 0-87923-648-1.
A combination of rebus riddles and photo collages are used for the letters of the alphabet.
ALL AGES.

Ehlert, Lois. *Eating the Alphabet: Fruits and Vegetables from A to Z.* San Diego, California: Harcourt Brace Jovanovich, 1989. ISBN 015-224435-2.
From apricot to zucchini, the reader learns all about fruits and vegetables.
ALL AGES. Upper and lower case.

Falls, Charles B. *ABC Book.* Garden City, New York: Doubleday & Co., Inc., 1923. ISBN 0-.85-08097-2.
From antelope to zebra, colorful illustrations introduce a variety of animals.
ALL AGES. Upper case.

Fisher, Leonard Everett. *The ABC Exhibit.* New York: Macmillan Publishing Co., 1991. ISBN 0-02-735251-X.
Fisher provides a collection of paintings portraying not only objects from A to Z, but also many elements of art such as shape, color, and layout.
ALL AGES. Upper case.

The Glorious ABC. Selected by Cooper Edens. New York: Atheneum, 1990. ISBN 0-689-31605-4.
Through artwork of the past (1874–1926), the letters of the alphabet are introduced.
ALL AGES. Upper case.

Grover, Max. *The Accidental Zucchini: An Unexpected Alphabet.* San Diego, California: Browndeer Press, 1993. ISBN 0-15-277695-8.
Grover uses brilliantly colored paintings to present a refreshing look at ordinary objects and words.
ALL AGES. Upper case.

Hoban, Tana. *A, B, See!* New York: Greenwillow Books, 1982. ISBN 0-688-00832-1; 0-688-00833-X (lib bdg).
Black and white photograms of familiar objects are used to present the alphabet.
ALL AGES.

———. *26 Letters and 99 Cents.* New York: Greenwillow Books, 1987. ISBN 0-688-06361-6; 0-688-06362-4 (lib bdg).
Brightly colored photographs and wordless text are used to introduce the alphabet, coins, and counting.
ALL AGES.

Korab, Balthazar. *Archabet: An Architectural Alphabet.* Washington, D.C.: Preservation Press, 1985. ISBN 0-89133-117-4.
The letters of the alphabet can be seen in, on, and around buildings in this look at architecture and the alphabet.
ALL AGES. Upper case.

Linscott, Judy. *Once Upon A to Z: An Alphabet Odyssey.* Illustrated by Claudia Porges Holland. New York: Doubleday, 1991. ISBN 0-385-41893-0; 0-385-41907-4 (lib bdg).
Andy and his amazing appetite meet Daisy the delivery girl and somehow they decide to form a musical group.

AGES 5 AND UP. Upper and lower case.

Lobel, Arnold. *On Market Street.* Pictures by Anita Lobel. New York: Greenwillow, 1981; Scholastic, 1981. ISBN 0-590-41004-0.

A young child goes shopping at the market and buys all kinds of things from A to Z.

ALL AGES. Upper case.

McMillan, Bruce. *The Alphabet Symphony: An ABC Book.* New York: Greenwillow Books, 1977. ISBN 0-688-80112-9; 0-688-84112-0 (lib bdg).

The letters of the alphabet are revealed through photographs of the instruments of the Portland Symphony Orchestra.

ALL AGES. Upper case.

Mayers, Florence Cassen. *ABC The Alef-Bet Book; The Israel Museum, Jerusalem.* New York: Harry N. Abrams, Inc., 1989. ISBN 0-8109-1885-4.

This bilingual book uses the English and Hebrew alphabets to introduce artifacts and art from the Israel Museum in Jerusalem.

ALL AGES. Upper and lower case.

———. *ABC Costume and Textiles from the Los Angeles County Museum of Art.* New York: Harry N. Abrams, Inc., 1988. ISBN 0-8109-1877.

From bridal shoes, mittens, and hats, the reader is treated to an alphabet of costumes and textiles.

ALL AGES. Upper and lower case.

———. *ABC Egyptian Art from the Brooklyn Museum.* New York: Harry N. Abrams, Inc. 1988. ISBN 0-8109-0888-3.

Mayers provides an alphabetical presentation of items from the civilization of ancient Egypt.

ALL AGES. Upper and lower case.

———. *ABC Museum of Fine Arts, Boston.* New York: Harry N. Abrams, 1986. ISBN 0-8109-1847-1.

The letters of the alphabet are illustrated with painting, sculpture, musical instruments, and decorative art from the Museum of Fine Arts.

ALL AGES. Upper and lower case.

———. *ABC The Museum of Modern Art, New York.* New York: Harry N. Abrams, Inc., 1988. ISBN 0-8109-1849-8.

This alphabet book is illustrated with painting, sculpture, and design from the Museum of Modern Art.

ALL AGES. Upper and lower case.

———. *ABC Musical Instruments from the Metropolitan Museum of Art.* New York: Harry N. Abrams, Inc., 1988. ISBN 0-8109-1878-1.

An ABC presentation of all kinds of musical instruments in this selection of items from the Metropolitan Museum of Art.

ALL AGES. Upper and lower case.

———. *ABC The National Air and Space Museum.* New York: Harry N. Abrams, Inc., 1987. ISBN 0-8109-1859-5.

From early aviation to the latest in space technology, this is an alphabetical guide to items from the air and space museum.

ALL AGES. Upper and lower case.

———. *ABC National Museum of American History.* New York: Harry N. Abrams, Inc., 1989. ISBN 0-8109-1875-7.

Examples of American history, craft, and ingenuity are shown in a special alphabet book.

ALL AGES. Upper and lower case.

———. *A Russian ABC: AEB Featuring Masterpieces from the Hermitage, St. Petersburg.* New York: Harry N. Abrams, 1992. ISBN 0-8109-1919-2.

Art from three Russian museums are used to illustrate the English alphabet and letters of the Cyrillic alphabet.

ALL AGES. Upper and lower case.

———. *ABC The Wild West: Buffalo Bill Historical Center, Cody, Wyoming.* New York: Harry N. Abrams, Inc., 1990. ISBN 0-8109-1903-6.

A guide to western art and memorabilia from collections of the Buffalo Bill Historical Center is shown in alphabetical sequence.

ALL AGES. Upper and lower case.

Micklethwait, Lucy. *I Spy: An Alphabet in Art.* New York: Greenwillow Books, 1992. ISBN 0-688-11679-5.

Using the paintings of famous artists, objects from A to Z are presented.

ALL AGES. Upper and lower case.

Munari, Bruno. *Bruno Munari's ABC.* Cleveland, Ohio: The World Publishing Co., 1960.

Watercolor illustrations are used to show objects for each letter of the alphabet.

ALL AGES. Upper case.

Nicholson, William. *An Alphabet.* London: William Heinemann, 1898; San Francisco, California: Alan Wofsy Fine Arts, 1975. ISBN 0-915246-02-8.

From A to Z, these 26 woodcut portraits represent a variety of jobs and occupations.

ALL AGES. Upper case.

Rubin, Cynthia Elyce. *ABC Americana from the National Gallery of Art*. New York: Harcourt Brace Jovanovich, Inc., 1989. ISBN 0-15-200660-5.
   Rubin presents an alphabetical list of 26 watercolor paintings from the Index of American design, a graphic archive of American Folk and Decorative Arts.
ALL AGES. Upper case.
Sarasas, Claude. *The ABCs of Origami: Paperfolding for Children*. Rutland, Vermont: Charles Tuttle Co., Inc., 1964, 1990. ISBN 0-8048-000-6.
   Using objects from A to Z, Sarasas gives explicit step-by-step directions for creating origami (paper folded) figures.
AGS 8 AND UP. Upper case.
Seuss, Dr. *Dr. Seuss's ABC*. New York: Beginner Books, 1963. ISBN 0-394-90030-8.
   In typical Seuss fashion, outlandish creatures are used to present the alphabet and appropriate objects.
ALL AGES. Upper and lower case.
Simpson, Gretchen Dow. *Gretchen's ABC*. New York: HarperCollins, 1991. ISBN 0-06-025645-1; 0-06-025646-X (lib bdg).
   Paintings of ordinary objects are used to present the letters of the alphabet.
ALL AGES. Lower case.
Sloat, Terri. *From Letter to Letter*. New York: E.P. Dutton, 1989. ISBN 0-525-44518-8.
   All kinds of objects fill up the capital letters that are connected to lower case letters on the facing page.
ALL AGES. Upper and lower case.
Stevenson, James. *Grandpa's Great City Tour: An Alphabet Book*. New York: Greenwillow Books, 1983. ISBN 0-688-02323-1; 0-688-02324-X (lib bdg).
   Grandpa takes MaryAnn and Louis on an aerial tour of the city to see all kinds of things from A to Z.
AGES 2 AND UP. Upper and lower case.
Sullivan, Charles. *Alphabet Animals*. New York: Rizzoli International Pub., Inc., 1991. ISBN 0-8478-1377-0.
   Sullivan combines light-hearted verse with illustrations of paintings, sculpture, and photographs to show the letters of the alphabet.
ALL AGES. Upper case.
Van Allsburg, Chris. *The Z Was Zapped*. Boston, Massachusetts: Houghton Mifflin Co., 1987. ISBN 0-395-44612-0.
   The twenty-six letters of the alphabet suffer a series of mishaps in this unique ABC book.
ALL AGES. Upper case.
Wildsmith, Brian. *Brian Wildsmith's ABC*. New York: Franklin Watts, 1963. ISBN 0-531-01525-4.
   Using simple text and rich bright colors, Wildsmith presents his simple version of the ABC's.
ALL AGES. Upper and lower case.

ART AND ILLUSTRATION IN ALPHABET BOOKS: ACTIVITIES

After going through *Arlene Alda's ABC: A New Way of Seeing* and *Archabet,* take the children outside (or even on a walk around the room). Encourage them to look at objects in a new light and try to locate letters of the alphabet in things around them. Another activity is to cut out pictures of things in old magazines. Look for photographs that resemble objects for all 26 letters of the alphabet. Mount the pictures on cardboard or paper and make your own ABC nature book.

Have the class create their own list of actions after sharing Beller's *A-B-C-ing: An Action Alphabet.* Let each child choose one of the actions to re-create in a freeze frame. Take photographs of the children and create an action ABC of your class.

Look at the paintings and designs of farm animals in *Erni Cabat's Magical ABCs.* Students can create their own crazy critters by drawing the outline of a familiar animal and filling in the body with wild designs, colors, and patterns. Use wallpaper, tissue paper, wrapping paper, etc. to create a textured effect.

Share Hoban's *A, B, See!* Then create your own photograms. Photograms are made by placing an object on a piece of photosensitive paper and then exposing the paper to sunlight. The object should have an easily discernable outline. Be sure that you include at least one object for each of the 26 letters. An alternative activity is to create a black and white silhouette picture. A silhouette is a solid outline drawing on a light background. The easiest way to create one is to have someone stand against a dark background, such as black construction paper. Use an overhead projector to throw light around the outline of the person.

A natural activity to follow the use of Florence Cassen Mayers' alphabet books is to take a field trip to a museum. Divide the class into groups of two to three and give each group a form to use to find things in the museum for each of the 26 letters. Be sure to note the artist, type of media, date, and other pertinent data.

Bruce McMillan uses the instruments of an orchestra in *The Alphabet Symphony* to present the letters of the alphabet. Go over each of the photographs in the alphabet book and discuss what they are and how they work. Using all kinds of scrap materials (boxes, spoons, pans, etc.) let the children create their own instruments and symphony.

Play "I Spy" alphabet-style with the children after sharing Lucy Micklethwait's book. Use slides or photographs of paintings for the game. Identify something in the painting (from A to Z, naturally) that you want the children to find. Discuss the artists and titles of paintings as you play the game.

Discuss the use of color and media in alphabet books. Have the children experiment with different types of media and techniques including: charcoal, pen and ink, pencil, colored chalk, crayons, paint (oil, gouache, tempera, splatter), cut paper, textured rubbings, photographs, collage, vegetable prints, and linoleum and woodcuts.

The combination of two or more art mediums is a popular technique in modern alphabet books like *An Alphabet in Five Acts, All About Arthur,* and *Once Upon A to Z.* Show and discuss these three titles before having your students create their own collage ABC books. Based on *An Alphabet in Five Acts,* have students select a sequence of four to six letters of the alphabet and write a sentence using one word (in sequence) for each letter. Use paint, chalk, crayon, or even textured material to make a background. Then cut out photographs of faces and things for each letter to apply to the background for a three dimensional effect much like that in *All About Arthur.* Students can use the same technique to create the layered colored paper technique used in *Once Upon A to Z.* Use all kinds of different colors and textured paper and cut them into the desired shapes and sizes and apply to some kind of background material.

On Market Street is a fun book to read aloud to children and have them try to guess what was bought for each succeeding letter. Discuss the characters and the items they wear. Identify the vegetables for V, the musical instruments for M, etc. Make a list of favorite ice cream flavors for I, or favorite books for B. Be imaginative in discussing the illustrations. Give the children a sheet of paper to divide into 26 sections, and have them write down some items that they could buy for each letter. Talk about the letter people in the book. What would you buy for each letter in your name? Have the children draw their own letter people and items that could be purchased. You can also play a shopping game with the children. Place 26 cards (one for each letter of the alphabet) in a bag. One at a time, a child pulls a card from the bag and names an item to buy that begins with that letter.

Linoleum cuts and woodcuts are difficult techniques for the beginning artist. However, you can create your own simple woodcuts by cutting designs in squares cut from styrofoam meat containers. Use tempera paint to cover the design and press it onto paper.

Ask your students to choose an artist/illustrator to research. Compare the work of different artists/illustrators of alphabet books. Locate information about the personal as well as professional lives of artists including the date and place of birth, family, childhood, education, career, etc. Some artists to study include: Brian Wildsmith, Bruno Munari, Dr. Seuss, Ed Emberley, Mary Azarian, Wanda Gag, Anita Lobel, Chris Van Allsburg, Lois Ehlert, Maurice Sendak, Leo & Diane Dillion, Roger Duvoisin, and others. Use the activity sheet as a guideline for information about the artist.

In her paintings Gretchen Simpson uses closeups of parts of objects and unusual angles to present the letters of the alphabet. After students study her technique have them create their own alphabet paintings imitating Simpson's style. For older readers use Simpson's paintings as story starters or for writing descriptive paragraphs.

Children can draw their own versions of connecting letters after looking at the ones in *From Letter to Letter*. Have them draw as many items as possible to fill up the upper case version of the featured letter. Each child should choose a letter of the alphabet to draw with the letter connecting to another letter.

Dr. Seuss is well known for his unusual characters, bold graphics, and alliterative text. Use *Dr. Seuss's ABC* as an introduction to both the alphabet and to Dr. Seuss. Let the students create their own unusual characters by creating "Glitter Critters." Divide the class into groups of two to four. Give each student a glitter stick. One student draws a part of the creature, then passes the paper to the next student who adds another part. Continue the cycle until the "Glitter Critter" is done. If desired, use paint or markers to add other details to the critters. Give each critter a name beginning with a letter of the alphabet and use the pictures for a display. Be sure to have the students create and name a critter for each letter of the alphabet.

After sharing *Brian Wildsmith's ABC*, make greeting cards or book jackets for a letter of the alphabet. Use lots of purples, greens, and blues to finger paint the designs.

The Z Was Zapped by Van Allsburg offers many unique opportunities for follow-up activities. Some of the things that students could do include:

1. Design a card inviting someone to a showing of the Alphabet theater's new production, or design a playbill for *The Z Was Zapped*.
2. Conduct an imaginary interview with one of the letters from *The Z Was Zapped*. Write an article about the interview and share it with the class.
3. Make a list of more verbs and nouns that describe mishaps that might have happened to the letters other than those that did happen. Imitate Chris Van Allsburg's art by writing Act 2 for *The Z Was Zapped*. Use the activity sheet as a guide to more misadventures for the letters.
4. Write or do an oral review of *The Z Was Zapped*. Imitate the style of reviewers such as Siskel and Ebert.
5. Write a reverse of the action in the play by creating good adventures for each letter of the alphabet. Have each student take a letter of the alphabet and create a pleasant event for it.

Museum Visit

As you go through the museum, try to find an item for each letter of the alphabet. Be sure to list the artist, date, and type of medium (painting, sculpture, etc.) for each item.

A -

B -

C -

D -

E -

F -

G -

H -

I -

J -

K -

L -

M -

N -

O -

P -

Q -

R -

S -

T -

U -

V -

W -

X -

Y -

Z -

What was your favorite piece?

Why?

What was your least favorite and why?

Illustrators

Choose an artist or illustrator of an alphabet book. Find out as much as you can about the artist and write a brief biographical sketch. Use the following questions to get you started and then think of more on your own.

Name of artist/illustrator:

Date and place of birth:

Family (brothers, sisters, etc.):

Education:

Career (When, why, and where did art career begin?):

Favorite type of art media:

Other types of media used:

Names of books written and/or illustrated:

Other information:

A Shopping Trip

Pretend that you have been sent to the market or mall to do some shopping. What items might you buy for each letter of the alphabet?

For example for P you might buy peanuts, popcorn, and peaches.

A -   P -

B -   Q -

C -   R -

D -   S -

E -   T -

F -   U -

G -   V -

H -   W -

I -   X -

J -   Y -

K -   Z -

L -

M -   What other items might you buy on
                      your shopping trip?

N -   What is your favorite item?

O -   What is your least favorite item?

Create more misadventures for the letters of the alphabet. Imitate the illustration techniques of Chris Van Allsburg as you make a series of misadventures for each letter.

An example might be: *"The I was impaled."*

11. POP CULTURE AND OTHER ABC ADVENTURES

Hundreds of alphabet books for children are on the market, and most of them fit into the categories already discussed. In addition to the informational ABC books and those for early learners, there are numerous titles featuring popular book and television characters as well as alphabet books featuring holidays, monsters, beginning readers, and other assorted alphabet adventures. Any of these books are good to use for letter and sound recognition, information resources, and just for plain reading fun.

Alphabet books can be used to introduce favorite characters such as Clifford, Paddington Bear, Harold, Mary Poppins, and the Beatrix Potter animals. Children become acquainted with these characters and can often be steered to other titles featuring further adventures of the character. Clifford, the big red dog, is particularly popular with very young children, and his *Clifford's ABC* is an excellent way to introduce this lovable dog to more readers. Dozens of words and objects for each letter are shown in the text along with Clifford and his owner, Emily Elizabeth. Be sure to have a stuffed animal version of Clifford handy when sharing his books. The impact is even greater when children can touch a stuffed version of a book character. The same holds true for *Peter Rabbit's ABC*. Beatrix Potter's characters and illustrations have been popular with children for decades, and this version uses reproductions from original illustrations of her characters to introduce the letters of the alphabet. The soft, pale yellow background and characters from Potter's well-known stories introduce familiar objects and the letters that they begin with. Winnie the Pooh is another character that has been loved by generations of children, and in *Pooh's Alphabet Book* the reader is taken by Pooh on an alphabetical tour. Quotations from A. A. Milne's work are used as the text, with key words in the quotations highlighted in color for the featured letter on the page. Pooh, his friends, and their problems are the subject of this special alphabet book.

Harold with his trusty purple crayon is another popular character who has his own alphabet book. Like the rest of the Harold stories, the ABC book is very small, just right for the little ones' hands. One evening Harold takes his ever-present purple crayon and goes on a walk. Along the way he encounters and draws all kinds of things from A to Z in an adventure that is not soon forgotten. Although *Mary Poppins from A to Z* is for older children, it too uses familiar characters to introduce the alphabet. Each page is a short story about someone in the Banks family and his or her adventure, using words beginning with the featured letter of the alphabet. The pen and ink drawings, with alternating blue and yellow backgrounds, face the page with the short story. Babar, Curious George, and Raggedy Ann and Andy are other characters from children's literature that have alphabet books of their own.

Folk and fairy tale characters are an integral part of two alphabet books. In *The Hole by the Apple Tree* by Polette, Harold digs a hole, his friends come by, and Harold and his imagination lead them through an adventure involving all kinds of familiar folk and fairy tale characters. Polette uses cartoonish characters to convey her message about the alphabet to the young reader. *Macmillan Fairy Tale Alphabet Book* by Hall uses the backdrop of dozens of characters from children's literature as a means of introducing the alphabet. Her book is definitely for an older group. Very detailed illustrations coupled with alliterative sentences mean that the reader will need many hours to identify all of the characters and books that are referred to in the text. Hall refers to characters from fairy tales, folklore, tall tales, and other famous children's literature while at the same time she presents the letters of the alphabet. For those who have difficulty recognizing all of the characters, an illustrated list in the back identifies the stories. Using the alphabet book as a means of introducing children to literary characters is an effective means to encourage reading and to promote literacy skills.

Alphabet books also feature pop culture or television characters such as the Sesame Street Gang, Garfield, the Care Bears, Smurfs, Snoopy, and Maggie Simpson. While some of the pop culture characters are long lasting, like the Muppets from Sesame Street, Snoopy, and Garfield, there are others like Maggie Simpson and the Norfin Trolls that will become dated. The Sesame Street Muppet gang has proved to be very effective with helping children grasp basic concepts, and there are several titles featuring one or more characters from Sesame Street. In *A Day in the Country: An Alphabet Story,* the entire gang go for a day in the country and find themselves playing the alphabet game. In *The Sesame Street ABC Storybook,* different Muppet characters tell a story for each letter of the alphabet. In some stories, only one character is used, such as Cookie Monster, while in others several Muppets are featured. One of the nicest alphabet books that uses pop culture characters is *Disney's Elegant ABC* by Vincent Jefferds. Rhyming poems introduce a variety of words and objects for each letter of the alphabet, and the illustrations all show one or more of the Disney characters demonstrating the word in action. Sometimes the characters themselves are used as part of the letter. For example, D is for Dumbo, M is for Mickey, P is for Pinocchio, and S is for Snow White. More than one character or object is used for each letter. The book also includes a section on letter construction and numbers. Rich vibrant colors on a stark white background accentuate the pictures, and Disney characters that are universally known make this alphabet book one that children will enjoy more than once.

The short-term pop culture characters are useful because of their current popularity and are one means of capturing attention in order to convey an important message. The Smurfs, Care Bears, Norfin Trolls, Fraggles, Maggie Simpson, and even Gumby are all characters that enjoy a surge in popularity that is oftentimes very shortlived. While the characters are popular, however, the market is flooded with all kinds of items featuring them, including alphabet books. The books often become dated quickly, so use them while the characters are popular as a means of capturing a child's attention and as a means of enticing children to read more and better quality materials.

OTHER ABC ADVENTURES

In addition to alphabet books that are useful in enriching science, art, and social studies, as well as pleasure reading, there are many other titles featuring monsters, holidays, elves, feelings, and assorted other topics. These alphabet books are often useful with both children and young adults. For some reason, children are enthralled with the topic of monsters, and there are several alphabet books that feature monsters. The friendly-looking, colorful monsters in *The Monster Alphabet* are shown doing all kinds of everyday activities as they go through the alphabet. A series of words from A to Z run across the bottom of the pages describing the activities. The scenes on the pages are interconnected to one another. In Alan Snow's *The Monster Book of ABC Sounds,* rats and monsters play a hide-and-seek game to the tune of the alphabet song. A border around the pictures and text includes the featured letter as well as a string of items that begin with that letter. The monsters are friendly-looking, and they make all kinds of sounds as a part of the game from Aaaaah!, Boo!, and kerplunk to pop, Vrroom and zzzzzzzzz. Brightly-colored cartoon illustrations and rhyming text make this book a perfect title to read aloud to a group of children or to share with an individual child as a bedtime story. One way to use this book at a storytime would be to pass out sound cards to the children as they are seated. As you read the story the child holding the appropriate sound card makes that sound. The cards should be in a monster shape and would serve as a great souvenir for the children. Monsters partying their way through the alphabet are the topic of *ABC of Monsters* by Deborah Niland. When a little girl decides to attend a party, little does she know that she will encounter all kinds of wild and crazy monsters prancing and cavorting their way through the alphabet with everything from annoying apes to inking inkspots. The illustrations are bright and colorful, and the text is simple enough for even the youngest reader. *Alphabrutes* by Dennis Nolan also uses friendly wild monsters who weave their way through the alphabet. While the story is told through pictures and not words, the friendly monsters do make fun sounds like "aargh" and "blurp" as they frolic and gather around a yellow basket trying to find out what is inside. The letters of the alphabet are painted on the white t-shirts that the monsters are wearing. Other monster alphabet books include *Little Critter's The Trip* and *Little Monster's Alphabet Book* by Mercer Mayer and *Magic Monsters Act the Alphabet* by Jane Belk Moncure. These three titles feature very simple text and an easy-to-follow plot line. Little Critter goes on a trip and discovers all kinds of A to Z words, Little Monster shares his alphabet collection, and the Magic Monsters put on an act to show off the alphabet. The monsters are not particularly scary, so the books can be used with very young children.

Along with the topic of monsters, there are two books on elves and forest creatures that are worth mentioning. Jane Yolen's *Elfabet: An ABC of Elves* is a clever book showing elves engaged in alphabetical activites and surrounded by an assortment of objects for each. The central drawings are detailed and whimsical portraits of the elves, with borders filled with flowers and other objects that begin with the featured letter. One example is on the R pages with "Rose Elf restfully reading." The elf is resting on a rose, reading a book, while the border includes a rabbit, a raccoon, a robin, a rose, a ruby ring, and a ragged robin. A glossary in the back of the book identifies the items in the borders. *Elfabit* by Steve Pilcher also includes elves as well as fairies, pixies, and other forest fantasy creatures. The cartoon-like illustrations and rhyming text accompany the creatures on an alphabetical trip.

Feelings and emotions are a topic that can be easily discussed with children. Boddy's *ABC Book of Feelings* and Hubbard's *C is for Curious* are both useful as means of discussing caring and feelings. Boddy presents an alphabet of emotions, as told from the Christian point of view. Bright colorful pictures accompany the words and explanations of the wide spectrum of emotions that range from afraid, bashful, and homesick to puzzled, surprised, and zany. Woodleigh Hubbard also presents a litany of emotions in *C is for Curious: An ABC of Feelings*. Colorful modernistic pictures and some unusual creatures dot the pages of this book on feelings. Judy Lalli presents a different slant in *Feelings Alphabet* by using black and white photographs of children as they show various emotions. Beneath each picture is a word describing the emotion in a typestyle representative of that emotion. For example, the picture of U shows a child with an unhappy face. The word unhappy is written with a tear dripping from it. N shows a picture of a child hanging from a monkey bar with the word nervous written in shaky handwriting. All of these books, as well as Sandra Boynton's *A is for Angry* (discussed elsewhere), are helpful for a discussion on emotions.

Children and their everyday activities are the subject of several alphabet books. *Day Care ABC* features children from a variety of cultures who share activities and toys at the same day care center. *Annie, Bea, and Chi Chi Dolores* shows three young children as they embark on a day of activities at school from all aboard the bus, counting, and making music to zipping up to go home. *Lucy and Tom's a.b.c.* is a visit through the alphabet as seen from the world of two small children, and while *A is for Annabelle* is not really about a child, the topic is dolls, which is one that children enjoy. The delicate and dainty illustrations show the world of Annabelle the doll and all her personal items.

Several alphabet books that feature holidays have already been mentioned in other sections, but there are four titles that have not been discussed. *B is for Bethlehem: A Christmas Alphabet* uses the letters of the alphabet to recount the events surrounding the birth of Jesus. The book was originally written as a play for second graders to perform during the holidays, and it is certainly an effective title to use with any grade level as a performance piece. The illustrations are a mixed media collage mixing watercolors with cut paper designs. The rhyming couplets are effective in telling the Christmas story. *The Christmas Tree Alphabet Book* is a look at Christmas traditions around the world, while *AlphaZoo Christmas* combines tongue twisters with animals engaged in alphabetical holiday activities. All kinds of familiar and not so familiar animals are dressed in Victorian style, including boisterious bluebirds, an elegant elk, quick stepping quetzals, and zigzagging zebras. *An Easter Alphabet* shares the signs and symbols of Easter through old-fashioned illustrations from artists of the past (1885–1933). For more holiday alphabet books, see the sections on story alphabet books, animals, and multiculturalism.

Alphabet books cover a multitude of topics, many of which have not been discussed in detailed fashion in this book. Alphabet books on mimes, baseball, silent letters, sounds, and simple objects are all listed in the annotated bibliography at the end of this chapter. Furthermore, dozens of other alphabet books are available on even more topics. The list is endless and so is the reader's pleasure in enjoying these books.

Alexander, Liza. *A Day in the Country: An Alphabet Story*. Illustrated by Rick Wetzel. Racine, Wisconsin: Western Publishing Co., Inc., 1988. ISBN 0-307-13106-8; 0-307-63106-0 (lib bdg).

The Sesame Street gang go off for a day in the country and wind up playing the alphabet game.

AGES 3–8. Upper and lower case.

Anglund, Joan Walsh. *A is For Always: An ABC Book*. New York: Harcourt, 1968.

Anglund provides an alphabetical guide to behavior, including fearless and generous.

AGES 4 AND UP. Upper and lower case.

Bernthal, Mark. *Baby Bop's ABC*. Barney Publishing, 1993. ISBN 0-7829-0377-0.

Brightly colored illustrations and rhyming text featuring Baby Bop (of *Barney* fame) introduce small children to the alphabet.

AGES 2–6.

Boddy, Marlys. *ABC Book of Feelings*. Illustrated by Joe Boddy. St. Louis, Missouri: Concordia, 1991. ISBN 0-570-04190-2.

From the Christian point of view, an alphabet of emotions from afraid to zany.

AGEG 4–8. Upper case.

Bond, Michael. *Paddington's ABC*. Illustrated by John Lobban. New York: Viking, 1990. ISBN 0-670-84104-8.

This book follows an ordinary day with Paddington bear, as he encounters all kinds of things from A to Z.

AGES 3–7. Upper and lower case.

Bridwell, Norman. *Clifford's ABC*. New York: Scholastic, 1983. ISBN 0-590-44286-4.

The beloved big red dog, Clifford, displays words from A to Z.

AGES 2 AND UP. Upper and lower case.

Bruna, Dick. *B is for Bear: An ABC*. London: Methuen Children's Books, 1971.

Using the traditional "A is for . . ." format, Bruna introduces the alphabet with simple objects and bright colors.

AGES 3–7. Lower case.

Brunhoff, Laurent de. *Babar's ABC*. New York: Random House, 1983. ISBN 0-394-85920-0.

All of the residents of Celesteville present the letters of the alphabet with words and sentences.

AGES 4 AND UP. Upper and case.

Burningham, John. *John Burningham's ABC*. Indianapolis, Indiana: The Bobbs-Merrill Co., Inc., 1964.

Ordinary objects from apple to zoo are presented in this simple alphabet book.

AGES 4–7.

————. *John Burningham's ABC*. New York: Crown Publishers, Inc., 1985. ISBN 0-517-55960-9.

A small boy introduces the alphabet with an alligator, juggler, newt, and other objects from A to Z.

AGES 4–7. Upper and lower case.

Calder, Lyn, and M. Hover. *The Sweetie Book of ABC*. Illustrated by John Costanza, Manuel & Rochelle Valdiva. Racine, Wisconsin: Western Publishing Company, Inc., 1991. ISBN 0-307-10182-7.

The Tiny Toons characters introduce the alphabet by showing objects for each letter.

AGES 2 AND UP. Upper and lower case.

Calmenson, Stephanie. *Sesame Street ABC*. Racine, Wisconsin: Western Publishing Co., 1986. ISBN 0-307-07016-6.

Popular Sesame Street characters demonstrate the letters of the alphabet.

AGES 2–6, Upper and lower case.

Dantzic, Cynthia Maris. *Stop Dropping Bread Crumbs on My Yacht: The Silent ABC*. Englewood Cliffs, New Jersey: Prentice Hall, Inc., 1974. ISBN 13-846998.

In this series of stories, words with silent letters are stressed.

ALL AGES.

Davis, Jim. *Garfield A to Z Zoo*. Illustrated by Mike Fentz and Dave Kunh. New York: Random House, 1984. ISBN 0-394-86483-2.

A grak bird startles Garfield as he goes to the zoo, causing him to hit his head and dream about all kinds of imaginary animals from Aquawalker to Zuni.

AGES 5–8.

An Easter Alphabet. From a poem by Nora Tarlow. New York: G.P. Putnam's Sons, 1991. ISBN 0-399-22194-8.

The alphabet is introduced through the signs and symbols of Easter.

ALL AGES. Upper case.

Eastman, P. D. *The Alphabet Book*. New York: Random House, 1974. ISBN 0-394-82818-6.

This easy-to-read alphabet book introduces all kinds of animals and people in humorous situations.

AGES 3–7. Upper case.

Floyd, Lucy, and Kathryn Laskey. *Agatha's Alphabet: With Her Very Own Dictionary*. Ilustrated by Dora Leder. New York: Rand-McNally, 1975.
Using a dictionary style, the authors provide lists of actions and objects for the letters of the alphabet.
AGES 6–9. Upper and lower case.

Fowler, Richard. *Mr. Little's Noisy ABC*. New York: Grosset & Dunlap, 1987. ISBN 0-448-19201-2.
In this humorous ABC book, the reader follows Mr. Little's noisy antics from A (Ahhh!) to Z (Zoom!).
AGES 4–8. Upper and lower case.

Fujikawa, George. *Gyo Fujikawa's A to Z Picture Book*. New York: Grosset & Dunlap, 1974. ISBN 0-448-11741-X; 0-448-13205-2 (lib bdg).
All kinds of objects are shown for each letter of the alphabet.
AGES 3–7. Upper and lower case.

Gasiorowicz, Nina, and Cathy Gasiorowicz. *The Mime Alphabet Book*. Minneapolis, Minnesota: Lerner Publications Co., 1974. ISBN 0-8225-0280-1.
In this unusual black and white alphabet book mimes act out the letters of the alphabet.
ALL AGES.

Groening, Maggie, and Matt Groening. *Maggie Simpson's Alphabet Book*. New York: HarperCollins Pub., 1991. ISBN 0-694-00318-2 (soft); 0-06-020236 (lib bdg).
Bright, colorful pictures and one-word text help the Simpson family introduce the alphabet.
AGES 3 AND UP. Upper case.

Hall, Nancy Christensen. *Macmillan Fairy Tale Alphabet Book*. Pictures by John O'Brien. New York: Macmillan Pub. Co., 1983. ISBN 0-02-741960-6.
The letters of the alphabet are presented against the background of scenes from fairy tales, tall tales, and other well-known children's works.
ALL AGES. Upper case.

Harada, Joyce. *It's the ABC Book*. Union City, California: Heian International, Inc., 1982. ISBN-89346-157-1.
Animals, objects, and plants are shown in bright colors with simple text.
AGES 4 AND UP. Upper and lower case.

Harrison, Susan. *AlphaZoo Christmas*. Nashville, Tennessee: Ideals Publishing Corp, 1993. ISBN 0-8249-8623-7; 0-8249-8632-6 (lib bdg).
Tongue twisting text and watercolor illustrations provide the reader with a new look at the Christmas season.
AGES 4–7. Upper and lower case.

Hayward, Linda and others. *My ABC's*. Racine, Wisconsin: Western Publishing Company, 1989. ISBN 0-8343-0075-3.
The Sesame Street characters use a variety of activities, stories, and songs to introduce the alphabet.
AGES 3 AND UP. Upper and lower case.

Hennessy, B. G. *A, B, C, D, Tummy, Toes, Hands, Knees*. Pictures by Wendy Watson. New York: Viking Penguin, 1989. ISBN 0-670-81703-1.
Although this is technically not an alphabet book, it shows a child's day with objects, actions, sounds, and concepts in rhyme.
AGES 3–7.

Hirsch, Lynn Armstrong, Illustrator. *Have You Met the Alphabet?* New York: Derrydale Books, 1991. ISBN 0-517-17393-5.
A collection of several items is used in the illustrations for each letter of the alphabet.
AGES 3–8. Upper case.

Holt, Virginia. *A My Name Is Alice*. Illustrated by Joe Mathieu. New York: Random House, 1989. ISBN 0-394-82241-2.
Based on a jump rope rhyme, the Muppets introduce short poems about apples, cookies, magic, umbrellas and other words representing letters of the alphabet.
AGES 3–8. Upper and lower case.

Hubbard, Woodleigh. *C is for Curious: An ABC of Feelings*. San Francisco, California: Chronicle Books, 1990. ISBN 0-87701-679-8.
An alphabet of feelings from angry to zealous is shown.
ALL AGES.

Hughes, Shirley. *Lucy and Tom's a.b.c.* New York: Viking Kestrel, 1984, 1986. ISBN 0-670-81256-0.
Brother and sister, Tom and Lucy, show off their world and the alphabet as they see it.
AGES 2–6. Upper and lower case.

Hyman, Jane. *The Gumby Book of Letters*. Garden City, New York: Doubleday & Co., Inc., 1986. ISBN 0-385-23456-2; 0-385-23846-0 (lib bdg).
The green clay figure, Gumby, introduces the sounds of the letters of the alphabet.
AGES 3 AND UP. Upper and lower case.

Jefferds, Vincent. *Disney's Elegant ABC*. New York: Simon and Schuster, 1983. ISBN 0-671-45571-0.
Disney characters are used to illustrate the rhyme and words for each letter of the alphabet.

AGE 3 AND UP. Upper case.

Johnson, Crockett. *Harold's ABC*. New York: Harper and Row, 1963.

Harold and his trusty purple crayon take a trip through the alphabet.

AGES 2 AND UP. Upper case.

Kahn, Peggy. *The Care Bears Book of ABC's*. Illustrated by Carolyn Bracken. New York: Random House, 1984. ISBN 0-394-95808-X.

Large letters and rhymes about Care Bears are used in this ABC book.

AGES 3–6. Upper case.

Korr, David. *ABC Toy Chest*. Illustrated by Nancy W. Stevenson. Racine, Wisconsin: Western Publishing Co., 1981. ISBN 0-307-23129-1.

Henry is searching for something in his toy chest and finds all sorts of items from accordion and barbell to underwear to zoo.

AGES 3–7. Upper case.

Kraus, Robert, et al. *The Old-Fashioned Raggedy Ann and Andy ABC Book*. Illustrated by Johnny Gruelle. New York: Little Simon, 1980. ISBN 0-671-42552-8.

Raggedy Ann and Andy introduce key words and objects.

AGES 5 AND UP. Upper case.

Kunin, Claudia. *My Christmas Alphabet*. Racine, Wisconsin: Western Publishing Co., 1993. ISBN 0-307-13720-1.

Traditional Christmas holiday items such as elves, holly and stockings are captured in photographs introducing the letters of the alphabet.

AGES 2–6.

———. *My Hanukkah Alphabet*. Racine, Wisconsin: Western Publishing Co., 1993. ISBN 0-307-13719-8.

Traditional objects associated with Hanukkah are shown in alphabetical sequence.

AGES 2–6.

Lalli, Judy. M. S. *Feelings Alphabet: An Album of Emotions from A to Z*. Rolling Hills Estates, California: B. L. Winch and Associates, 1984. ISBN 0-935266-151 (soft).

The letters of the alphabet are represented by captioned pictures of a feeling or emotion.

AGES 3 AND UP. Upper case.

LaZebnik, Ken, and Steve Lehman. *A is for At Bat: Baseball Primer*. Illustrations by Andy Nelson. Siren, Wisconsin: Culpepper Press, 1988. ISBN 0-929636-00-7.

The reader is taken on a rhyming trip through the alphabet via the world of baseball.

ALL AGES. Upper and lower case.

Lukas, Noah. *Tiny Trolls ABC*. Illustrated by S. D. Schindler. New York: Random House, 1993. ISBN 0-679-84797-9.

Tiny trolls are into everything from apple to zipper.

AGES 3–7. Upper and lower case.

Martin, Rodney. *The Monster Alphabet*. Illustrated by Yvonne Ashby. Nashville, Tennessee: Ideals Childrens Books, 1984. ISBN 0-8249-8205-3.

All kinds of friendly monsters are shown doing activites and sharing items from A to Z.

AGES 4 AND UP. Upper and lower case.

Maurer, Donna. *Annie, Bea, and Chi Chi Dolores: A School Day Alphabet*. Pictures by Denys Cazet. New York: Orchard Books, 1993. ISBN 0-531-05467-5; 0-531-08617-8 (lib bdg).

Three young children share an alphabetical day at school.

AGES 3 AND UP. Upper and lower case.

Mayer, Mercer. *Little Critter's The Trip*. Racine, Wisconsin: Western Publishing Co., Inc., 1988. ISBN 0-307-11661-1; 0-307-60661-9 (lib bdg).

Little Critter and his family set off on a trip that includes all kinds of things from A to Z.

AGES 4–8.

———. *Little Monster's Alphabet Book*. New York: Golden Press, 1978.

Little Monster shares his alphabet collection including a brown grump apple and fireflies to red rubber raft and zipperump-a-zoo.

AGES 5–8. Upper and lower case.

Mendoza, George. *The Christmas Tree Alphabet Book*. Illustrated by Bernadette. New York: World Publishing Co., 1971.

Children from around the world celebrate Christmas with a variety of traditions from A to Z.

ALL AGES. Upper case.

———. *The Marcel Marceau Alphabet Book*. Photographs by Milton H. Greene. Garden City, New York: Doubleday, 1970.

Black and white photographs of Marcel Marceau miming words are used for each letter of the alphabet.

ALL AGES. Upper case.

Milne, A. A. *Pooh's Alphabet Book*. Illustrated by Ernest Howard Shepard. New York: E.P. Dutton, Inc., 1975. ISBN 0-525-37370-5.
   The reader is introduced to the land of Pooh and his friends in this alphabetical tour.
AGES 4 AND UP. Upper case.

Moncure, Jane Belk. *Magic Monsters Act the Alphabet*. Illustrated by Helen Endres. Elgin, Illinois: The Child's World, 1980. ISBN 0-89565-116-5.
   The magic monsters put on an act to show off the alphabet.
AGES 3 AND UP. Upper and lower case.

Muntean, Michaela. *A My Name Is Annabel: A Sesame Street Alphabet Book*. Illustrated by Tom Brannon. Racine, Wisconsin: Western Publishing Co., 1986. ISBN 0-307-21356-0.
   The gang from Sesame Street show off the alphabet and their favorite things that begin with each letter.
AGES 4 AND UP. Upper case.

Niland, Deborah. *ABC of Monsters*. New York: McGraw-Hill, 1976. ISBN 0-07-046560-6.
   A little girl attends a party where all kinds of monsters are partying their way through the alphabet.
AGES 3–7. Upper and lower case.

Nolan, Dennis. *Alphabrutes*. Englewood Cliffs, New Jersey: Prentice-Hall, 1977.
   Brutes and beasts of all shapes and sizes romp across the pages trying to discover what is in the yellow basket.
AGES 3–7. Upper case.

Oechsli, Kelly. *The Monkey's ABC Word Book*. New York: Golden Press, 1982. ISBN 0-307-11953-X; 0-307-61953-2.
   A group of monkeys show all kinds of objects for each letter of the alphabet.
AGES 3–9. Upper case.

Parker, Jessie. *The Norfin Trolls from A to Z*. New York: Scholastic, Inc., 1993. ISBN 0-590-46957-6.
   The Norfin trolls use action and words to show their ABC's in their photographs.
AGES 3 AND UP. Upper case.

Peyo. *The Smurf ABC Book*. New York: Random House, 1983. ISBN 0-394-96073-4.
   Blue Smurfs and their daily activities are used to introduce objects, names, and the letters of the alphabet.
AGES 2 AND UP. Upper and lower case.

Peter Rabbit's ABC. London, England: Frederick Warne Co., 1987. ISBN 0-7232-3423-X.
   By combining familiar objects and letters, the alphabet is introduced by favorite characters from Beatrix Potter stories.
AGES 2 AND UP. Upper and lower case.

Phillips, Tamara. *Day Care ABC*. Pictures by Dora Leder. Niles, Illinois: Albert Whitman & Co., 1989. ISBN 0-8075-1483-7.
   From A to Z, children show the activites that take place in a day care center.
AGES 3–7. Upper and lower case.

Pilcher, Steve. *Elfabit*. Burlington, Ontario: Hayes Publishing Ltd., 1982. ISBN 0-88625-042-0.
   Pilcher takes the reader on an alphabetical trip through the world of forest fantasy creatures.
AGES 3–9 Upper case.

Polette, Nancy. *The Hole by the Apple Tree: An A–Z Discovery Tale*. Pictures by Nishan Akgulian. New York: Greenwillow Books, 1992. ISBN 0-688-10557-2; 0-688-10558-0 (lib bdg).
   As Harold digs a hole, his imagination takes him and his friends on an alphabet trip with many familiar storybook friends.
AGES 5–8. Upper case.

Rey, H. A. *Curious George Learns the Alphabet*. Boston, Massachusetts: Houghton Mifflin Co., 1963. ISBN 0-395-16031-6; 0-395-1718-7 (soft).
   The man in the yellow hat teaches Curious George all about the letters of the alphabet.
AGES 6–10.

Ross, Harry. *The Fraggles Alphabet Pie*. Illustrated by Larry Di Fiori. Chicago, Illinois: Childrens Press, 1988. ISBN 0-516-09073-9.
   The Fraggles have an exciting adventure with an alphabet pie.
AGES 4 AND UP. Upper case.

The Sesame Street ABC Book of Words. Illustrated by Harry McNaught. New York: Random House, 1988. ISBN 0-394-8880-4; 0-394-98880-9 (lib bdg).
   Busy scenes involving characters from Sesame Street introduce the letters of the alphabet and objects that begin with each letter.
ALL AGES. Upper and lower case.

The Sesame Street ABC Storybook. New York: Random House, 1974. ISBN 0-394-82921-2; 0-394-92921-7 (lib bdg).
   The Muppets present a story for each letter of the alphabet.
ALL AGES. Upper and lower case.

The Sesame Street Book of Letters. Boston, Massachusetts: Little, Brown, 1970.
    Comic pictures and funny word combinations illustrate the letters of the alphabet.
AGES 3 AND UP. Upper and lower case.

Smee, Nicola. *ABC*. New York: HarperCollins, 1990. ISBN 0-00-195465-2.
    Twenty-six children are engaged in a series of alphabet activities.
AGES 3–8. Upper and lower case.

Smith-Moore, J. J. *Abigail's Alphabet*. Los Angeles: Price Stern Sloan, Inc., 1987. ISBN 0-8431-2217-X.
    Energetic Abigail introduces the letters of the alphabet while showing the reader all the things that happen during her busy day.
AGES 3–8. Upper case.

Snoopy's ABC. Racine, Wisconsin: Western Publishing Co., 1987. ISBN 307-0927-5; 0-307-60927-8.
    The Peanuts gang introduce all sorts of A to Z words.
ALL AGES. Upper and lower case.

Snow, Alan. *The Monster Book of ABC Sounds*. New York: Dial Books for Young Readers, 1991. ISBN 0-8037-0935-8.
    Rats and monsters play a hide-and-seek game to the tune of the alphabet song.
ALL AGES. Upper and lower case.

Taylor, Kenneth N. *Big Thoughts for Little People*. Illustrated by Kathryn E. Shoemaker. Wheaton, Illinois: Tyndale House
    Publishing, Inc., 1971, 1983. ISBN 0-8423-0164-X.
    Rhyming text, Bible verses, and questions about the pictures are all a part of this religious alphabet book.
AGES 5–8.

Travers, P. L. *Mary Poppins from A to Z*. Illustrated by Mary Shepard. New York: Harcourt Brace & World, Inc., 1962. ISBN
    0-15-252590-4.
    Mary Poppins and members of the Banks family are featured in alphabet stories.
AGES 6–12.

Tudor, Tasha. *A is for Annabelle*. New York: Walch, 1954. ISBN 0-02-688534-4.
    A is Annabelle the doll, and all the items and activites that she has.
AGES 4–8. Upper case.

Wersba, Barbara. *26 Starlings Will Fly Through Your Mind*. Illustrated by David Palladini. New York: Harper & Row, 1980.
    ISBN 0-06-026376-8; 0-06-026377-6 (lib bdg).
    Using the imagination of a little girl and a myriad of words, images, and colors, the letters of the alphabet are presented.
AGES 5 AND UP.

Wilner, Isabel. *B is for Bethlehem: A Christmas Alphabet*. Illustrated by Elisa Kleven. New York: Dutton, 1990. ISBN 0-525-
    44622-2.
    The events of the birth of Jesus are conveyed with letters of the alphabet.
ALL AGES. Upper case.

Yolen, Jane. *Elfabet: An ABC of Elves*. Illustrated by Lauren Mills. Boston, Massachusetts: Little, Brown & Co., 1990. ISBN
    0-316-96900-1.
    In this ingenious ABC book, an assortment of elves engage in all kinds of activities surrounded by objects of the same letter.
AGE 3 AND UP. Upper and lower case.

POP CULTURE AND OTHER ABC ADVENTURES: ACTIVITIES

After sharing *Harold's ABC,* have the students write their own Harold alphabet adventure using the trusty purple crayon (or any color of their choice). If you don't want to use Harold, have them use their own name. Use the activity sheet and have the children draw a "color" ABC adventure of their own.

Use *Macmillan Fairy Tale Alphabet Book* with older children (grades 3 and up) and have them write their own alphabet adventure sentences and stories using characters from fairy tales, folklore, and other children's storybooks. High school students can use characters from literature such as Huck Finn, Tom Sawyer, and Lady Macbeth.

Use either precut monster shapes (for preschoolers) or have the children create their own monsters. Cut out the shapes from construction paper or lightweight cardboard and decorate with markers, crayons, paint, fabric, or any other items to complete the monsters. Add craft sticks to the backs of the monsters to create monster puppets.

After sharing Snow's *The Monster Book of ABC Sounds,* give the children an activity sheet of rats and monsters trying to find their ABCs. Make a list of other sounds that the monsters might have made as they chased the rats around.

After sharing *Annie, Bea, and Chi Chi Dolores* and *Day Care ABC,* have the children make a list of other activites that take place in a school setting. Play follow the leader and do some of the activities that were discussed in the books or on the lists that the children created.

Share any of the four ABC books dealing with feelings and emotions. In addition to those used in the books, have the children make a list of other emotions. Talk about some of the emotions and how we all have different feelings at one time or another. Write the names of the emotions/feelings on cards and drop in a box. Have each child take a turn at choosing and pantomiming that emotion while the rest of the group try to guess what it is. Other activities might include: 1. Give each student an emotion to write a description of and to draw a picture of someone showing that feeling; 2. Divide a piece of cardboard into four squares. Have the children draw pictures of themselves showing four of the emotions expressed in the books.

B is for Bethlehem was originally designed as a performance piece for second graders, and it is a natural to use during the holiday season. Give each child a letter and rhyme to learn for their performance of this unique alphabet book. As part of the performance, have the child create their own mixed media collage rendition of the event that they are going to recite. You can use watercolors, fabric, cut paper, or any kind of art materials to make a collage.

129

ABC Adventure

Choose a color and draw your own ABC adventure just as Harold did with his trusty purple crayon.

Rats and Monsters and ABCs

In *The Monster Book of ABC Sounds* the rats and monsters had a wild adventure with the alphabet. Trace the path the monsters made through the alphabet.

What a Feeling!!!

Draw pictures of 4 of the feelings discussed in the alphabet books about emotions and feelings.

APPENDIX: ALPHABET BOOKS

1. *A is for Apple*
2. *ABC*. ill. by Colin Twinn
3. *ABC*
4. *ABC in English and French*
5. *ABC in the Woods*
6. *ABC Just for Me*
7. *ABC's and Other Learning Rhymes*
8. Ackerman, Karen. *Flannery Row*
9. Adams, Pam. *Mr. Lion's I-Spy ABC*
10. *Agard, John. The Calypso Alphabet*
11. Alda, Arlene. *Arlene Alda's ABC*
12. Alden, Laura. *Cat's Adventure in Alphabet Town*
13. Alden, Laura. *Elfin's Adventure in Alphabet Town*
14. Alden, Laura. *Nightingale's Adventure in Alphabet Town*
15. Alden, Laura. *Owl's Adventure in Alphabet Town*
16. Alden, Laura. *Penguin's Adventure in Alphabet Town*
17. Alden, Laura. *Squirrel's Adventure in Alphabet Town*
18. Alden, Laura. *Umpire's Adventure in Alphabet Town*
19. Alexander, Liza. *A Day in the Country*
20. *Alpha-Bakery Children's Cookbook*
21. Amery, Heather. *The Stephen Cartwright ABC*
22. Andersen, Karen Born. *An Alphabet in Five Acts*
23. Anderson, Kat. *Alpha-Blocks*
24. Angel, Marie. *Marie Angel's Exotic Alphabet*
25. Anglund, Joan Walsh. *A is for Always: an ABC Book*
26. Anglund, Joan Walsh. *In a Pumpkin Shell: A Mother Goose ABC*
27. *The Animal's ABC*
28. Anno, Mitsumasa. *Anno's Alphabet*
29. Anno, Mitsumasa. *Anno's Magical ABC*
30. Argent, Kerry. *Animal Capers*
31. Arnosky, Jim. *Mouse Numbers and Letters*
32. Arnosky, Jim. *Mouse Writing*
33. Asch, Frank. *Little Devil's ABC*
34. Ashton, Elizabeth. *An Old-Fashioned ABC Book*
35. Asimov, Isaac. *ABC's of the Earth*
36. Asimov, Isaac. *ABC's of the Ocean*
37. Awdry, Rev. W. *Thomas's ABC Book*
38. Aylesworth, Jim. *The Folks in the Valley*
39. Aylesworth, Jim. *Old Black Fly*
40. Azarian, Mary. *The Farmer's Alphabet*

41. *Baby's ABC*
42. *Baby's ABC*. ill. by Bettina Paterson
43. *Baby's First ABC*
44. Balian, Lorna. *Humbug Potion*
45. Banks, Kate. *Alphabet Soup*
46. Bannatyne-Cugnet, Jo. *A Prairie Alphabet*
47. Barker, Cicely Mark. *A Flower Fairy Alphabet*
48. Barnes, Djuna. *Creatures in an Alphabet*
49. Barry, Katherine. *A is for Anything*
50. Barry, Robert. *Animals Around the World*
51. Base, Graeme. *Animalia*
52. Baskin, Leonard. *Hosie's Alphabet*
53. Bayer, Jane. *A My Name Is Alice*
54. Beisner, Monica. *A Folding Alphabet Book*
55. Beller, Janet. *A-B-C-ing An Action Alphabet*
56. Berenstain, Stan and Jan. *The Berenstain's B Book*
57. Berenstain, Stan and Jan. *"C" is for Clown*
58. Berger, Terry. *Ben's ABC Day*
59. Bernhard, Durga. *Alphabeasts*
60. Bernthal, Mark. *Baby Bop's ABC*
61. Biondi, Janet. *D is for Dolphin*
62. Birmingham, Duncan. *"M" is for Mirror*
63. Bishop, Ann. *Riddle-iculous-Rid Alphabet Book*
64. Black, Floyd. *Alphabet Cat*
65. Blackwell, Deborah. *An ABC Bestiary*
66. Blake, Quentin. *Quentin Blake's ABC*
67. Boddy, Marlys. *ABC Book of Feelings*
68. Boettcher, Sue. *Sue Boettcher's Black Cat ABC*
69. Bond, Michael. *Paddington's ABC*
70. Borlenchi, Patricia. *From Albatross to Zoo*
71. Bowen, Betsy. *Antler, Bear, Canoe*
72. Bowman, Clare. *Busy Bodies*
73. Boynton, Sandra. *A is for Angry*
74. Boynton, Sandra. *A to Z*
75. Brent, Isabelle. *An Alphabet of Animals*
76. Bridwell, Norman. *Clifford's ABC*
77. Broomfield, Robert. *The Baby Animal ABC*
78. Brown, Marcia. *All Butterflies*
79. Brown, Marcia. *Peter Piper's Alphabet*
80. Brown, Ruth. *Alphabet Times Four*
81. Bruce, Lisa. *Oliver's Alphabet*
82. Bruna, Dick. *B is for Bear*
83. Brunhoff, Laurent de. *Babar's ABC*
84. Buckman, Mary. *The Alphagate*
85. Budd, Lillian. *The Pie Wagon*
86. *Bunnies' ABC*
87. Bunting, Jane. *My First ABC Book*
88. Burningham, John. *John Burningham's ABC*
89. Burton, Marlee. *Aaron Awoke*

90. Cabat, Erni. *Erni Cabat's Magical ABC's*
91. Calder, Lyn & M. Hover. *The Sweetie Book of ABC*
92. Calmenson, Stephanie. *It Begins with an A*

93. Calmenson, Stephanie. *Sesame Street ABC*
94. Carle, Eric. *All About Arthur*
95. Carter, Angela. *Comic and Curious Cats*
96. Cassedy, Sylvia. *Roomrimes*
97. Cassedy, Sylvia. *Zoomrimes*
98. Chaplin, Susan. *I Can Sign My ABC's*
99. Chardiet, Bernice. *C is for Circus*
100. Charles, Donald. *Letters from Calico Cat*
101. Charles, Donald. *Shaggy Dog's Animal Alphabet*
102. Chess, Victoria. *Alfred's Alphabet Walk*
103. Chouinard, Roger and Mariko. *The Amazing Animal Alphabet Book*
104. Chwast, Seymour. *The Alphabet Parade*
105. Chwast, Seymour. *Still Another Alphabet Book*
106. Cleary, Beverly. *The Hullabaloo ABC*
107. Cleaver, Elizabeth. *ABC*
108. Clifton, Lucille. *The Black BC's*
109. Clise, Michele Durkson. *Animal Alphabet Folding Screen*
110. Coats, Laura Jane. *Alphabet Garden.*
111. Cohen, Nora. *From Apple to Zipper*
112. Colletta, Irene & Hallie. *From A to Z*
113. Cook, Doris. *Dinosaur's Adventure in Alphabet Town*
114. Cook, Lyn. *A Canadian ABC*
115. Cooney, Barbara. *A Garland of Games and Other Diversions*
116. Cox, Lynne. *Crazy Alphabet*
117. Crews, Donald. *We Read: A to Z*
118. Crowther, Robert. *The Most Amazing Hide-and-Seek Alphabet Book*
119. Cushman, Doug. *The ABC Mystery*

120. Dantzic, Cynthia Maris. *Stop Dropping Bread Crumbs.*
121. Dareff, Hal. *Fun with ABC and 123*
122. Davis, Jim. *Garfield A to Z Zoo*
123. Deasy, Michael. *City ABC's*
124. DeLage, Ida. *ABC Easter Bunny*
125. DeLage, Ida. *ABC Halloween Witch*
126. DeLage, Ida. *ABC Triplets at the Zoo*
127. Delaunay, Sonia. *Sonia Delaunay's Alphabet*
128. DeMejo, Oscar. *Oscar de Mejo's ABC*
129. Demi. *Demi's Find the Animal ABC*
130. Demi. *The Peek-a-Boo ABC*
131. DerManuelian, Peter. *Hieroglyphs from A to Z*
132. Diaz, Jorge. *The Rebellious Alphabet*
133. *Disney Babies A to Z*
134. Domanska, Janina. *A Was an Angler*
135. Doolitte, Eileen. *The Ark in the Attic*
136. Doubilet, Anne. *Under the Sea from A to Z*
137. Downie, Jill. *Alphabet Puzzle*
138. Dragonwagon, Crescent. *Alligator Arrived with Apples*
139. Dreamer, Sue. *Circus ABC*
140. Drucker, Malka. *A Jewish Holiday ABC*
141. Dubin, Jill. *Little Bitties ABC*
142. Duke, Kate. *The Guinea Pig ABC*
143. Duvoisin, Roger. *A for the Ark*

144. *An Easter Alphabet*
145. Eastman, P.D. *The Alphabet Book*
146. Edens, Cooper. *An ABC of Fashionable Animals*
147. Edwards, Michelle. *Alef-bet: A Hebrew Alphabet Book*
148. Ehlert, Lois. *Eating the Alphabet*
149. Eichenberg, Fritz. *Ape in a Cape*
150. Elliott, David. *An Alphabet of Rotten Kids*
151. Elting, Mary & Michael Folsom. *Q is for Duck*
152. Emberley, Ed. *Ed Emberley's ABC*

153. Falls, Charles B. *ABC Book*
154. Farber, Norma. *As I Was Crossing Boston Common*
155. Farber, Norma. *This is the Ambulance Leaving the Zoo*
156. Feelings, Muriel. *Jambo Means Hello*
157. Feeney, Stephanie. *A is for Aloha*
158. Feldman, Judy. *The Alphabet in Nature*
159. Felix, Monica. *The Alphabet*
160. Ferguson, Don. *Winnie the Pooh's A to Zzzz*
161. Fife, Dale. *Adam's ABC*
162. Fisher, Leonard Everett. *The ABC Exhibit*
163. Fisher, Leonard Everett. *Alphabet Art*
164. Floyd, Lucy. *Agatha's Alphabet*
165. Folsom, Marcia. *Easy as Pie*
166. Fortey, Richard. *The Dinosaur's Alphabet*
167. Fowler, Richard. *Mr. Little's Noisy ABC*
168. Freeman, Don. *Add-A-Line Alphabet*
169. Fujikawa, Gyo. *Gyo Fujikawa's A to Z Picture Book*

170. Gabler, Mirko. *The Alphabet Soup*
171. Gag, Wanda. *The ABC Bunny*
172. Gardner, Beau. *Have You Ever Seen?*
173. Garten, Jan. *The Alphabet Tale*
174. Gasiorowicz, Nina. *The Mime Alphabet Book*
175. Geisert, Arthur. *Pigs from A to Z*
176. Geringer, Laura. *The Cow is Mooing Anyway*
177. *The Glorious ABC*
178. Goennel, Heidi. *Heidi's Zoo*
179. Gorey, Edward. *The Eclectic Abecedarium*
180. Greenaway, Kate. *A Apple Pie*
181. Gretz, Susanna. *Teddy Bear's ABC*
182. Groening, Maggie. *Maggie Simpson's Alphabet Book*
183. Grossbart, Francine. *A Big City*
184. Grover, Max. *The Accidental Zucchini*
185. Gundersheimer, Karen. *ABC Say with Me*
186. Gustafson, Scott. *Alphabet Soup*

187. Hague, Kathleen. *Alphabears*
188. Hall, Mahji. *"T" is for Terrific*
189. Hall, Nancy Christensen. *Macmillan Fairy Tale Alphabet Book*
190. Harada, Joyce. *It's the ABC Book*
191. Harrison, Susan. *AlphaZoo Christmas*
192. Harrison, Ted. *A Northern Alphabet*
193. Hatay, Nona. *Charlie's ABC*
194. Hawkins, Colin and Jacqui. *Busy ABC*

195. Hawkins, Colin and Jacqui. *I Spy*
196. Hayward, Linda. *Alphabet School*
197. Hayward, Linda. *My ABC's*
198. Heide, Florence. *Alphabet Zoop*
199. Hennessy, B. G. *ABCD, Tummy, Toes, Hands, Knees*
200. Hepworth, Cathi. *Antics!*
201. Hillman, Priscilla. *A Merry Mouse Christmas ABC*
202. Hirsch, Lynn Armstrong. *Have You Met the Alphabet*
203. Hoban, Tana. *A, B, See*
204. Hoban, Tana. *26 Letters and 99 Cents*
205. Hoberman, Mary Ann. *Nuts to You and Nuts to Me*
206. Hoguet, Susan Ramsey. *I Unpacked My Grandmother's Trunk*
207. Holabird, Katharine. *The Little Mouse ABC*
208. Holl, Adelaide. *The ABC of Cars, Trucks and Machines*
209. Holt, Virginia. *A My Name Is Alice*
210. Hubbard, Woodleigh. *C is for Curious*
211. Hudson, Cheryl Willis. *Afro-Bets*
212. Hughes, Shirley. *Lucy and Tom's a.b.c.*
213. Hunt, Jonathan. *Illuminations*
214. Hyman, Jane. *The Gumby Book of Letters.*
215. Hyman, Trina. *A Little Alphabet*

216. Ilsley, Velma. *M is for Moving*
217. *Incredible Animals A to Z*
218. Ipcar, Dahlov. *I Love My Anteater with an A*
219. Isadora, Rachel. *City Seen from A to Z*

220. Jacobs, Leland. *Alphabet of Girls*
221. Jeffares, Jeanne. *An Around the World Alphabet*
222. Jefferds, Vincent. *Disney's Elegant ABC*
223. Jernigan, Gisela. *Agave Blooms Just Once.*
224. Jewell, Nancy. *ABC Cat*
225. Johannson, Anna. *The Great ABC Search*
226. Johnson, Audean. *A to Z Look and See*
227. Johnson, Crockett. *Harold's ABC*
228. Johnson, Jean. *Firefighters A to Z*
229. Johnson, Jean. *Librarians A to Z*
230. Johnson, Jean. *Police Officers A to Z*
231. Johnson, Jean. *Postal Workers A to Z*
232. Johnson, Jean. *Sanitation Workers A to Z*
233. Johnson, Jean. *Teachers A to Z*
234. Johnson, Laura. *The Teddy Bear ABC*
235. Johnson, Odett. *Apples, Alligators and Also Alphabets*
236. Jonas, Ann. *Aardvarks Disembark*
237. Jones, Lily. *Baby Kermit's Playtime ABC*

238. Kahn, Peggy. *The Care Bears Book of ABC's*
239. Kahn, Ruth. *My Daddy's ABC's*
240. Kellogg, Steven. *Aster Aardvarks' Alphabet Adventures*
241. Kennedy, X. L. *Did Adam Name the Vinegarroon?*
242. Kightley, Rosalinda. *ABC*
243. Kingdom, Jill. *The ABC Dinosaur Book*
244. King-Smith, Dick. *Alphabeasts.*

245. Kitamura, Satoshi. *From Acorn to Zoo*
246. Kitamura, Satoshi. *What's Inside?*
247. Kitchen, Bert. *Animal Alphabet*
248. Korab, Balthazar. *Archabet*
249. Korr, David. *ABC Toy Chest*
250. Kraus, Robert. *The Old Fashioned Raggedy Ann & Andy ABC Book*
251. Kreeger, Charlene. *The Alaska ABC Book.*
252. Kunin, Claudia. *My Christmas Alphabet*
253. Kunin, Claudia. *My Hanukkah Alphabet*
254. Kurz, Ann. *Cranberries From A to Z*

255. Lalicki, Barbara. *If There Were Dreams*
256. Lalli, Judy. *Feelings Alphabet*
257. LaZebnik, Ken. *A is for At Bat*
258. Lear, Edward. *A Was Once an Apple Pie*
259. Lear, Edward. *A New Nonsense Alphabet*
260. Lear, Edward. *An Edward Lear Alphabet*
261. Lecourt, Nancy. *Abracadabra to Zigzag*
262. Leedy, Loreen. *The Dragon ABC Hunt*
263. LeSieg, Theo L. *Hooper Humperdink . . . ? Not Him!*
264. Lillie, Patricia. *One Very, Very Quiet Afternoon*
265. Linscott, Jody. *Once Upon A to Z*
266. *A Little ABC Book*
267. Lobel, Anita. *Alison's Zinnia*
268. Lobel, Anita. *Pierrot's ABC Garden*
269. Lobel, Arnold. *On Market Street*
270. Lopshire, Robert. *ABC Games*
271. Lucero, Faustina. *Little Indian's ABC*
272. Lukas, Noah. *Tiny Trolls ABC*
273. Lyon, George Ella. *ABCedar*

274. MacDonald, Suse. *Alphabetics*
275. McDonnell, Janet. *Ape's Adventure in Alphabet Town*
276. McDonnell, Janet. *Bear's Adventure in Alphabet Town*
277. McDonnell, Janet. *Fox's Adventure in Alphabet Town*
278. McDonnell, Janet. *Goat's Adventure in Alphabet Town*
279. McDonnell, Janet. *Hippo's Adventure in Alphabet Town*
280. McDonnell, Janet. *Ichabod's Adventure in Alphabet Town*
281. McDonnell, Janet. *Kangaroo's Adventure in Alphabet Town*
282. McDonnell, Janet. *Mouse's Adventure in Alphabet Town*
283. McDonnell, Janet. *Quarterback's Adventure in Alphabet Town*
284. McDonnell, Janet. *Raccoon's Adventure in Alphabet Town*
285. McDonnell, Janet. *Turtle's Adventure in Alphabet Town*
286. McDonnell, Janet. *Victor's Adventure in Alphabet town*
287. McDonnell, Janet. *XYZ's Adventure in Alphabet Town*
288. McGinley, Phyllis. *All Around the Town*
289. Mack, Stan. *The King's Cat is Coming*
290. MacKinnon, Debbie. *My First ABC*
291. McKissack, Patricia. *The Big Bug Book of the Alphabet*
292. McKissack, Patricia. *The Children's ABC Christmas*
293. McMillan, Bruce. *The Alphabet Symphony*
294. McPhail, David. *David McPhail's Animals A to Z*
295. Maddex, Diane. *Architects Make Zigzags*

296. Maddex, Diane. *Built in the USA*
297. Magee, Doug. *All Aboard ABC*
298. Magee, Doug. *Let's Fly from A to Z*
299. Magel, John. *Dr. Moggle's Alphabet Challenge*
300. Marolda, Maria. *Cuisenaire Alphabet Book*
301. Martin, Bill. *Chicka Chicka Boom Boom*
302. Martin, Cyd. *A Yellowstone ABC*
303. Martin, Rodney. *The Monster Alphabet*
304. Mattiesen, Thomas. *ABC: An Alphabet Book*
305. Maurer, Donna. *Annie, Bea and Chi Chi Dolores*
306. Mayer, Marianna. *The Unicorn Alphabet*
307. Mayer, Marianna & Gerald McDermott. *The Brambleberry's Animal Alphabet*
308. Mayer, Mercer. *Little Critter's The Trip*
309. Mayer, Mercer. *Little Monster's Alphabet Book*
310. Mayers, Florence Cassen. *ABC The Alef Bet Book*
311. Mayers, Florence Cassen. *ABC Costume and Textiles*
312. Mayers, Florence Cassen. *ABC Egyptian Art*
313. Mayers, Florence Cassen. *ABC Museum of Fine Arts, Boston*
314. Mayers, Florence Cassen. *ABC The Museum of Modern Art*
315. Mayers, Florence Cassen. *ABC Musical Instruments*
316. Mayers, Florence Cassen. *ABC The National Air and Space Museum*
317. Mayers, Florence Cassen. *ABC National Museum of American History*
318. Mayers, Florence Cassen. *ABC The Wild West*
319. Mayers, Florence Cassen. *A Russian ABC*
320. Mazzarella, Mimi. *Alphabatty Animals and Funny Foods*
321. Mendoza, George. *Alphabet Sheep*
322. Mendoza, George. *A Beastly Alphabet*
323. Mendoza, George. *The Christmas Tree Alphabet Book*
324. Mendoza, George. *The Marcel Marceau Alphabet Book*
325. Merriam, Eve. *Goodnight to Annie*
326. Merriam, Eve. *Halloween ABC*
327. Merriam, Eve. *Where Is Everybody?*
328. *Mickey's Daytime-Nighttime ABC*
329. Micklethwait, Lucy. *I Spy*
330. Miles, Miska. *Apricot ABC*
331. Miller, Edna. *Mousekin's ABC*
332. Miller, Elizabeth. *Cat and Dog and the ABC's*
333. Miller, Jane. *Farm Alphabet Book*
334. Miller, Robert. *Richard Scarry's Chipmunk ABC*
335. Milne, A. A. *Pooh's Alphabet Book*
336. Modesitt, Jeanne. *The Story of Z*
337. Moncure, Jane Belk. *Magic Monsters Act the Alphabet*
338. Moncure, Jane Belk. *My "a" Sound Box*
339. Moncure, Jane Belk. *My "b" Sound Box*
340. Moncure, Jane Belk. *My "c" Sound Box*
341. Moncure, Jane Belk. *My "d" Sound Box*
342. Moncure, Jane Belk. *My "e" Sound Box*
343. Moncure, Jane Belk. *My "f" Sound Box*
344. Moncure, Jane Belk. *My "g" Sound Box*
345. Moncure, Jane Belk. *My "h" Sound Box*
346. Moncure, Jane Belk. *My "i" Sound Box*
347. Moncure, Jane Belk. *My "j" Sound Box*
348. Moncure, Jane Belk. *My "k" Sound Box*

349. Moncure, Jane Belk. *My "l" Sound Box*
350. Moncure, Jane Belk. *My "m" Sound Box*
351. Moncure, Jane Belk. *My "n" Sound Box*
352. Moncure, Jane Belk. *My "o" Sound Box*
353. Moncure, Jane Belk. *My "p" Sound Box*
354. Moncure, Jane Belk. *My "q" Sound Box*
355. Moncure, Jane Belk. *My "r" Sound Box*
356. Moncure, Jane Belk. *My "s" Sound Box*
357. Moncure, Jane Belk. *My "t" Sound Box*
358. Moncure, Jane Belk. *My "u" Sound Box*
359. Moncure, Jane Belk. *My "v" Sound Box*
360. Moncure, Jane Belk. *My "w" Sound Box*
361. Moncure, Jane Belk. *My "xyz" Sound Box*
362. Moore, Frank J. *The Magic Moving Alphabet Book*
363. Munari, Bruno. *Bruno Munari's ABC*
364. Muntean, Michaela. *A My Name Is Annabel.*
365. *The Muppet Babies ABC*
366. Murphy, Chuck. *My First Book of the Alphabet*
367. Musgrove, Margaret. *Ashanti to Zulu*
368. *My ABC*
369. *My ABC's at Home*

370. Nedobeck, Don. *Nedobeck's Alphabet Book*
371. Neumeier, Marty. *Action Alphabet*
372. Newberry, Clare Turlay. *The Kittens ABC*
373. Nicholson, William. *An Alphabet*
374. Niland, Deborah. *ABC of Monsters*
375. Nolan, Dennis. *Alphabrutes*

376. Obligado, Lilian. *Faint Frogs Feeling Feverish . . .*
377. Oechsli, Kelly. *The Monkey's ABC Word Book*
378. Olesky, Patti. *The ABC of Living Things*
379. Oliver, Robert S. *Cornucopia*
380. Onyefulu, Ifeoma. *A is for Africa*
381. Owen, Annie. *Annie's ABC*
382. Owens, Mary Beth. *A Caribou Alphabet*
383. Owoo, Ife Nii. *A is for Africa*
384. Oxenbury, Helen. *Helen Oxenbury's ABC of Things*

385. Palazzo, Tony. *A Cat Alphabet*
386. Palazzo, Tony. *A Monkey Alphabet*
387. Pallotta, Jerry. *The Bird Alphabet Book*
388. Pallotta, Jerry. *The Dinosaur Alphabet Book*
389. Pallotta, Jerry. *The Extinct Alphabet Book*
390. Pallotta, Jerry. *The Flower Alphabet Book*
391. Pallotta, Jerry. *The Frog Alphabet Book . . and Other Awesome Amphibians*
392. Pallotta, Jerry. *The Furry Alphabet Book*
393. Pallotta, Jerry. *The Icky Bug Alphabet Book*
394. Pallotta, Jerry. *The Ocean Alphabet Book*
395. Pallotta, Jerry. *The Underwater Alphabet Book*
396. Pallotta, Jerry. *The Victory Garden Alphabet Book*
397. Pallotta, Jerry. *The Yucky Reptile Alphabet Book*
398. Parker, Jessie. *The Norfin Trolls from A to Z*

399. Patrick, Denise Lewis. *Animal ABC's*
400. Patterson, Bettina. *Merry ABCs*
401. Paul, Ann Whitford. *Eight Hands Round*
402. Pearson, Tracy Campbell. *A Apple Pie*
403. Pelham, David. *A is for Animals*
404. Peppe, Rodney. *Rodney Peppe: The ABC Index*
405. *Peter Rabbit's ABC*
406. Petersham, Maud & Miska. *An American ABC*
407. Peyo. *The Smurf ABC Book*
408. Phillips, Tamara. *Day Care ABC*
409. Piatti, Celestino. *Celestino Piatti's Animal ABC*
410. Pienkowski, Jan. *ABC*
411. Pienkowski, Jan. *ABC Dinosaurs and Other Prehistoric Creatures*
412. Pilcher, Steve. *Elfabit*
413. Piper, Watty. *The Little Engine That Could: Let's Sing ABC*
414. Pittman, Helena Clare. *Miss Hindy's Cats*
415. Polette, Nancy. *The Hole by the Apple Tree*
416. Porter, Gail A. *Hugo Hippo's ABC Fun Book in Africa*
417. Pragoff, Fiona. *Alphabet From a-Apple to z-Zipper*
418. Pratt, Kristin Joy. *A Walk in the Rainforest*
419. Preiss, Leah Palmer. *The Pigs' Alphabet*
420. Provensen, Alice & Martin. *A Peaceable Kingdom*
421. Purviance, Susan. *Alphabet Annie Announces an All-American Album*

422. Rankin, Laura. *The Handmade Alphabet*
423. *The Real Mother Goose ABC's*
424. Reasoner, Charles. *Alphabite!*
425. Reasoner, Charles. *A Big Alphabet Book*
426. Red Hawk, Richard. *ABC's The American Indian Way*
427. Reese, Bob. *ABC*
428. Reeves, James. *Ragged Robin*
429. Reit, Seymour. *Things That Go: A Traveling Alphabet*
430. Ressmeyer, Roger. *Astronaut to Zodiac*
431. Rey, H.A. *Curious George Learns the Alphabet*
432. Rice, James. *Cajun Alphabet*
433. Rice, James. *Cowboy Alphabet*
434. Rice, James. *Texas Alphabet*
435. Ricklen, Neil. *Baby's ABC*
436. Riehecky, Janet. *Little Lady's Adventure in Alphabet Town*
437. Riehecky, Janet. *Walrus's Adventure in Alphabet Town*
438. Rockwell, Anne. *Albert B. Cub and Zebra*
439. Rockwell, Norman. *Norman Rockwell's Americana ABC*
440. Roe, Richard. *Animal ABC.*
441. Rojankovsky, Feodor. *Animals in the Zoo*
442. Rosario, Idalia. *Idalia's Project ABC*
443. Rosenberg, Amye. *A to Z Busy Word Book*
444. Ross, Anna. *Little Ernie's ABC*
445. Ross, Harry. *The Fraggles Alphabet Pie*
446. Rourke, Linda. *Eye Spy: A Mysterious Alphabet*
447. Royston, Angela. *The A to Z Book of Cars*
448. Ruben, Patricia. *Apples to Zippers*
449. Rubin, Cynthia Elyce. *ABC Americana from the National Gallery of Art*
450. Ryden, Hope. *Wild Animals of Africa ABC*

451. Ryden, Hope. *Wild Animals of America ABC*

452. Samton, Sheila. *Amazing Aunt Agatha*
453. Sarasas, Claude. *The ABC's of Origami*
454. Scarry, Richard. *Richard Scarry's ABC Word Book*
455. Scarry, Richard. *Richard Scarry's ABC's*
456. Scarry, Richard. *Richard Scarry's Cars and Trucks from A to Z*
457. Scarry, Richard. *Richard Scarry's Find Your ABC's*
458. Schmid-Belk, Donna D. *The Arizona Alphabet Book*
459. Schmidered, Dorothy. *The Alphabeast Book*
460. Sedgwick, Paulita. *Circus ABC*
461. Seeley, Laura L. *The Book of Shadowboxes*
462. Sendak, Maurice. *Alligators All Around*
463. *The Sesame Street ABC Book of Words*
464. *The Sesame Street ABC Storybook*
465. *The Sesame Street Book of Letters*
466. Seuss, Dr. *Dr. Seuss's ABC*
467. Shelby, Anne. *Potluck*
468. Shirley, Gayle C. *A is for Animals*
469. Shirley, Gayle C. *C is for Colorado*
470. Shirley, Gayle C. *M is for Montana*
471. Shuttlesworth, Dorothy. *ABC of Buses*
472. Silverman, Marcia. *Baby's Book of ABC*
473. Silverman, Marcia. *Bunny's ABC Box*
474. Simon, Seymour. *Space Words*
475. Simpson, Gretchen. *Gretchen's ABC*
476. Sloane, Eric. *ABC Book of Early Americana*
477. Sloat, Terri. *From Letter to Letter*
478. Small, Terry. *Tails, Claws, Fangs and Paws*
479. Smee, Nicola. *ABC*
480. Smith, Harry W. *ABC's of Maine*
481. Smith-Moore, J. J. *Abigail's Alphabet*
482. *Snoopy's ABC*
483. Snow, Alan. *The Monster Book of ABC Sounds*
484. Somes, Laurie. *ABC's of Washington State*
485. Steig, Jeanne. *Alpha Beta Chowder*
486. Steiner, Charlotte. *Annie's ABC Kitten*
487. Stevenson, James. *Grandpa's Great City Tour*
488. Stock, Catherine. *Alexander's Midnight Snack*
489. Stutson, Caroline. *On the River ABC*
490. Sullivan, Charles. *Alphabet Animals*
491. Sutton, Rosalind. *The Mouse Family ABC*
492. Szekeres, Cyndy. *Cyndy Szekeres' ABC*

493. Tada, Jona Eareckson & Steve Jensen. *The Great Alphabet Fight*
494. Tallarico, Tony. *Preschool Can You Find ABC*
495. Tallon, Robert. *Zoophabets*
496. Taylor, Kenneth. *Big Thought for Little People*
497. *Teddy Bears ABC*
498. Thornhill, Jan. *The Wildlife ABC*
499. Torrence, Susan & Leslie Polansky. *The California Alphabet Book*
500. Torrence, Susan & Leslie Polansky. *The Oregon Alphabet Book*
501. Torrence, Susan & Leslie Polansky. *The Washington Alphabet Book*

502. Travers, P.L. *Mary Poppins from A to Z*
503. Tryon, Leslie. *Albert's Alphabet*
504. Tudor, Tasha. *A Is for Annabelle*

505. Van Allsburg, Chris. *The Z Was Zapped*

506. Walters, Marguerite. *The City-Country ABC*
507. Warren, Cathy. *Victoria's ABC Adventure*
508. Watson, Clyde. *Applebet: An ABC*
509. Weeks, Sarah. *Hurricane City*
510. Weil, Lisl. *Owl and Other Scrambles*
511. Wells, Ruth. *A to Zen*
512. Wersba, Barbara. *26 Starlings Will Fly Through Your Mind*
513. Whitehead, Patricia. *Arnold Plays Baseball*
514. Whitehead, Patricia. *Best Halloween Book*
515. Whitehead, Patricia. *Best Thanksgiving Book*
516. Whitehead, Patricia. *Best Valentine Book*
517. Whitehead, Patricia. *Christmas Alphabet Book*
518. Whitehead, Patricia. *Dinosaur Alphabet Book*
519. Whitehead, Patricia. *Here Comes Hungry Albert*
520. Whitehead, Patricia. *Let's Go to the Farm*
521. Whitehead, Patricia. *Let's Go to the Zoo*
522. Whitehead, Patricia. *What a Funny Bunny*
523. Wildsmith, Brian. *Brian Wildsmith's ABC*
524. Wilks, Mike. *The Annotated Ultimate Alphabet Book*
525. Williams, Garth. *The Big Golden Animal ABC*
526. Williams, Jenny. *Everyday ABC*
527. Wilner, Isabel. *B is for Bethlehem*
528. Wilner, Isabel. *A Garden Alphabet*
529. Wilson, Ron. *100 Dinosaurs from Z to A*
530. Winik, J. T. *Fun from A to Z*
531. Wolf, Janet. *Adelaide to Zeke*
532. Wood, Jakki. *Animal Parade*
533. Wormell, Christopher. *An Alphabet of Animals*
534. Wylie, Joanne & David. *A Fishy Alphabet Story*
535. Wynne, Patricia. *The Animal ABC*

536. Yolen, Jane. *All in the Woodland Early*
537. Yolen, Jane. *Elfabet*

538. Zabar, Abbie. *Alphabet Soup*
539. Zacks, Irene. *Space Alphabet*
540. *Zen ABC*
541. Zimmer, Velma E. *Come with Me from Z to Z*

446. Ross, Harry. *The Fraggles Alphabet Pie*
447. Rourke, Linda. *Eye Spy: A Mysterious Alphabet*
448. Royston, Angela. *The A to Z Book of Cars*
449. Ruben, Patricia. *Apples to Zippers*
450. Rubin, Cynthia Elyce. *ABC Americana From the National Gallery of Art*
451. Ryden, Hope. *Wild Animals of Africa ABC*
452. Ryden, Hope. *Wild Animals of America ABC*

453. Samton, Sheila. *Amazing Aunt Agatha*
454. Sarasas, Claude. *The ABC's of Origami*
455. Scarry, Richard. *Richard Scarry's ABC Word Book*
456. Scarry, Richard. *Richard Scarry's ABC's*
457. Scarry, Richard. *Richard Scarry's Cars and Trucks From A to Z*
458. Scarry, Richard. *Richard Scarry's Find Your ABC's*
459. Schmid-Belk, Donna D. *The Arizona Alphabet Book*
460. Schmidered, Dorothy. *The Alphabeast Book*
461. Sedgwick, Paulita. *Circus ABC*
462. Seeley, Laura L. *The Book of Shadowboxes*
463. Sendak, Maurice. *Alligators All Around*
464. *The Sesame Street ABC Book of Words*
465. *The Sesame Street ABC Storybook*
466. *The Sesame Street Book of Letters*
467. Seuss, Dr. *Dr. Seuss's ABC*
468. Shelby, Anne. *Potluck*
469. Shirley, Gayle C. *A is for Animals*
470. Shirley, Gayle C. *C is for Colorado*
471. Shirley, Gayle C. *M is for Montana*
472. Shuttlesworth, Dorothy. *ABC of Buses*
473. Silverman, Marcia. *Baby's Book of ABC*
474. Silverman, Marcia. *Bunny's ABC Box*
475. Simon, Seymour. *Space Words*
476. Simpson, Gretchen. *Gretchen's ABC*
477. Sloane, Eric. *ABC Book of Early Americana*
478. Sloat, Terri. *From Letter to Letter*
479. Small, Terry. *Tails, Claws, Fangs and Paws*
480. Smee, Nicola. *ABC*
481. Smith, Harry W. *ABC's of Maine*
482. Smith-Moore, J. J. *Abigail's Alphabet*
483. *Snoopy's ABC*
484. Snow, Alan. *The Monster Book of ABC Sounds*
485. Somes, Laurie. *ABC's of Washington State*
486. Steig, Jeanne. *Alpha Beta Chowder*
487. Steiner, Charlotte. *Annie's ABC Kitten*
488. Stevenson, James. *Grandpa's Great City Tour*
489. Stock, Catherine. *Alexander's Midnight Snack*
490. Stutson, Caroline. *On the River ABC*
491. Sullivan, Charles. *Alphabet Animals*
492. Sutton, Rosalind. *The Mouse Family ABC*
493. Szekeres, Cyndy. *Cyndy Szekeres' ABC*

494. Tada, Jona Eareckson & Steve Jensen. *The Great Alphabet Fight*
495. Tallarico, Tony. *Preschool Can You Find ABC*
496. Tallon, Robert. *Zoophabets*

BIBLIOGRAPHY

Bader, Barbara. *American Picturebooks from Noah's Ark to the Beast Within*. New York: Macmillan Publishing Co., Inc., 1976.

Baldwin, Ruth M. *100 Nineteenth-Century Rhyming Alphabets in English*. Carbondale, Illinois: Southern Illinois University Press, 1972.

Barr, Marilynn G. *ABC Art*. Palo Alto, California: Monday Morning Books, Inc., 1989.

Burie, Audrey Ann, and Mary Ann Heltsche. *Reading with a Smile*. Washington, D.C.: Acropolis Books, Ltd., 1981.

Camp, Donna J., and Gail E. Thompkins. "The Abecedarius: Soldier of Literacy." *Childhood Education* vol. 66, no. 5 (1990): 298–302.

Canavan, Diane D., and Lavonna H. Sanborn. *Using Children's Books in Reading/Language Arts Programs*. New York: Neal-Schuman Pub., Inc., 1992.

Cefali, Leslie. "Alphabet Books Grown Up!" *Book Links* (May 1993): 41–45.

Chenfeld, Mimi Brodsky. *Creative Activites for Young Children*. San Diego, California: Harcourt Brace Jovanovich, 1983.

Coudron, Jill. M. *Alphabet Activities*. Carthage, Illinois: Fearon Teacher Aids, 1983.

DeSalvo, Nancy N. *Beginning with Books: Library Programming for Infants, Toddlers, and Preschoolers*. Hamden, Connecticut: The Shoe String Press, 1993.

Fagalla, Kathy. *Building on Books: Integrating Children's Literature into the Curriculum*. Bridgeport, Connecticut: First Teacher Press, 1987.

————. *Crayons Crafts and Concepts: Learning Concepts Through Art*. Bridgeport, Connecticut: First Teacher, Inc., 1985.

Glazer, Joan I. *Introduction to Children's Literature*. New York: McGraw-Hill, 1979.

Herbeck, Joyce. "Alphabet Books in Middle School and High School? New Alphabet Books Appeal to Readers of All Ages." *The NERA Journal* vol. 28, no. 1 (1992).

Huck, Charlotte, Susan Hepler, and Janet Hickman. *Children's Literature in the Elementary School*. 4th ed. New York: Holt, Rinehart Winston, 1979.

Invitation to Read: More Children's Literature in Reading Program. Edited by Bernice Cullinan. Newark, Delaware: International Reading Association, 1992.

Krause, Claudia. *Alphabetivities: 175 Ready-to-Use Activities from A to Z*. West Nyack, New York: The Center for Applied Research in Education, Inc., 1986.

Laughlin, Mildred Knight, and Letty S. Watt. *Developing Learning Skills Through Children's Literature: An Idea Book for K–5 Classrooms and Libraries*. Phoenix, Arizona: Oryx Press, 1986.

Lieberman, Lillian. *ABC Board Games: Patterns for Easy to Do Reading Games*. Palo Alto, California: Monday Morning Books, 1991.

Lieberman, Lillian. *ABC Box Games: Patterns for Easy to Do Reading Games*. Palo Alto, California: Monday Morning Books, 1991.

Lieberman, Lillian. *ABC Folder Games: Patterns for Easy to Do Reading Games*. Palo Alto, California: Monday Morning Books, 1991.

McElmeel, Sharron L. *An Author a Month (For Nickels)*. Englewood, Colorado: Teacher Ideas Press, 1990.

McElmeel, Sharron L. *An Author a Month (For Pennies)*. Englewood, Colorado: Teacher Ideas Press, 1988.

McGee, Lea M., and Donald J. Richgels. " 'K is Kristen's': Learning the Alphabet From a Child's Perspective." *The Reading Teacher* (December 1989): 216–225.

Mesrobian, Joyce. "Alphabet Books." *Day Care and Early Education* (Winter 1992): 37–39.

Miletta, Maureen M. "Picture Books for Older Children: Reading and Writing Connections." *The Reading Teacher* (March 1992): 555–556.

Moore, Jo Ellen, Kathleen Morgan, and Joy Evans. *Fun with the Alphabet*. Monterey, California: Evan–Moor Corp., 1987.

Morgan, Kathleen. *Simple Games for Practicing Basic Skills*. Monterey, California: Evan-Moor Corp., 1987.

Muncy, Patricia Tyler. *Complete Book of Illustrated K–3 Alphabet Games and Activities*. West Nyack, New York: The Center for Applied Research for Education, Inc., 1980.

Norton, Donna E. *Through the Eyes of a Child: An Introduction to Children's Literature*. Columbus, Ohio: Charles E. Merrill Publishing Co., 1983.

Ohanian, Susan. "Across the Curriculum from A to Z." *Learning 87* (April 1987): 34–40.

Paulen, Mary Ann. *Creative Uses of Children's Literature*. Hamden, Connecticut: Library Professional Publications, 1982.

Polette, Keith. "Using ABC Books for Vocabulary Development in the Secondary School." *English Journal* (January 1989): 78–80.

Roberts, Patricia L. *Alphabet: A Handbook of ABC Books and Activities for the Elementary Classroom*. Metuchen, New Jersey: The Scarecrow Press, Inc., 1984.

Roberts, Patricia L. "Alphabet Books: Activities from A to Z." *Reading Teacher* (September 1990): 84–85.

Roberts, Patricia L. *Alphabet Books as a Key to Language Patterns: An Annotated Action Bibliography*. Hamden, Connecticut: Library Professional Publications, 1987.

Smith, Elva S. *The History of Children's Literature*. Chicago, Illinois: American Library Association, 1980.

Smolkin, Laura B., and David B. Yaden, Jr. "O is for Mouse: First Encounters With The Alphabet Book." *Language Arts* (October 1992): 432–441.

Sutherland, Zena. *Children and Books*. 8th ed. New York: HarperCollins Publishing, 1991.

Thompson, Deborah L. "The Alphabet Book as a Content Area Resource." *The Reading Teacher* (November 1992): 266–267.

Warren, Jean. *ABC Circus: The Great Big Fun Unit with Alphabet Cards*. Everett, Washington: Warren Publishing House, Inc., 1991.

Warren, Jean. *ABC Farm: The Great Big Fun Unit with Alphabet Cards*. Everett, Washington: Warren Publishing House, Inc., 1991.

Warren, Jean. *ABC Space: The Great Big Fun Unit with Alphabet Cards*. Everett, Washington: Warren Publishing House, Inc., 1991.

Warren, Jean. *1-2-3 Reading and Writing*. Everett, Washington: Warren Publishing House, Inc., 1992.

Yaden, David B., Jr., Laura B. Smolkin, and Laurie MacGillivray. "A Psychogenetic Perspective on Children's Understanding About Letter Associations During Alphabet Book Readings." *Journal of Reading Behavior* vol. 25, no. 1 (1993): 45–68.

INDEX

ABOUT THE AUTHOR

Cathie Hilterbran Cooper (B.S. Ohio University; M.L.S. Kent State University) is the district media specialist for Adena Local School District in Frankfort, Ohio. She has been a library/media specialist for 18 years with both high school and primary grades. In addition, she has worked as a branch director and children's and reference librarian for a public library. She has published several articles in professional journals and currently serves on the review board for *Ohio Media Spectrum*. Her first book was *The Storyteller's Cornucopia* (Alleyside Press, 1992). She resides in Columbus, Ohio with her husband and son.